FREEDOM AT RISK

FREEDOM AT RISK

Reflections on

POLITICS, LIBERTY, AND THE STATE

James L. Buckley

Encounter Books New York • London

First American edition published in 2010 by Encounter Books,
an activity of Encounter for Culture and Education, Inc.,
a nonprofit, tax exempt corporation.
Encounter Books website address: www.encounterbooks.com

Manufactured in the United States and printed on
acid-free paper. The paper used in this publication meets
the minimum requirements of ANSI/NISO Z39.48 1992
(R 1997) (*Permanence of Paper*).

FIRST AMERICAN EDITION

LIBRARY OF CONGRESS CATALOGING-IN-PUBLICATION DATA
Buckley, James Lane, 1923–
Freedom at risk: reflections on politics, liberty, and the state/
by James L. Buckley.
p. cm.
Includes bibliographical references and index.
ISBN-13: 978-1-59403-478-7 (hardcover: alk. paper)
ISBN-10: 1-59403-478-8 (hardcover: alk. paper) 1. United States—Politics
and government—1945–1989. 2. United States—Economic policy. 3. United
States—Social policy. 4. Federal government—United States. 5. Judges—
United States. 6. Constitutional history—United States. I. Title.
E839.5.B83 2010
973.92—dc22
2010008536

10 9 8 7 6 5 4 3 2 1

FOR MY SISTER AND OLDEST FRIEND
Priscilla Langford Buckley

Contents

CONTENTS

Introduction

As I wrote in my "memoir of sorts," *Gleanings from an Unplanned Life*, my life has largely been shaped by chance. While in the Navy in World War II, I decided to pursue the tranquil life of a country lawyer. But after I had spent four years of practice with a New Haven law firm in preparation for a move to the country, my father lured me to New York City to work for a group of companies engaged in oil exploration outside the United States.

Over the next seventeen years, I led a contented and highly private life with my wife, Ann, and our six children. Then something wholly unexpected occurred. I had never—ever—given any thought to public service. Nevertheless, for reasons too complicated to explain here, in 1968 I was recruited by New York's Conservative Party to run as a pro forma candidate for election to the United States Senate. Having tested the waters, I ran again two years later and was swept into office in a three-way race with a vote of 40 percent (a margin of victory just three points lower than Bill Clinton's in 1992). Although rejected by an ungrateful electorate in 1976, I was later tapped by the Reagan administration, first for a position in the State Department and then for one in the federal judiciary. And so, through no planning of my own, I wound up serving in all three branches of the federal government: six years as a senator, two as an under secretary of state, and fifteen as a federal appellate judge.

Over those years, I had occasion to produce articles, speeches, and radio commentaries on a wide range of public issues. I recently started going through my files with the thought that my family might like a collection of my writings as a supplement to *Gleanings from an Unplanned Life*. But as I started reading these pieces, I found that although most of them were written years ago, many of them remain strikingly relevant to such current concerns as the intrusive growth of the federal government, environmental regulation, the place of religion in public life, energy policies, campaign financing, and judicial activism. And so I believe this collection may be of interest to a wider audience. The one new essay in this book is the first, "On Liberty and the State." In it, I express my concerns over the dramatic expansion of federal authority in recent years and its implications for a free society, concerns that reflect my own experiences in government.

I was a member of the Senate during a turbulent period, one marked by often violent protests against the Vietnam War, major controversies over a host of domestic and foreign policy questions, and the Watergate scandals. To the *New York Times*'s disappointment, I failed to "grow" during my six years in office. Instead, I brought a consistently conservative perspective to my analyses of the issues of those rocky days. Much of the material collected in this volume dates back to that period.

My State Department responsibilities (as the under secretary of state in charge of military and economic aid programs) dealt largely with technical subjects of only contemporary interest. As a consequence, I have included only one of my writings in that capacity. This book contains, however, several essays dealing with the foreign arena. These include discussions of our abandonment of South Vietnam, the importance of Radio Free Europe and Radio Liberty, and my experience as head of an American delegation to a United Nations conference.

I served on the U.S. Court of Appeals for the District of Columbia Circuit from 1985 until my retirement in 2000. Because judicial reasoning is inherently mind-numbing, I have included none of the several hundred opinions I wrote as a circuit judge. During those years, however, I had ample opportunity to address questions involving the Constitution and the role of federal judges that have been raised in the disgracefully politicized judicial confirmation hearings of recent times.

In the course of my years engaged in the writing, administration, or interpretation of federal laws, I have had more than the average citizen's opportunity to observe their effects. My experience suggests that the most useful, but least honored, law is one not to be found in the statute books—the Law of Unintended Consequences. It was formulated by an astute observer of the human condition who noted the frequency with which governmental remedies inflict greater harm than the ills they are intended to cure (e.g., the loss of low-income housing caused by rent control; the loss of lives resulting from the lighter cars built in response to automobile fuel-efficiency standards; the adverse impact of minimum-wage laws on minority teenage employment). This suggests that we should move with extreme caution before attempting to correct any more of our social and economic ills through government action. We have neither the wealth nor the resilience to cope with more than one or two panaceas at a time.

Finally, a word of explanation for occasional acts of self-plagiarism. Anyone whose job has entailed repeated talks to a variety of audiences will understand why certain passages will appear in more than one selection. If you have spent a fair amount of time getting words to say just what you want them to, you lose any sense of shame in repeating them in another context. I take comfort from the fact that Johann Sebastian Bach was frequently guilty of the same offense in his musical compositions.

OVERVIEW

It is considered unseemly these days to speak of American exceptionalism, yet how else can one describe our extraordinary success? We are the heirs of the most productive, prosperous, innovative, generous, and free society the earth has known, one that has transformed the world. This suggests that we should take particular care not to abandon the political insights and civic virtues that have made us, well, exceptional.

On Liberty and the State

In 1976, when I was running for re-election to the United States Senate, it was my misfortune to have Daniel Patrick Moynihan for an opponent. (He beat me handily.) During our first encounter, Pat told the audience that although I was a fine fellow, I was stuck in the eighteenth century. In response, I confessed that I was guilty as charged and acknowledged my total commitment to the values and principles imbedded in the Declaration of Independence and the Constitution. I neglected to mention my fealty to the economic insights contained in Adam Smith's *Wealth of Nations*. The relevant question, of course, is whether those eighteenth-century values, principles, and insights remain relevant to the problems and needs of the vastly changed world in which we now live. I believe they do.

American independence was won and the Republic created by a remarkable generation of men who turned a rebellion against the British crown into a transforming moment in human history, one based on the revolutionary proposition that all men are created equal and are endowed by their Creator with fundamental rights that no government has the moral authority to set aside. But with the gaining of independence, the Founders faced the formidable task of creating a government that could operate effectively while respecting and protecting the liberties for which the

Revolution had been fought. As James Madison described the challenge in *The Federalist Papers*:

> In framing a government which is to be administered by men over men, the great difficulty lies in this: you must first enable the government to control the governed; and in the next place oblige it to control itself. A dependence on the people is, no doubt, the primary control on the government; but experience has taught mankind the necessity of auxiliary precautions.

The Founders had no illusions about human nature; they understood that the drive to accumulate power, whether by an individual despot or a parliamentary majority, was the historic enemy of individual freedom. So they incorporated two "precautions" into the Constitution: its system of checks and balances and the principle of federalism. In describing the latter, Madison explained:

> The powers delegated by the proposed Constitution to the federal government are few and defined. . . . The powers reserved to the several States will extend to all the objects which, in the ordinary course of affairs, concern the lives, liberties, and properties of the people, and the internal order, improvement, and prosperity of the State.

During the debates over the Constitution's ratification, many expressed a concern that this division of responsibilities was not clear enough in the document itself. As a result, the first Congress made the division explicit in the Bill of Rights, whose Tenth Amendment reads as follows: "The powers not delegated to the United States by the Constitution, nor prohibited by it to the States, are reserved to the States respectively, or to the people."

Even with those safeguards in place, the Founders understood that the preservation of our liberties ultimately depended on the American people's continuing exercise of what was then referred to as "republican virtue"—the subordination of personal advantage to the public good. Hence Benjamin Franklin's answer to the woman who, at the close of the Constitutional Convention in Philadelphia, asked him what form of government the American people were to have: "A republic, madam, if you can keep it." The ultimate responsibility for preserving the Republic would lie with the people.

The Founders' division of governmental labors accords with the venerable principle of subsidiarity, which recognizes a hierarchy of responsibilities, beginning with the individual. Thus, under that principle, you and I are expected to earn our own livings and provide for our own families, and governmental responsibilities are allocated to the lowest levels able to exercise them. Thus, the governmental decisions most immediately affecting people's lives are to be made by those who are the closest to them and have the most intimate knowledge of the relevant facts and conditions.

This design served us well during the first 150 years of our national existence—so well that in commenting on the American Constitution, the eminent British historian Lord Acton declared that "by the development of the principle of federalism, it has produced a community more powerful, more prosperous, more intelligent, and more free than any other which the world has seen." The Supreme Court, however, has proven an unreliable guardian of constitutional virtue. Over the years, decisions expanding the reach of the Constitution's Commerce Clause have effectively repealed the Tenth Amendment. As a consequence, our nation has been converted into an administrative state overseen by a fourth, extra-constitutional branch of government in which unelected officials write rules that reach into every corner of American life.

Few appreciate the speed with which this transformation has taken place. Federal statutory law is to be found in the United States Code. In 1935, at the outset of the New Deal, the Code consisted of a single volume containing 2,275 pages of statutes. This was the work product of Congress since it first met in 1789. Today, the Code consists of thirty volumes of statutory law. But the expansion of the Code's Title 42 provides the most telling evidence of the nature of the changes that have been taking place. In 1935, Title 42 was labeled "Public Education" and contained just eighteen pages. Eleven years later, Title 42 had been renamed "Public Education and Welfare" and had grown to 128 pages. Thanks to Lyndon Johnson's Great Society, by the time the 1970 edition was published, Title 42 had exploded to 3,022 pages.

Over the next thirty years, that number more than doubled—and that is just the tip of the iceberg. Those and a host of other federal statutes are administered by bureaus and agencies that in turn issue streams of marching orders that have the force of law. By 2010, the Code of Federal Regulations consisted of 225 volumes containing 35,367 pages of detailed, fine-print regulations. This expansion of federal controls has reached a point where I sometimes indulge a fantasy in which America's extraordinarily productive society wakes up one day, like a latter-day Gulliver, to find itself immobilized by the last regulatory strands that bureaucratic Lilliputians have spun over it during the night.

What is of particular interest is the degree to which the federal government has intruded on the responsibilities of the states. In the ten years from 1966 to 1976, for example, federal grants to state and local governments, each with its own set of marching orders, grew from $13 billion to $56 billion. By 2010, these grants-in-aid programs cost over $236 billion. Worse still are the unfunded mandates by which Congress commands the states to spend their own money to meet Washington's priorities rather than their own.

It is hard to conceive of a more dramatic departure from the Founders' plan. But setting aside the propriety of the Supreme Court decisions that made these intrusions on state authority possible, the question before us is whether transforming the federal government into a European-style administrative state will lead to a better life for most Americans. In arriving at an answer, we need to consider three things: first, the competence of a central government to handle other than the kinds of core responsibilities contemplated by the Constitution; second, the financial consequences; and third, the impact on Congress's ability to do anything that can be described as truly thoughtful.

In addressing the first, one must keep in mind that government is by nature monopolistic, rigid, and political. A federal bureau or agency is immune to the disciplines of the marketplace that, in the private sector, promote efficiency and weed out losers. If costs exceed budget, government will raise taxes or borrow money to pay for the overruns; and if a program fails to achieve its goals, the congressional response is to throw more money at it. Congress will rarely admit that a program was ill advised and cancel it: to the contrary, even the worst of them is protected by the "iron triangle" consisting of the legislators who created it, the bureaucrats who administer it, and the groups that benefit from the status quo, however flawed. Moreover, while private enterprises and individuals are able to respond overnight to new circumstances and act quickly to correct errors in judgment, once a regulatory regimen is locked in place, it is enormously difficult to change. All federal programs are subject to congressional oversight, of course, but Congress is too preoccupied with current agendas to scrutinize the management of more than a fraction of the programs it has created.

Then there is the matter of politics. Because Congress is a political animal, it is inevitable that where there is a conflict between politics and common sense or Economics 101, politics will usually decide the issue. Career legislators are extremely reluctant to take any action that would offend important constituencies. To cite some typical examples: It is conceded (and the experience of states like Texas confirms) that tort reform would reduce medical costs by tens of billions of dollars, but, lest tort lawyers be offended, that most obvious reform was ignored by congressional committees intent on a trillion-dollar restructuring of our health-care system; sugar-beet farmers are kept in business by restrictions on the importation of cane sugar that cost 300 million American consumers over $1.9 billion a year; and to protect manufacturers in their constituencies, Republican and Democratic congressmen exhibit rare bipartisanship in continuing the production of weapons that the Pentagon no longer needs or wants.

Misguided political decisions are to be found, of course, in state governments as well as in Washington, D.C.; but one of the virtues of federalism is that the states serve as laboratories that are able to test a variety of approaches to shared problems. If one state makes a costly mistake, only its own citizens will suffer the consequences. On the other hand, if an initiative proves successful, other states can profit from the example. Furthermore while Washington issues one-size-fits-all regulations to states as diverse as North Dakota and Hawaii, state governments are able to tailor their directives to the specific conditions that obtain in their states.

The 2008 housing meltdown is a classic example of what the costs can be when Congress imposes an ill-conceived policy on the entire nation. Under the original understanding of our federal system, a concern for expanding home ownership might be appropriate for the states, but it is not appropriate for the federal government. A few years ago, however, Congress decided this should be a national priority and enacted a succession of laws that pressured lenders into making improvident loans while providing them, courtesy of Fannie Mae and Freddie Mac, with an open-ended market for the high-risk mortgages they had financed. Imaginative Wall Street marketers in turn packaged the obligations and distributed them around the globe. As Harvard economist Jeffrey Miron notes, "[P]rivate forces jumped willingly on a runaway train, but it was government that built the train and drove it off the cliff." Such are the costs that can be imposed when government interferes with the workings of Adam Smith's "invisible hand" on a national scale.

Unfortunately, Congress's failure to anticipate the practical consequences of its actions is not surprising. Few of those drawn to elective office have had any significant personal exposure to the disciplines of the marketplace. Thirty-odd years ago, when I was in the Senate, I witnessed such an astonishing display of economic innocence in a floor debate that I checked the biographies of my colleagues in the *Congressional Directory*. I could find only eighteen who had had any significant experience in business or agriculture. Sixty-three of the hundred senators were lawyers who had moved into one government position or another within a half-dozen years of graduating from law school. So it is hardly surprising that they should exhibit so little understanding of economic causes and effects. Thus, while lawmakers will castigate corporations that relocate overseas, they refuse to bring taxes on American businesses in line with those paid by their foreign competitors; nor will they recognize that when marginal tax rates rise beyond a certain point, those who make the high-risk investments that launch the new enterprises that have revolutionized our economy will instead devote their ingenuity to sheltering their incomes from taxation.

The second reason for declining to ask Washington to take over matters that lie within the competence of the states is financial. The states have limited borrowing powers, and so they are ultimately restrained by the willingness of their citizens to be taxed. The federal government, however, has virtually limitless borrowing power, which it is now exercising to a dangerous degree. And unlike the states, it is ultimately able to lighten the burden by debasing the dollars with which it will meet its debt obligations and, in the process, impoverishing its citizens.

During the 1960s, when Lyndon Johnson's Great Society programs were being unveiled, Senator Everett Dirksen of Illinois observed, "A billion here, a billion there—pretty soon you're talking real money." Now, it seems, the word that trips off political tongues is "trillion." Within a few months in 2008–09, Presidents George W. Bush and Barack Obama commandeered more than $1.5 trillion in order to restore liquidity to the financial markets and jump-start a recovery. Obama added about a trillion to what had been Bush's record-setting half-trillion-dollar deficit. Meanwhile, after a year of contentious debate, Congress bulldozed a trillion-dollar health-care bill into law. All of this required Congress to raise the debt ceiling to $14.3 trillion, on top of an unfunded Medicare/Medicaid/Social Security liability of $107 trillion. No doubt about it, we're talking real money. What *is* in doubt is whether we will ever be able to pay this debt; and if so, at what cost to future generations and the resilience of our economy. This runaway spending has to be contained, but that will happen only if we change some now deeply ingrained political habits.

Finally, there is the cost to Congress and the quality of government itself. Once upon a time, the Senate could be referred to, with reason, as the world's greatest deliberative body. But that was long, long ago, when Congress was in session no more than six or seven months a year and its members worked at a leisurely pace. They had the time to study the bills under consideration and discuss them with their colleagues, and they were routinely in their respective chambers to hear the merits debated. They could do so because Congress pretty well limited itself to the half-dozen areas of responsibility assigned to it by the Constitution. And when their work in Washington was over, they would return to their home communities and resume their normal lives. They were essentially citizen legislators.

The situation today is radically different. Congress's compulsion to scratch every itch on the body politic has so overwhelmed congressional dockets that members live on a treadmill. Although they may be reasonably informed on the legislation generated by their own committees, that represents only a fraction of the bills on which they will be called upon to vote. So, on most matters, they will cast their votes on a largely reflexive political basis; and because nearly all of today's members of Congress are career legislators, a member's calculus will inevitably include an assessment of the impact of a particular vote on his chances for re-election rather than being based solely on his best judgment as to where the public interest lies.

It is that calculation, I suspect, that has encouraged the changes we have seen in the scope of our social programs. What began as a system of safety nets for our most needy citizens (e.g., welfare, Medicaid, food stamps) has evolved into a broader concern for the comfort of the electorate at large. Witness the promises to ease the lives of the middle class that are now a routine part of presidential campaigns. This trend is reflected in the striking changes that have taken place in the obligation to pay federal income taxes. In 2000, *before* the first George W. Bush tax cuts took effect, 25.2 percent of those filing federal income-tax returns had no tax liability. By 2007, that figure had risen to 43.4 percent. Over the same period, the share of income-tax receipts contributed by the wealthiest 1 percent increased from 20.8 to 40.4 percent. So much for the notorious tax cuts for the rich.

These costly distortions of the original constitutional plan need to be reversed. But how do we go about it? How do we wean the public of the illusion that money that comes from Washington is somehow free? My recitation of the costs of doing things Washington's way is hardly new. The problem has been that too few Americans have been sufficiently aware of the profound changes that have taken place in how we govern ourselves. Call it the frog-in-a-pot-of-slowly-warming-water phenomenon: until very recently, the increases in economic and other regulations, the intrusions on the authority of state and local governments, have been too gradual to alarm the public at large.

Fortunately (if that is the proper word!), the excesses of the Obama administration may have turned the heat up fast enough to ignite a public rebellion against the dramatic expansion of federal power that is now occurring. In its first year in office, the administration persuaded Congress to enact a $787-billion stimulus package that to date has stimulated little more than a growth in government jobs; took over two car companies and a fistful of banks; nationalized large segments of our health-care system; and launched programs that will increase our national debt from 40 percent of our gross domestic product to a projected 80 percent within the next ten years. This should be shock therapy enough to induce the American people to return to constitutional virtue, and there are signs that that might in fact be happening—witness a mid-2009 poll of independent voters which found that 56 percent of those polled favored "smaller government with fewer services," three times the number who had held that position just one year earlier. A mid-2010 poll of likely voters found 63 percent holding that position.

I am not such a romantic as to believe that we can return to the division of governmental labors that obtained even fifty years ago. Too many federal programs are too deeply imbedded in our society, and too many institutional adjustments have been made to accommodate them. What we can do is consciously establish strict standards for the adoption of new federal initiatives, standards based on the spirit if not the letter of the Constitution. In the first instance, we must call a halt to all new grants-in-aid programs and then see which of the existing ones we can pare away. By definition, these do not relate to national imperatives, because the states retain the option of declining them. In the second instance, before Congress adopts a new program that is within the competence of state governments, we must require that it first explain why the program must be of universal application.

To illustrate how these standards would work in practice, I cite two relatively recent expansions of federal authority. Washington's assumption of responsibility for the environment clearly meets the test. Air, water, and wildlife move across state boundaries, acid emissions generated by industrial plants in the Midwest will kill fish in New England lakes, and the conversion of Carolina wetlands into trailer parks can affect fisheries up and down the Atlantic coast. On the other hand, George W. Bush's "No Child Left Behind" program and earlier interventions into the field of education by previous administrations are out of bounds. As bad as too many of our public schools are, they clearly fall within the competence of state and local officials; and, although that point alone is sufficient to rule out federal intervention, there is no reason to believe Washington can do a better job of managing the schools: witness the District of Columbia school system, for which the federal government is constitutionally responsible.

My proposed reform, therefore, would retain federal responsibility for the health of the environment, but it would shutter the Department of Education. The weeding out of unwarranted federal programs, of course, can't be accomplished overnight. Phasing out the myriad grants-in-aid programs, for example, will take time because of the commitments that state and local governments have been required to make in order to qualify for federal dollars. This must be done, however, if we are to restore to state and local governments the autonomy and authority they need to deal with their own responsibilities in their own ways, and if we are to free the federal government to concentrate on concerns that require attention at the national level.

The argument will be made that many of these programs are justified because poorer states don't have the resources to provide their citizens with the level of services that every American ought to have. Education and welfare will be cited as examples. If this is indeed true (and we should note, for example, that the amount of money spent per student is an uncertain measure of educational quality), and if the need to help the poorest states provide these services can be considered a legitimate national obligation, there is a far better approach to that problem than the creation of federal education, welfare, or whatever programs that are imposed on all the states, rich or poor. My brother William F. Buckley Jr. had the answer to that problem in a book, *Four Reforms*, that was published in 1973. In it he suggested that the efficient way to meet those objectives would be through a system of block grants limited to the have-not states. The only requirement would be that those funds be used for the broad purposes (education, welfare, etc.) for which the grants were made. Under this approach, Washington would not be telling the recipients how to educate their citizens or how to look after their needy—in short, would not be telling them how to meet their own responsibilities under the Constitution. Nor could it use the presumed needs of the poorer states to impose federal regulations on the wealthier states, which have the resources to meet the needs of their own citizens.

The problem with this proposal is that Congress finds it almost impossible to dispense funds without encumbering them with detailed instructions on how they are to be used. I say "almost" because in 1972 Congress initiated a "revenue sharing" program in which grants with minimal strings attached were made to states and localities, rich and poor alike. But these represented only a tiny portion of federal transfers to the states, and the program has since been discarded. Revenue sharing was a nod to the spirit of federalism, but no more than that.

A return to federalism, of course, won't guarantee that we will end up with less intrusive, less costly government, because states are quite capable of smothering their citizens (and economies) with expensive care. What it will do is enable the people of each state to determine for themselves whether the benefits of particular programs warrant their cost. In making those judgments, they will have the advantage of being able to compare the results of their state's initiatives with those of others. And if they make those comparisons, they might ask why the most politically conservative states had the lowest rates of unemployment during the 2008–09 recession, or why the wealthiest, most heavily taxed, and most liberal ones, such as New York, New Jersey, and Connecticut, should have suffered such devastating deficits. They might also compare different approaches to health-care reform, such as Indiana's health-savings-account option for state employees, Texas's curbs on tort-litigation recoveries, and Massachusetts's mandatory insurance requirements, to see which best serves the cause of affordable health care. If they decide that the human and financial costs of their own programs are unacceptable, it will be far easier for them to modify those state programs than to secure a revision of the federal rule book.

But it will take more than a return to federalism to safeguard our individual freedoms. In the first and last analysis, this requires that our people continue to prize their liberties, continue to assume responsibility for their own well-being, continue to understand (as recent polls indicate a majority of them still do) that a more limited, frugal government is in the public interest as well as in their own. Unfortunately, however, the siren song of "entitlement" is having its effects. That Americans believe they have a right to promised Social Security benefits is understandable, because they have been required to pay into the system throughout their working lives. But too many are beginning to believe they have a right to have government provide a buffer against the vicissitudes of life that earlier generations believed it was their own responsibility to cope with.

The rights guaranteed by the Bill of Rights all take the form of limitations on government action: Congress is forbidden to pass any law that will infringe on our rights to express our views, to worship as we please, to enjoy the privacy of our homes. Today, however, there is a tendency to conjure up new rights that add up to a right to pick one's neighbors' pockets. I witnessed that mindset on a recent trip in Alaska. During a discussion of health care, a bright young naturalist remarked that he had chosen a low-paying profession, the implication being that because he had elected to earn less than he was capable of doing, he had a right to expect others to help him pay his medical bills.

My healthy young friend's concern over the cost of his future care is hardly an isolated one. Although most Americans were satisfied with their own medical insurance, the escalating cost of the same and the fact that a significant proportion of our population is uninsured placed the issue at the top of the 2009–10 political agenda. As is all too typical these days, the cures offered by President Obama and enacted by Congress focus on further government interventions in the medical marketplace rather than on getting rid of impediments to the free-market competition that could bring us more effective care at a lower cost. As such, they provide insights into the political class's approach to a problem.

This one began with a particularly unfortunate unintended consequence of World War II's wage controls. Industries competing for labor were not allowed to do so by offering higher pay, but they were permitted to sweeten the employment pie with fringe benefits. The cost of these benefits was deductible in computing the employer's taxes, but, for reasons unfathomable, it was not treated as income in computing the beneficiaries' taxes. This was the reason American companies began to purchase health insurance for their employees. And so today, 61 percent of working Americans have employer-provided health insurance. But because the users of the policies haven't purchased them themselves and have no incentive to shop around for the most economical medical services when they need them, the insurers who create health-insurance packages and the professionals who deliver medical services are not subject to the competitive pressures that bring about greater efficiency and lower prices.

To compound the injury, state governments have been in the habit of requiring policies to cover more and more procedures, many of them discretionary, thus adding to the cost of insurance while denying their citizens the right to purchase more reasonably priced policies that may be available in other states. So instead of harnessing the efficiency of the marketplace by converting the cost of employer-provided policies into extra pay and allowing individuals to buy their own medical insurance and deduct the cost in calculating their personal income taxes, instead of allowing them to purchase policies offered in any state, and instead of approaching reform in stages so that we might assess how each worked in practice, the political class's answer to our medical problems was to extend federal regulation over the entire field—with the horrendous unintended consequences that will inevitably occur when the federal government takes over one-sixth of the economy in a single act of legislative and executive hubris.

Where the marketplace *has* been allowed to work is in the development of medical devices and pharmaceuticals. As a consequence, and in part because the top individual tax rates have been low enough to provide incentives for the very substantial risks that entrepreneurs must be prepared to take to bring new medical technology and medicines to the market, the United States has been producing the lion's share of the innovations that have transformed medical care here and around the world. Yet Congress has chosen to help pay for its trillion-dollar health-care bill by imposing higher taxes on the medical industry and on the individuals who help to finance it.

We won't be able to bring our expanding administrative state under control and avoid national bankruptcy until the American people insist that we do so. This requires that our citizens rediscover that the price of cradle-to-grave security is the ultimate erosion of their freedoms. This is the hard lesson that history has to teach. When I contemplate current trends, I am haunted by Edward Gibbon's description of democracy's demise in ancient Athens:

> In the end, more than they wanted freedom, they wanted security. They wanted a comfortable life and they lost it all—security, comfort, and freedom. When the Athenians finally wanted not to give to society, but for society to give

to them, when the freedom they wished for was freedom from responsibility, then Athens ceased to be free and was never free again.

It was this experience, and that of countless other failed democracies, that the architects of the American Republic took into account in writing their "auxiliary precautions" into the Constitution. They were not ivory-tower theorists. Rather, they had scrutinized the historical record and knew that the one constant in human affairs is human nature itself, and that, left unchecked, its drives and weaknesses will inevitably undermine free institutions. They gave us a Constitution designed to contain those destructive impulses, a governmental structure that remains as applicable to today's world as it was to theirs.

I pray that Gibbon's epitaph will never be read over the American Republic, but time is running out. What we desperately need today is the leadership to focus our people's attention on the consequences of the present drift. I am convinced that a majority of Americans remain capable of understanding what is at stake, and the success of Newt Gingrich's "Contract with America" in bringing about the Republican revolution of 1994 demonstrates that that understanding can be translated into effective political action. Unfortunately, once in power, the Republican congressional majorities fell victim to the seductions of office and betrayed their own revolution. But if an indulgent Providence gives us another chance—and President Obama and the congressional leadership may have unwittingly hastened that possibility through their arrogant overreaching—perhaps the next time reformers gain control they will have learned from this very recent history.

There are signs that that may prove to be the case. The tea-party phenomenon and the polls suggest that a significant number of Americans now understand both the seriousness and the nature of the threat to their freedoms, and that they are determined to do something about it. In a very few years, we will know whether they have succeeded—or whether we have slipped irretrievably into the suffocating embrace of an all-caring state, with all that that implies.

In the meantime, we can take comfort from the old saying that God takes care of fools, drunks, and the United States of America.

In Sum:
A Political Credo

The following is taken from a statement I issued during my failed bid for re-election to the Senate in 1976. If I were issuing it today, I would modify it in only one respect. I would revise the second sentence to suggest that today's ideologues are reluctant to allow Americans to make even the most trivial decisions affecting their lives.

For too many years, the ideologues in Washington have been in the driver's seat. They don't believe that free men and women can be trusted to govern themselves, and so they insist that the truly important decisions be moved as far away from the people as possible. These are the ideologues who for years have been imposing their goals, their priorities on the people of New York.

I believe that New Yorkers can be trusted to run their own affairs through the levels of government that are closest to them.

I believe that the free-enterprise system, operating in freedom and without the shackles of over-regulation from Washington, can do what it has done: create more jobs and prosperity and comfort and individual happiness than any other economic system in the world.

I believe that the controls we are most in need of in Washington are controls on the bureaucracy's desire to control our lives.

I believe that we cannot afford one penny less for defense than the amount required to maintain our unquestioned ability to protect our legitimate interests wherever they are challenged.

I believe that our commitment to the proposition that all men are created equal is a commitment to the equal dignity and equal rights of each American as an individual, and not as a member of one sex or the other, or of one category or another.

I believe that the United States Constitution, with its principle of federalism designed to prevent a concentration of power in a central government and its Bill of Rights designed to protect the individual against the abuse of government power, remains the best protection of our freedoms.

I believe, finally, that in a free society, the role of government is to serve, not to rule.

GOVERNANCE

The *American Heritage Dictionary* defines "governance" as "the act, process, or power of governing; government." While most of what follows falls within that definition, I have stretched it to include ruminations on the role of families and communities in shaping individuals for responsible citizenship in a self-governing society.

On Becoming a United States Senator

The following article first appeared in the February 2, 1973, issue of National Review. *After it had been reprinted under the title of "Notes of an Earnest Freshman" (I fear I was), I received a note from Senator Hubert Humphrey of Minnesota, who was kind enough to call it "one of the most revealing and frank commentaries on the Senate and what happens in that august body that I've ever read."*

On January 20, 1971, Jacob Javits, pursuant to custom, escorted me down the center aisle of the United States Senate chamber. Vice President Agnew swore me in, and I was handed a pen, with which I entered my name in the books of the Senate. I then walked a few steps to my desk on the Republican side of the aisle. I had become the Junior Senator from the State of New York. Or, as senatorial courtesy puts it, the distinguished and honorable Senator from the great State of New York.

Rarely has anyone, distinguished and honorable or otherwise, entered the United States Senate so innocent of the mechanisms of a legislative body or of the impact of politics on the legislative process. Prior to my election, I had never held public office or participated in any organized political effort other than the third-party mayoralty and senatorial campaigns of the brothers Buckley.

Shortly after my election, Clif White, my campaign manager and guide to the political world, organized a private dinner with a few of the senior Republican senators so that I might acquire a better feel for the life I was about to enter. I had hoped to get specific advice on how to go about the job of being an effective senator. What I got instead were affable assurances to the effect that anyone capable of winning election to the Senate would find no difficulty in getting along once in it. This was all, in its own way, reassuring; but I did not emerge from the dinner with the mother lode of hard, practical information that would help me to thread my way through the complexities of senatorial life.

The first formal business for a senator-elect is the meeting with the sergeant at arms and the secretary of the Senate, who give you the basic housekeeping instructions, take sample signatures for franking privileges, and explain a senator's insurance and retirement benefits. I also learned where I would stand in the Senate pecking order. I would rank ninety-ninth, because I had no prior service as a congressman or governor, which is taken into account in the calculation of seniority. (I beat out Lawton Chiles of Florida because New York has the larger population.) At that meeting I was presented with three books: *The Rules and Manual of the United States Senate*; an exegesis thereof by the chief parliamentarian, Dr. Floyd Riddick; and the *Congressional Directory* for the second session of the prior Congress. I was determined to spend the next few weeks mastering the parliamentary rules, but I was soon bogged down in their intricacy. To my relief, however, I quickly learned that the Senate operates in a reasonably free and tolerant manner, and that much of its business is conducted not by the rule book but by continuing recourse to unanimous-consent agreements. Those who do know the rule book, however, are equipped, at critical moments, to take the parliamentary advantage.

New senators learn that they are expected to carry the principal burden of presiding over the Senate. For someone like me, who had never presided over any official function or even read *Robert's Rules of Order*, the prospect seemed ominous. It isn't all that difficult, however, because sitting immediately in front of the Chair is one of the three parliamentarians, who whispers up the appropriate instruction. The most difficult task is to learn the identity of eighty or ninety brand-new faces, together with state of origin, so that one can recognize the Senator from Such-and-Such without any obvious fumbling.

During this orientation period, I introduced myself to the Senate Republican leadership—to Minority Leader Hugh Scott, Minority Whip Bob Griffin, Chairman Gordon Allott of the Republican Policy Committee, and Chairman Margaret Chase Smith of the Republican Conference.

One important call was at the office of Senator Wallace Bennett, chairman of the Republican Committee on Committees, in order to learn how committee assignments were made and to register my preferences. The process is in fact mechanical. Once the majority and minority vacancies on the various committees become known, the members of each party in the incoming class line up in order of seniority to take their pick. Each senator is appointed to two major committees, and often to one or more minor ones. My own initial assignments were to Public Works, Space, and the District of Columbia.

It was in committee work that I first came to appreciate the enormous volume of business that courses through Congress, and its implications. It is not unusual to find meetings or hearings involving as many as three committees or subcommittees of which one is a member scheduled for the same time, each involving business of some importance. A senator either spreads himself thin by putting in token appearances at each or devotes himself to one meeting, relying on overworked staff members to keep abreast of what is going on in the other two. I have yet to be convinced that there isn't somewhere in the bowels of the Capitol a computer programmed to arrange as many conflicting meetings as possible.

The committee system constitutes a delegation of responsibility for legislative work in designated areas. It should not be assumed, however, that a given committee will be representative of the Senate as a whole. Senators naturally tend to gravitate to those committees that interest them the most or whose work is most important to their particular constituencies, and a committee can become as "mission oriented" as an executive agency. Given the broad range of viewpoints represented on each side of the aisle, the requirement that each committee have a majority and minority membership roughly comparable to that of the Senate as a whole is no guarantee that it will reflect the political spectrum in any other sense. Thus committee reports are too often "selling documents" that do not provide other senators with the kind of balanced information that would be needed to help them reach a reasonably educated opinion regarding a bill's merits.

It isn't long—especially if controversial and complex legislation is being worked on—before a newcomer senses the enormous influence wielded by committee staffs. These are usually heavily loaded in favor of the majority party in terms of both outlook and availability to committee members. Time and again, after new points are raised in committee, the staff will disappear, to return the next day with what is often a considerably refocused bit of legislation.

It can be extraordinarily difficult for committee members, even those who are particularly concerned with the legislation in question, to keep up with what is happening to it. There simply isn't time for a member to rethink and reconsider every interlocking provision of a complex bill each time a substantive change is made; hence the heavy reliance on staff. Furthermore, committees often work under enormous pressures to report out particular pieces of legislation by deadlines that are often set not so much by the natural rhythm of the legislative process as by political considerations.

Thus major legislation is often rushed through committee, reported out on the floor of the Senate, and put to a vote with few senators fully understanding it. It is, in fact, virtually impossible for a senator to keep up with most, let alone all, of the significant legislation being considered by committees other than his own. I do not refer to legislation that grabs the headlines and occasions national debate: a senator has to examine such legislation in some detail if only to answer his mail and reply to reporters' questions. It is, after all, by his positions on conspicuous legislation that he establishes his political identity.

Most of the bills considered by the Senate are relatively inconspicuous, though by no means unimportant. They may establish new programs that will have an enormous impact on American society, on the states, or on the economy; programs that in time may grow into multi-billion-dollar commitments. Yet many of these bills will be enacted with little real examination by most of the senators who will have to vote yea or nay on them, and with less than adequate comprehension of what such bills involve.

A senator simply does not have sufficient legislative help to get a proper analysis of every bill that issues from the legislative mill. Too many bills are called to a vote before the ink has dried on the explanatory report. Thus, all too often a senator's vote is based simply on a summary description of the bill (which can be totally inadequate), plus whispered conversations with colleagues who may or may not have detailed information as to its content—all in the fifteen-minute period allowed for voting after the bells have started ringing to summon him to the floor.

Technically speaking, any senator can ensure that adequate time is allowed for debate of any bill. He can simply register his refusal to sign on to a unanimous-consent agreement limiting the time allotted for debate. This presupposes, however, that he has had enough advance warning of the particular mischief at hand to record a timely objection to any agreement to which he is not a party. It also presupposes that he will be able to educate and energize a sufficient number of his all-too-preoccupied colleagues to assure himself of sufficient floor support to make the effort worthwhile.

I recall two cases in my own experience—although there are, unfortunately, many more—that dramatize the pressures under which the Senate operates.

In early 1971, Governor Daniel Evans of Washington suggested the need for legislation to cope with economic disasters, similar to existing legislation designed to cope with natural disasters. The law he proposed would be narrow in its focus, providing relief on a short-term, emergency basis to help communities ride out sudden economic catastrophes.

Two bills incorporating this approach were introduced, and hearings on them were held by the Public Works Committee. Several months later, the committee met in executive session to consider the legislation as revised by staff after the hearings. To the astonishment of at least some members, the draft bill differed in fundamental respects from both of the measures that had been introduced. The basic concept had shifted drastically. Instead of a tightly focused bill to bring maximum effort to bear on specific emergency situations, it had become an amorphous one that would also cover areas of chronic unemployment or chronically low economic activity, for which there already existed thirty or forty other federal programs. The definition of areas that could be eligible for relief under the legislation was such that even a neighborhood could qualify for the most exotic kinds of federal help.

Nevertheless, this basically new legislation was approved in a single day by the full committee and reported out. The legislation was then rushed to the floor of the Senate, debated before a largely empty chamber, and put to a vote—all within a day or two of the time printed copies of the bill and of the accompanying committee report had become available to the senators. This legislation opened up a whole new area of federal intervention. It carried no price tag, and it was approved by senators only a few of whom had any grasp of its scope.

The second example concerned a new program of a truly sweeping nature that was enacted by an overwhelming majority of senators, many of whom I am convinced had little understanding of the real issues involved. Just before the August recess in 1971, the Committee on Labor and Public Welfare reported out a measure innocuously titled "A Bill to Extend the Economic Opportunity Act of 1968 and Other Purposes." The "other purposes" turned out to be the inauguration of a comprehensive federal program for "child development" services designed ultimately to embrace a very large proportion of pre-school-aged children regardless of financial need. Whereas in its first year the new program would cost a mere $100 million (chicken feed these days), the committee report placed the figure for the second year at $2 billion—an amount significantly greater than the projected cost of all the rest of the Office of Economic Opportunity's activities. Furthermore, the report stated that the cost of the child-development program would double every two years thereafter for some time hence. Secretary of Health, Education, and Welfare Elliot Richardson estimated that the annual cost of the new program would come to $20 billion before the end of the decade.

Thanks to an interested housewife who had followed the progress of the bill in committee, my office was alerted to its implications. Because of the recess, we had time to examine its horrors, and I was in a position to argue, on the basis of expert opinion, against the child-development section. The bill, however, had been scheduled as the first order of business on the day Congress returned and was to be voted on in the Senate the next day, "other purposes" and all. As a consequence, there was little opportunity to educate my colleagues about those "other purposes."

Any senators who happened to be on the floor to hear the debate would have learned that there was substantial controversy among professionals over the child-development section, a fact they would not have discovered from reading the committee report. They would have learned that a number of experts questioned the need for such a vast undertaking and, in fact, warned that permanent harm could be done to younger children placed in the impersonal "warehouse" environment of the kind of day-care facility that was apt to result from the legislation. They would have learned also that the expert opinion heard in committee was entirely one-sided; and that even among the experts who favored the program, one had remarked that its far-reaching provisions would revolutionize the concept of the family in American life.

Unfortunately, almost no one besides the sponsors of the bill and the two or three senators arguing for the elimination or modification of the child-development section was on hand to hear the debate. Thus, when the time came to vote, most senators voted aye on the assumption that nothing significant was involved in the bill beyond a simple two-year extension of existing OEO programs. (This bill was later vetoed by President Nixon.)

This rush to enact legislation with little or no time allowed for pause, thought, or deliberation brings to mind another aspect of the Senate's current way of conducting its affairs. I speak of the phenomenon of the amendment—printed or unprinted—offered from the floor with little or no notice. Amendments can range from purely technical corrections of the statutory language to the most far-reaching changes in the legislation under consideration.

There is usually little check on the scope of amendments that can be offered from the floor, and no opportunity for the relevant committees and their staffs to study them so that some measure of expert analysis might be brought to bear in arguing their merits for the benefit of the Senate as a whole—always assuming that other senators are on hand to hear the debate. Thus all too often, especially when the Senate is operating under unanimous-consent agreements severely limiting the time for debate, amendments are apt to be adopted or rejected on the basis of their emotional or political appeal. So it was with the amendments that in October 1972 added $4 billion, or more than 27 percent, to the cost of the Welfare/Social Security bill reported out by the Senate Finance Committee; and with the amendments that added, in one day's time the previous June, almost $2 billion to the HEW/Labor appropriations bill. Surely there is a better way to conduct the nation's vital legislative business short of the highly restrictive rules that obtain in the House.

All of which brings me to certain observations about the Senate today.

At the root of most of the problems with the Senate is the enormous expansion of federal activities in recent years. A recent study by the Association of the Bar of the City of New York found that the workload of members of Congress had doubled every five years since 1935. Congress is simply trying to handle more business than it can manage. The results too often are waste, conflicts, inconsistencies, and superficiality.

Once upon a time Congress was in session only six or seven months a year. There is every reason to believe that during those months there was time and opportunity to think, to study, to argue, and to come to educated conclusions. As the volume of work increased, Congress was at first able to cope by extending the length of its sessions. But now, as a result of the explosion of federal activity resulting from the War on Poverty and other programs established in the 1960s, it is conceded that Congress is in session essentially on a year-round basis. And even with the increased length of congressional sessions, senators, as I have outlined above, have more legislation to consider in any given week than they can possibly digest.

One consequence of these increasing demands on senators' time is that it can no longer be said of the Senate that it is a club, exclusive or otherwise. Not so many years ago, members were able to spend unhurried time together, to get to know one another and develop a sense of fraternity while working towards common goals in a highly civil environment. I do not mean to suggest that all of this has disappeared. Real friendships and a sense of belonging do develop. But the sense of community that must once have existed has certainly been dissipated by the preoccupations that tend to keep senators concentrating on their own separate concerns except as their work requires them to come together. It is difficult, in fact, to come to know members of the opposition party who do not happen to serve on one's committees.

Whether the situation can be changed, only time and a differently constituted Congress will tell. But even assuming that the volume of business can be held at present levels, there remains the fact that each senator has only so many hours per day to devote to his job. A senator must be able not only to bring effective judgment to bear on his legislative duties, but also to maintain contact with his own constituency so as to find out what are the real problems people are faced with, and what are the real effects of the legislation he has helped enact.

All this, in turn, requires adequate staff and office space. Mundane as these considerations may seem, staffing and space can become important factors in determining just how good a job a senator is going to be able to do.

A new senator from a state like New York quickly learns that the Senate places great emphasis on the equal sovereign dignity of each individual state, which is a polite way of saying that when it comes to allocating rooms and funds, senators from the largest states invariably feel shortchanged. It should be kept in mind that the volume of work that must be handled by a senator's office depends significantly on the size of his constituency. I speak of answering mail and addressing constituents' problems (the so-called case work), which have been increasing at an enormous rate as the federal government has intruded more and more into its citizens' lives.

Case work involves such things as assisting with immigration problems, chasing down Social Security checks, helping municipalities process their applications for this or that program, helping businesses thread their way through red tape—you name it. While the office workload for a senator from New York may not be sixty times as heavy as that for a senator from Alaska, it is significantly more than two or three times as heavy. Yet when I entered the Senate in 1971, the smallest number of rooms assigned to any senator was five and the largest (for California and New York), seven. As I started out with a staff of thirty-five and needed one room for myself, this created a degree of congestion. In like manner, my allowance for hiring staff was less than twice the allowance for the smallest state. It is of course true that each senator bears an equal legislative responsibility and needs equal facilities to keep track of legislative matters and to help him do his individual and committee work. But this doesn't explain the disparity (or lack thereof) in space and staff allowances. In my own case, for example, staff members directly involved in legislative matters are less than one-fifth of the total.

Committee problems, time problems, space problems . . . it would seem from my descriptions that a senator's lot is not entirely a happy one. There are, of course, compensations, not the least of which is the pervasive air of civility and mutual respect with which the business of the Senate is conducted. But even the extraordinary civility and respect that are the hallmarks of the institution cannot overcome organizational and structural complexities that make a difficult job even more difficult.

I have often been asked whether I find my work in the Senate frustrating, and whether I have had any surprises. I have not found the work particularly frustrating, because I had few illusions as to what a very junior member of the minority party could accomplish on his own. Nor have I experienced any really major surprises, although I was not at all prepared for the enormous demands that would be made on my time, seven days a week, or for my loss of anonymity (the unsurprising result of six hundred or so thousand well-deployed dollars spent on television advertising during my campaign, reinforced by periodic meetings with the press).

Early on, I was struck by the number of extracurricular demands on a senator's time, especially for one who lives as close to millions of constituents as does a senator from New York: invitations to speak which for one good reason or another cannot be declined; ceremonial visits; people with problems whom one must see oneself and cannot refer to staff; people in the federal government one needs to get to know; and so on. The day is splintered into all kinds of pieces, even before the business of legislative work begins.

One thing that in my innocence I had not anticipated was the intensely political atmosphere that prevails within the Senate, the great impact of purely political considerations on specific actions taken by individual senators. It may well be, of course, that mine was an unusual introduction to the institution, as at least a half-dozen of my colleagues were beginning to jockey for position in the presidential race within months of when I was sworn in. This had an inevitable influence on how they orchestrated their performance in the Senate. Also there was the fact that both houses of Congress were controlled by one party and the White House by the other; and as the presidential primaries approached, the political atmosphere palpably intensified.

But these unusual considerations notwithstanding, I soon learned that many senators tend to cast their votes with a view towards minimizing future political controversy or embarrassment. When a senator's vote is clearly not critical to the fate of a bill, it is often deployed for future political convenience on the ground that it "wouldn't count anyway." Thus the Senate vote will often be quite lopsided on questions on which public opinion and the real opinion within the Senate are much more evenly divided.

This protecting of political flanks may seem harmless enough, but it vitiates what I believe should be an important educational function of the Senate. If citizens see that members of that body have voted overwhelmingly in favor of this or that piece of legislation, many who are not entirely certain of their own grounds for opposing it may decide that they have in fact been wrong, or backward, or insensitive. Yet if on such issues each member of the Senate had voted his true convictions, the breakdown might have been, say, fifty-five to forty-five instead of seventy to thirty. I can't help but wonder to what extent this form of political expediency may affect the public's perception of the issues.

There may be another reason why the opinion of the Senate—even when accurately recorded—is very often at odds with what I, at least, take to be the current mood of the American people. Without having researched the point, I suspect that the Senate incorporates a cultural lag of ten or fifteen years; that it is out of phase with the people by a period approximately equivalent to the average tenure of its membership.

A decade or so ago, the Senate was considered by some to be a backward, conservative body whose Republican–Southern Democrat coalition lay athwart progress and the will of the people. Others viewed it as a necessary brake on the rasher impulses of the House of Representatives. Today the situation is quite the reverse. The liberals are clearly in the majority in the Senate, and they do not reflect the growing public skepticism about federal initiatives; and it is the House that tends to blow the whistle on the excessive spending approved by the Senate.

If I am right about this cultural lag, there is a reason for it. A member of the House of Representatives is up for election every two years and thus needs to keep abreast of the views of his constituency. Also, because each member of the House represents a relatively compact area, his constituency tends to be more homogeneous than a senator's, and there is less of an impulse to cater to the fringe groups within it. A member of the Senate, on the other hand, represents an entire state, incorporating a multitude of conflicting claims and interests. For better or for worse (I suspect the latter) a senator tends to pay a disproportionate amount of attention to the loudest voices—editorial writers, television commentators, pressure groups. Furthermore, once in office, he is there for at least six years. Thus a senator may be less sensitive than a representative to basic shifts in the underlying mood of the electorate as a whole.

I make this comment by way of observation and not of criticism. The Founding Fathers intended, after all, that the Senate be a balance wheel that would moderate the impulses of the moment. This function it in fact performs, even though at any given time those who believe that the current impulses are the correct ones may tend to impatience. The Senate, however, is not an institution to which the impatient should gravitate. It has its own pace; and, under the present rules, it takes a little maturing on the vine of seniority to be in a position to have a large impact on the institution.

It would be inaccurate, however, and unfair to suggest that the newest members are without the power to do more than register their 1 percent of the Senate's total vote. The ancient tradition that freshman senators were to be seen and not heard has disappeared. Somewhat to my surprise, on my initial rounds I was encouraged by senior members to speak out when I felt I had learned the ropes and had something to say—which was not, I hasten to say, an invitation to be brash.

In point of fact, I soon learned that there are a number of ways in which even Number 99 can make his imprint on the law. If he is willing to do the necessary homework on the bills before his committee, if he attends meetings, if he presents arguments for or against specific provisions, he does have a chance to mold their final form. I have found that my own views will be given as careful a hearing as those of any other member of the committees on which I have served; again, the essential courtesy of the Senate comes to the fore. It is also possible, by submitting appropriate amendments, to shape legislation after it has reached the floor.

It will also occasionally be the lot of a senator to come across an idea of such universal appeal that it will whisk through the legislative process in record time; witness two bills I introduced involving certain benefits for prisoners of war and those missing in action in Indochina. Each immediately attracted more than sixty co-sponsors, and each has since been signed into law.

Finally, there are the educational opportunities that the Senate opens up even to the newest of senators. These had not occurred to me when I first decided to run for office, but it did not take long for me to appreciate the skill with which some of the more liberal members were utilizing their office to reach the public. They would schedule time on the Senate floor, often in tandem, to deliver themselves of learned or impassioned speeches to an empty chamber. Their wisdom might be wasted on the Senate air, but they were able to alert the press that Senator So-and-So would deliver remarks on such-and-such a topic at a particular time. Copies of the speech would be distributed, and the gist of the senator's argument and the points he wished to make would become part of the nation's informational bloodstream. I also noticed that conservative-minded senators were generally less alert to the possibilities presented by this exercise.

Whether utilized or not, the opportunity does exist for a senator to present his views on the important issues with some reasonable assurance that they will not be totally lost. Only by exploiting such opportunities for public education can he expect to help the electorate become more adequately informed on the basic issues. This in turn bears on the legislative process, because, in the last analysis, public opinion dictates the outside limits of the options available to Congress. By joining in the public debate and articulating the arguments in support of his own positions, a new senator—even one labeled "Conservative-Republican" (my official designation, since I was elected on the Conservative Party ticket but was accepted by the Republican caucus)—can contribute to the educational process that ultimately finds its reflection in national policy.

These, then, are the random impressions of the United States Senate by one of its newest members: It is a deliberative body in which there is too little time to deliberate. It is a place where a member is entitled to free haircuts (although he is expected to tip the barber one dollar) in a barber shop that keeps a shaving mug with his name on it. It is a place where on each desk there is a little inkwell, a wooden pen with a steel nib, and a glass bottle filled with sand with which to blot one's writing, and where on one side of the presiding officer's desk is a spittoon and on the other a box of snuff.

Yet it is also a place where the rules of civility are still observed, and the rights and independence of each individual still respected. It is a place where many of the major decisions affecting the shape of our times are made; a place where even the least of its members may have a hand in making them.

It is, all in all, a good place to be.

The one fundamental change that has occurred in the Senate since my departure more than three decades ago is the disappearance of the pervasive civility that so impressed me when I arrived there. Otherwise, the treadmill merely runs faster. Staffs have grown, but not in pace with the growth of the government agencies Congress is supposed to oversee. Major pieces of legislation now weigh in at wrist-snapping lengths of 500, 800, or even the 2,700 pages of Obamacare, and no senator will have read the entire document or the corresponding committee report before voting on it. Meanwhile, the recent tightening of campaign-finance screws has compelled senators to devote even more of their evenings and weekends to the task of raising money.

Overloading the Federal Horse

I delivered the first version of this speech towards the end of my Senate term and modified it from time to time as I gained experience in the Executive and Judicial Branches of government. Its underlying theme is that Washington, D.C., is no longer capable of truly thoughtful, effective government because it is overwhelmed with responsibilities that the Constitution had reserved to the states—and which the states are fully capable of handling. The following variation on this defense of federalism was delivered at the Northwestern University Law School in November 1990.

It has been my lot, over the past twenty years, to serve in each of the three branches of the federal government. So rather than give you a learned summary of recent trends in administrative law, I thought I would unburden myself of some observations on the institutional gridlock that is beginning to paralyze important areas of that government.

Over the years, the basic structure of our government put in place by the Founding Fathers has served us well; so well, in fact, that, in the two hundred years of its existence, we have found it unnecessary to make any significant change in its constitutional design. This is an extraordinary record of stability, and Americans have every reason to be proud of their charter; but at times they need to be reminded that it consists of more than its first ten amendments.

As is evident from recent Supreme Court confirmation hearings, there is a tendency these days to equate the Constitution with the Bill of Rights, which, however majestic an affirmation of fundamental values, is nonetheless a constitutional afterthought. The fact is that the principal concern of the Constitution's authors was with structure: how to frame a government that would be effective, but never threatening. The grand design that emerged from the constitutional debates proved a brilliant answer to the challenge that James Madison posed in the following terms: "In framing a government which is to be administered by men over men, the great difficulty lies in this: you must first enable the government to control the governed; and in the next place oblige it to control itself."

The Framers met that challenge in two ways: first, by dividing the powers delegated to the new government among three separate but equal branches; and second, by reserving to the sovereign states all authority not delegated to the national government. The first, of course, embodied the doctrine of the separation of powers; the second, the principle of federalism.

It was this last element of our constitutional design that commanded the admiration of the British historian Lord Acton. In a turn-of-the-century lecture on the American Revolution, in which he catalogued what he believed to be the Constitution's significant failings, Lord Acton nevertheless concluded that "by the development of the principle of federalism, it has produced a community more powerful, more prosperous, more intelligent, and more free than any other which the world has seen."

Two centuries have now elapsed since the Founding, and notwithstanding the jockeying that constantly occurs between the legislative and executive branches to establish which is the more equal, the separation of powers remains an integral part of our governmental system. On the other hand, the three branches of the federal government have, over the years, engaged in massive raids on the constitutional prerogatives of the states, to the point where, today, there is virtually no governmental responsibility that the Supreme Court will find beyond the reach of federal authority.

In the process, we have seen so great a transfer of power, authority, and initiative from state capitals to Washington, D.C., that the former have in many areas been reduced to the role of mere executors of federal policies. At the same time, we have so overloaded the federal horse that its ability to bear its expanded responsibilities is increasingly in doubt.

In January 1971, when I arrived in Washington as a newly elected senator, I came armed with a recent study of the inner workings of Congress. Its authors had concluded that the workload of the average congressional office had doubled every five years since 1935. Given the fact that, in simpler times, Congress worked at a leisurely pace and was in session for only six or seven months a year, its members could take the initial increases in stride simply by devoting more hours per day and more months per year to their work. Over time, however, the available hours and months were exhausted, and the increasing demands could be accommodated only by fundamental changes in the manner in which Congress went about its business. Inevitably, every new federal initiative will trigger a chain reaction of constituent questions and complaints, consultations with bureaucrats and special pleaders, and oversight hearings by an expanding number of committees and subcommittees—all at the expense of legislative quality.

I can certify that during my own six years in office, I witnessed both a sharp increase in the already frenetic pace of the Senate and an equally sharp decline in its ability to get very much done that could honestly be labeled "thoughtful." By all accounts, these two trends have continued unabated. It may well be that the Senate remains "the world's greatest deliberative body"—I can't make that judgment because I don't know enough about the others. But I believe it must be said that the Senate can no longer claim to be a *great* deliberative body, and this is no reflection on the quality of its current members. The simple fact is that their days are so fractured by competing claims on finite time that they, as well as their colleagues in the House, have too often found themselves incapable of handling many of their most fundamental obligations, such as the timely enactment of the annual appropriations required to provide for the orderly funding of the federal government's activities.

In recent years, we have seen the spectacle of Congress racing against the clock as a handful of senators and representatives patch together multi-thousand-page, mega-billion-dollar continuing resolutions that are then rushed into law, unread by their colleagues, so that the federal machinery will not grind to a complete halt. In every instance, boondoggles have later been discovered in the fine print—legislative contraband smuggled in by one or another senator or representative who could not possibly have secured its approval through open hearings and debate.

This year's protracted exercise has confirmed the worst we have come to expect. After heroic huffing and puffing, the congressional leadership managed to produce a deficit-reduction bill that increases overall spending by 8 to 10 percent despite the cuts in defense spending. And, yes, the boondoggles are still there. While it is too early to tell how many billions in pork are stashed away, preliminary digging by columnist James Jackson Kilpatrick has uncovered a $19-million appropriation to study the contribution of bovine flatulence to the greenhouse effect—yes, cows produce methane. What makes this example particularly intriguing is that the study had twice been eliminated from Senate legislation, and had not been included in any House bill. Yet the $19-million study reappeared, presumably by spontaneous generation, in the final bill that both houses rubber-stamped into law in the final hours of the 101st Congress.

While the pace and pressures of life on Capitol Hill appear to have destroyed its capacity for deliberative lawmaking, committee and subcommittee chairmen are nonetheless able to find the time to micromanage the Executive Branch's conduct of a host of federal programs and, in the case of the Senate, to convert confirmation hearings into political inquisitions.

But I am being unfair. Congress's erratic performance is to a large degree the result of a workload that has grown too great to permit either reflection or attention to detail, so it is not surprising that its members will turn instead to government by political reflex and political theater. What is clear from the experience of the past few years is that fundamental changes will have to be made before Congress can once again provide the thoughtful service the nation needs.

The problems besetting the Executive Branch are of a different order. The overloading of a legislative body will ultimately lead to paralysis, because each of its members is required, in theory if not always in practice, to reach an informed judgment on each item of business to come before it for a vote. Yet there is a limit to the number of issues an individual can master at any one time. By contrast, in the Executive Branch, new office space can be built and new staffs hired to handle new or expanded responsibilities. At a certain point, however, the proliferation of programs will outstrip the ability of any president to provide the bureaus and agencies under his titular control with meaningful direction.

Today, the sheer size of the federal establishment defies coherent oversight. To compound a president's problems, Congress has entrusted the management of a host of executive responsibilities to bureaus and agencies that together form a de facto fourth branch of government. These are staffed by essentially irremovable civil servants who exercise enormous influence over just about every facet of American life. And as a practical matter, they operate largely beyond the reach of even the most determined president.

Even in the case of cabinet departments headed by his own appointees, a president is apt to face almost insurmountable problems in getting his programs implemented. White House policy directives have a way of disappearing into bureaucratic black holes, and the cabinet secretaries themselves are often so caught up in detail that they lose sight of some of their administration's most pressing goals.

A president, of course, is still free to exercise energetic leadership during periods of international crisis. The fact remains, however, that, like Congress, the Executive Branch is experiencing its own institutional gridlock. No matter how large his margin of victory, the most a new president can expect in four or even eight years in office is to nibble away at the edges of his agenda.

The third branch has not fared so badly, even though litigation in federal courts has become one of the great growth industries of the past twenty-five years. Thanks to the proliferation of federal laws and regulations, the continuing discovery of hitherto-unsuspected constitutional rights, and the disposition of Americans to have a court decide almost any dispute, the number of appeals filed in federal courts has skyrocketed from 3,900 in 1962 to 37,000 in 1987. [*By 2009, they had risen to 57,740.*] The ninefold increase has had its inevitable impact on both the workload and the quality of the work of federal appellate judges, whose numbers have only doubled over the same period.

Nevertheless—and there are those who would consider this a very mixed blessing—the judiciary appears to have suffered neither gridlock nor paralysis. In a sense, the federal judiciary has proven a prime beneficiary of the expansion of federal authority. Thanks to the exploding body of law federal judges are called upon to decipher and apply, they are exercising more power today than could ever have been imagined two hundred years ago; and some are exercising it in remarkably creative ways. Take, for example, the federal district judge who, among other things, ordered a school district in Kansas City, Missouri, to build indoor Olympic-sized swimming pools, operate a twenty-five-acre farm, and install greenhouses and amphitheaters; the judge then directed the district to increase its tax rates to help pay for it all.

Whatever complaints one may lay at the feet of federal courts these days, judicial paralysis is certainly not one of them. On the contrary, the focus of the current debate is over judicial activism. One observation I would make on this prickly subject is that to the degree that federal judges treat the Constitution as no more than a repository of values to be applied without reference to original meaning, to that degree do they undercut the legitimacy of judicial review in the constitutional arena. Instead of interpreting laws, they dispense them.

In *Marbury* v. *Madison*, John Marshall asserted the Supreme Court's right to invalidate an act of Congress by affirming that the Constitution was "superior, paramount law," and that "it is emphatically the province and duty of the judicial department to say what the law is." Thus, when the Court concludes that the Constitution and an act of Congress are in conflict, the latter must yield. This seems to me a rather straightforward proposition: The Constitution is law, and, like any other law, it has a meaning that judges are trained to ascertain and apply.

I find it hard, therefore, to reconcile John Marshall's approach with that suggested by Justice Brennan in a 1985 address at Georgetown University. On that occasion he observed that "the genius of the Constitution rests not in any static meaning it might have had in a world that is dead and gone, but in the adaptability of its great principles to cope with current problems and current needs." He stated that "The act of interpretation must be undertaken with full consciousness that it is, in a very real sense, the community's interpretation that is sought." This statement, it seems to me, begs the question of a Supreme Court justice's competence to speak for the community at large.

Justice Brennan also spoke of the Bill of Rights as "a sparkling vision of the supremacy of the human dignity of every individual," and stated that it is the function of federal courts to bring that vision to full fruition in the light of "the evolution of our concepts of human dignity." Once again, I am troubled by his implicit assumptions. On the matter of capital punishment, for example, Justice Brennan acknowledged that his own views were shared by neither a majority of the Court nor a majority of his fellow countrymen. Nonetheless, he asserted that "On this issue, the death penalty, I hope to embody a community striving for human dignity for all, although perhaps not yet arrived." Thus Justice Brennan seems to be saying that he found the authority for his votes on this issue—and, one wonders, on how many others as well—not in the explicit language of the Constitution, nor in community sentiment, but in his own perception of what is required by an enlightened understanding of human dignity. It seems to me that this is the thinking not so much of a jurist as it is of a philosopher king.

Unfortunately, it is the unstated premise of much of the debate over recent Supreme Court nominees that Supreme Court justices *ought* to serve as philosopher kings. I submit that if the view of a judge as law*maker* is allowed to take root, we will have politicized the selection process and jeopardized the Court's independence. I fear, from the questions asked at confirmation hearings, that that process is well advanced, as a number of senators seem far more interested in how the nominee might vote on politically sensitive issues than in how he would approach the task of determining what vote the Constitution requires.

This is about as far as I can appropriately go in dealing with the judiciary, so let me return to the problems I see facing the Legislative and Executive Branches. Here, I must confess, I am profoundly worried. I believe that at the national level, we are rapidly losing our capacity for effective government: government in which politically difficult decisions can still be made, problems thought through to ultimate solutions, and long-term commitments undertaken in the confidence that they will be honored; government in which each branch will respect the prerogatives of the others and understand the limits of its own.

As the problems afflicting both Congress and the Executive are essentially structural, they are not prone to easy solution. There are no doubt many causes of the paralysis I see creeping over Washington, but I feel by far the most significant of these has been the virtual abandonment of the principle of federalism. Accordingly, I believe the surest road to true reform is to rediscover and reapply that principle, and, in that way, to reduce the scope of federal responsibilities to manageable size.

I do not suggest that it is possible or even desirable to replicate the division between state and federal authority that once obtained in this country, and that until relatively recently was thought to be constitutionally mandated. Too much water has gone over the dam; too many fundamental changes have occurred in American life. What I do urge is that we reaffirm the wisdom of the original constitutional design, in which only those functions that are deemed essential to the effective conduct of truly national business are assigned to the federal government, while all others are reserved as the exclusive province of the states; and that we then determine, in the light of today's conditions, which level of government should be doing what.

There will always be an argument as to where the line is to be drawn. But I think that where it is drawn is less important than the principle that a line must be drawn that leaves no question as to the outer limits of federal authority. Of course, having done this, all parties would have to take a blood oath to abide by the new dispensation.

This means that if the more enlightened folk who gravitate to Washington do not like the way the citizens of Illinois, or Hawaii, or Arkansas choose to manage their own affairs, they will have to suppress the impulse to impose enlightenment on them. But perhaps, in the fullness of time, Washington might learn to set aside the arrogance that assumes that the citizens of the several states cannot be trusted to govern themselves.

I recognize that my modest proposal would require an uncommon substitution of philosophy for politics; but ours, after all, is a system uniquely based on a philosophical conception of the nature of man and of the limits of human institutions. Those limits are now being tested; and perhaps it is not altogether romantic to hope that necessity, if not philosophy, will lead us to rediscover the robust federalism that in times past provided this nation with such extraordinary strength, and flexibility, and freedom.

As political philosophers, the delegates to the Constitutional Convention understood that they had accomplished something profoundly important. As realists, they also understood that the protection of the new Constitution would be a never-ending task. As Benjamin Franklin left Independence Hall on the last day of the convention, a woman asked him: "Dr. Franklin, what kind of government have you given us?" He answered, "A republic, madam, if you can keep it." That is the challenge that each generation of Americans has had to face. That challenge will soon be yours.

Good luck.

When I first raised these concerns, the federal government was about half as large as it is today, as measured by real dollars spent. The size of the Executive Branch has long since made a mockery of the notion of congressional oversight. There are simply too many people making too many decisions and spending too many dollars for 535 overworked members of Congress to possibly keep track of what they are doing. One can only hope that Washington's breathtaking responses to the 2008–09 financial meltdown—the frenetic enactment of zillion-dollar bailout and stimulus bills, the takeover of car manufacturers and insurance companies, the doubling of the national debt—will shock the public into demanding reductions in both the size and the cost of the federal establishment. The tea-party phenomenon suggests that this may in fact be happening.

The Federal Bureaucracy:
Servant or Master?

During my last years in the Senate, my staff and I were inundated with growing constituent complaints about the scope and arbitrary application of federal regulations. As a result, I became increasingly concerned over the enormous powers that have been entrusted to federal agencies and their potential abuse. I delivered these remarks to a meeting of the American Academy of Orthopaedic Surgeons in February 1980.

Last November, the state of Washington became the twentieth in just a year and a half in which the voters adopted a measure limiting how much their state would be allowed to tax or spend. A few months earlier, New Hampshire became the thirtieth state to call for a constitutional amendment requiring the federal government to live within its income.

All of this reflects a growing sense of political impotence and distrust. Millions of Americans feel they are being overwhelmed by events they can no longer influence, and that voting to replace one government official with another is an act of futility. There is no single cause for this disintegration of confidence, but as a veteran of six years on Capitol Hill who has had to wrestle with hundreds of constituent concerns, I am persuaded that a major source of the current discontent stems from the accelerating expansion of federal authority and the way that authority is being exercised.

In years past, citizens who had complaints with government could usually take them up with reasonably accessible state or local officials who had the authority to address them. With the explosive growth of the federal role, however, these officials have been converted in significant degree into mere administrators of programs and policies designed in Washington. Thus, today, a citizen with a grievance must be prepared to thread his way through the intimidating thickets of a federal bureaucracy that in practical effect now constitutes a fourth, extra-constitutional branch of government.

This bureaucracy is the creation of a Congress that has abdicated far too many of its legislative responsibilities. It is manned by insulated and sometimes imperious officials who wield an enormous influence over virtually every facet of American life. As they are not elected, they are not directly responsible to the people; and as they are protected by the civil-service laws, they are virtually immune to discipline by a president or by Congress. We have, in short, managed to vest these individuals with a degree of authority over others that the Founders of the Republic went to great pains to prevent anyone from acquiring.

Members of the business community have long been aware of the striking growth of bureaucratic power in the United States. But it is only recently that large numbers of Americans have come to feel themselves hemmed in and pushed around in their personal lives by tenured civil servants who seem to be responsible to no one. This is so because it is only recently that federal authority has been extended in a major way into areas having a direct and visible impact on very large numbers of ordinary citizens. Today, federal zealots are reaching into local schools, where they affect the interests of every child, and hence of every parent. Millions of workers now feel threatened by federally imposed affirmative-action programs requiring employers to hire and promote not on the basis of individual merit but on the basis of race, sex, or national origin. Small employers throughout America fear the knock on the door of one of the ubiquitous inspectors of the Occupational Safety and Health Administration.

Few agencies can match OSHA for the sheer rage and frustration its agents generate as they go about their appointed rounds. In its ten years of existence, the agency has become the symbol of the substitution of red tape for due process, and the way it has operated is instructive. The stated purposes of OSHA are laudable enough. To cite the language of the Occupational Safety and Health Act of 1970, they are "to assure so far as possible every working man and woman in the nation safe and healthful working conditions and to preserve our human resources."

Although there are those, such as I, who ask whether the same purposes could not be met as well by action at the state level, it has been the way OSHA has gone about preserving our human resources that has raised hackles to such a degree. Virtually every business enterprise in the country, from the smallest corner grocer to General Motors, is subject to OSHA; and to be subject to OSHA means that you can be visited by one of its investigators at any time without notice and fined on the spot for violations of regulations you not only have never heard about but in some instances couldn't find the text of even if you had.

A few years ago, the *Daily Camera* in Boulder, Colorado, published an editorial recording a vignette of life with OSHA. A local businessman, the employer of six, had a visitation from an inspector who discovered a violation for which the businessman was fined $1.16. When he asked for a copy of the regulation he had allegedly violated, he was told that none was available. For the ending of this real-life drama, let me read from the editorial:

Two weeks later he received a 248-page list of OSHA regulations. There was nothing in the document about the violation he was charged with, so again he asked for a copy of pertinent regulation. After a month he received a 48-page supplement to the 248-page rule book. The new document covered his situation but did not indicate that he was violating any rule.

So the small businessman appealed the case. After four hours of hearings with seven federal officials, the charge was dismissed—in a 19-page decision.

Now, the average individual will not go to court to protest a fine of $1.16, or even $1,600. He has no practical recourse but to pay it and mutter about high-handed bureaucrats, especially where the regulatory action is patently outrageous, as in the case of a former constituent of mine. He complained to me about being fined because he had constructed a guard rail that did not meet OSHA specifications. In fact, the iron piping he had used happened to be stronger, and therefore safer, than the wooden rails stipulated in the OSHA regulation he was fined for violating.

It occurs to me that I have been using the word "bureaucrat" in a somewhat pejorative manner, for which I apologize. Federal agencies and bureaus are manned, by and large, by able men and women most of whom work hard, are dedicated, and seek to serve the public good. They often face an impossible job in trying to make sense out of sweeping congressional directives; and given Congress's wholesale abdication of the responsibility to define precisely what it is that these people are supposed to do and how, they often have no choice but to draft and enforce rules in what is essentially a legislative vacuum. But the net impact of the federal bureaucracy has been to move us away from a system of government by laws to which every citizen has equal access, and towards one in which some men and women are empowered by government to exercise broad discretionary authority over other men and women.

As I contemplate the vast numbers of civil servants we have loosed upon the land, I am reminded of one of the grievances listed by Thomas Jefferson in the Declaration of Independence as justifying so serious an act as rebellion. Speaking of George III, he wrote: "He has erected a multitude of new offices, and sent hither swarms of officers to harass our people, and eat out their substance." It would appear we have come full circle in just two hundred years.

I am not suggesting that we take up arms and march on Washington, but I do suggest that we take seriously the dangers to individual liberties and to truly representative government that are posed by these latest swarms of non-elected officers. We were taught long ago that the power to tax is the power to destroy. So is the power to regulate, especially when so many essential activities are now made subject to official action or approval. It is a power that should never have been handed out without the most careful safeguards. As with any other power, it is subject to abuse; and I know of no change in human nature that would suggest that today's bureaucrat is immune to Lord Acton's famous dictum on the corruptive influence of power.

The old Department of Health, Education, and Welfare (which has now been spun off into two federal bureaucracies, the Department of Health and Human Services and the Education Department) could and did coerce schools into acceding to the most outrageous proposals through the simple expedient of withholding funds for programs that happened to have nothing to do with the matter in controversy; and there is no reason to believe that its successors will abandon this practice. The Securities and Exchange Commission is able to force compliance with demands of doubtful legality because a critical corporate financing cannot be postponed, or because an accounting firm cannot afford to be declared persona non grata by members of an agency with which it must continue to deal. The list of bureaucratic sins of commission and omission is endless, and in most cases the victims have little choice but to capitulate to orders they may believe to be outrageous, or irrational, or beyond the legal authority of the agency in question.

They do so because they are engaged in an unequal struggle. The laws governing the relationship between the regulator and the regulated simply reverse the normal legal presumptions. A citizen found by an agency to be in violation of its regulations is deemed to be guilty unless he can prove his innocence. A federal regulator is presumed to be acting within his authority unless the aggrieved party is able to demonstrate that he is acting in an arbitrary or capricious manner. This is a burden that is difficult and expensive to meet; and the issue too often is not merely whether the regulator is right, but whether he can be said to have abused his broadly defined discretion.

Regulatory bodies are clothed with the full authority of the federal government and have access to its resources. Most individuals and businesses, on the other hand, have limited funds and can ill afford the cost of a protracted fight. This is an advantage that some regulators consciously exploit, deliberately adopting dilatory tactics that are designed to spend their victims into submission. This practice is common enough, in fact, to have acquired a name. It is called "deep pocketing." Rather than fight an issue on its merits, an agency will wage a war of procedural attrition that will force an opponent to reach deeper and deeper into his pockets, until his resources are exhausted.

Bureaucratic abuse does not stop with money-whipping citizens who attempt to protect their rights. Some agencies have fallen into the hands of zealots who pursue ideological goals that bear little relationship to the clear intent of the legislation they are supposed to be implementing. Witness the Federal Trade Commission's recent antitrust suit against DuPont. Its purpose is to stop the company from expanding production of a paint pigment, titanium oxide, by a new process that has cut its cost so sharply that DuPont now supplies 40 percent of the domestic market. The company is being prosecuted for trying to make these savings available to more consumers, and all in the name of a statute that was specifically designed to enjoin the *restraint* of trade, not its expansion. As University of Chicago economist Yale Brozen has put it, in this action the FTC is standing the antitrust law on its head. It nevertheless has the power to charge off in hot pursuit of its own vision of what the antitrust law ought to be.

To cite another example of bureaucratic lawlessness, the Internal Revenue Service recently engaged in a power play that, if successful, would have threatened the existence of thousands of private schools, all in pursuit of a goal which, however exemplary on the face of it, was nevertheless none of the IRS's cotton-picking business. A year ago, the IRS dropped into the Federal Register a set of proposed regulations for revoking the tax-exempt status of certain private schools. If the proposed rules had been allowed to go into effect, any private school that happened to be founded or substantially expanded at or about the time a public-school system in the surrounding area was desegregated would be presumed to be engaged in discrimination on a simple finding that its enrollment failed to meet the racial and ethnic quotas stipulated in the regulations. In order to preserve the tax deductibility of the gifts essential to its survival, a school failing to meet that test would be required to adopt a detailed, costly affirmative-action program entailing the establishment of scholarships, minority-recruitment programs, and a host of other arbitrary requirements that could break the financial back of a new institution.

Fortunately, an alert citizen spotted the proposed regulations and sounded alarms that forced the Internal Revenue Service to hold the public hearings it had hoped to avoid by labeling its proposals as merely procedural. Hearings were held; and although the IRS modified some of its proposed language to mollify the swarms of protesting educators, Congress recognized these as cosmetic only and, in a rare show of courage, adopted legislation killing this particular venture in bureaucratic imperialism.

I say it was an act of courage because members of Congress are usually very careful not to offend the shapers of respectable opinion. In this particular case, the *New York Times* had declared itself to be totally delighted by the new role the IRS had volunteered to assume without a shred of statutory authority. The *Times* wasn't the least disturbed over the fact that the agency was out to arm itself with the power to force private schools out of existence on a mere allegation of discrimination.

One can reasonably ask why it should take an act of courage for Congress or a president to do something to keep the more spontaneously creative bureaucracies in line. I don't know why this should be so—which may explain why I come before you as a former senator. All I can do is point out that once an interpretation of a statute commands the praise of the *Times*, the *Washington Post*, the American Civil Liberties Union, and all the other gentry who have co-opted the market for the good and the compassionate and the right and the just, pressures are created that are truly paralyzing, even though the public at large and the great majority of a given legislator's constituents may have a rather different view of what is good, compassionate, right, and just.

Be that as it may, the fact remains that we have created, in our urge to regulate and in the way we have gone about the business of regulating, a new force in American life that undermines the safeguards the Founders so carefully wrote into our Constitution, one that threatens to destroy the sense of consensus that representative government must continue to cultivate if it is to survive. In my view, this aspect of our regulatory problem poses far greater dangers to the future well-being of the American Republic than all the waste and inefficiencies and economic dislocations that are now so abundantly documented.

We have created a professional civil service which we have endowed with an exceptional degree of power. Its members are elected by no one and, as a practical matter, are accountable to no one. Yet because so many private interests are now subject to governmental supervision and authority, the bureaucracy can exercise a fearsome power to intimidate that any president can turn to his own advantage.

An article that appeared a few months ago in the *Wall Street Journal* reminds us that this particular form of abuse did not end with Watergate. The article describes some of the pressures the Carter administration was able to bring to bear in order to muzzle corporate criticism of a proposed natural-gas bill. After a meeting with President Carter, the chief executives of some of our largest gas-consuming companies suddenly dropped their open opposition to the bill. According to the article, what the executives had heard from the president was some "not-so-subtle threats" involving matters pending before such agencies as the FTC and the SEC. The article noted that "the excuse for such [corporate] pusillanimity is that the fifteen-foot shelf of federal regulations passed by Congress has put a vast arsenal of weapons for punishment in any administration's hands."

It seems to me that any comprehensive program for regulatory reform must include, as a matter of first priority, a specific plan for pruning back the size of that arsenal while providing citizens with more effective weapons to protect themselves against bureaucratic aggression. Let me suggest just a few ways in which we can begin to achieve those goals.

First, we can narrow the scope of administrative discretion by sharpening the focus of congressional mandates and requiring that they be strictly interpreted. We can also harness economic incentives and disincentives to achieve specific goals. The Environmental Protection Agency is now finalizing a study to examine this alternative, which was mandated by an amendment I authored to the Clean Air Act. Among the EPA's conclusions is that a system of pollution taxes or permits should be able to control nitrogen-oxide emissions from stationary sources at a tenth to a quarter the cost of the conventional regulatory approach.

Second, we should recognize that a civil servant is as capable of abusing authority as any other human being. Therefore, we should provide individuals and businesses that are subject to regulation with the kinds of procedural protections that are conjured up by the words "due process." A taxpayer, for example, ought not to be presumed guilty until proven innocent, and a federal bureaucracy or agency ought to be required to prove its case before it can invoke the sanctions at its disposal.

Third, we should require government agencies to be as accountable for their actions as anyone else in our society. This would require the waiver of sovereign immunity so that anyone suffering a loss as a result of bureaucratic negligence or abuse could sue the federal government for damages.

And fourth, we can, to a degree, mitigate the element of cost as a deterrent to challenging the actions of a federal agency. This can be done by enacting legislation entitling any successful contestant in a civil or administrative action to reimbursement of any reasonable costs incurred in presenting his case. This would encourage those who feel they have a legitimate grievance to defend or enforce their rights against the federal government, and, in the process, it would help define the limits of governmental authority, which ought to be a major goal of any free society.

These and other reforms designed to curb the abuse of regulatory power will of course be resisted by all who in their heart of hearts applaud the fact that we have empowered a Washington-based elite to impose its enlightened views on a benighted citizenry. But citizens are growing tired of being pushed around by so-called public servants who are hellbent on imposing policies on the public that the public doesn't want, and who are adept at throwing needless roadblocks in the way of productive citizens trying to make a living in an increasingly regulated world.

There is an enormous body of support for the kinds of measures I have suggested, some of it in surprising places. I know this because I was able to persuade two Senate committees to incorporate important elements of two of them in pending legislation. The 1976 law extending the life of the Consumer Product Safety Commission provides, on an experimental basis, for the payment of damages for losses resulting from gross negligence on the part of the commission. That same year, the Public Works Committee adopted my proposal for the reimbursement of costs incurred by anyone successfully challenging the EPA under amendments to the Clean Air Act. I was able to succeed in each instance because even regulation-prone senators had come to recognize, through the sheer volume of constituent complaints, the extent of a citizen's helplessness in the face of even the most obvious examples of bureaucratic muddle-headedness, or indifference, or downright bullying.

It is on the basis of this experience that I so firmly believe that the reforms I speak of are politically attainable. Given the necessary effort, the power of a runaway bureaucracy can be curbed and elementary fairness restored to the regulatory process. If we make progress on this one front, we will have gone some way towards renewing the American people's confidence that ours is a system in which the citizen continues to count, one in which public servants will remain precisely that: servants, not masters.

As might be expected in this imperfect world, the regulatory reforms I urged in these remarks have not been enacted, and, despite the efforts of Presidents Reagan and Bushes I and II to roll back the regulatory tide, the fifteen feet of fine-print federal regulations to which I referred have grown to twenty-five feet—and these do not include the additional yard or so that will be added to implement Obamacare. To compound the injury, Congress has developed the habit of imposing criminal penalties for breaches of regulations, however obscure; and to make matters even worse, it has dispensed at times with the common-law requirement that the accused know he has violated the law. We are all familiar, of course, with the principle that a person is presumed to know the law. Fair enough in the days when crimes consisted, essentially, of offenses against variations on the Ten Commandments. But today, citizens cannot rationally be presumed to know the intricacies of all the regulations that increasingly affect their lives—and can land them in jail.

The New York City Fiscal Crisis

New York's chronic mismanagement caught up with City Hall in early 1975, when Mayor Abraham Beame acknowledged that the city was on the brink of bankruptcy. As has become all too customary when any significant part of the American body politic is faced with a fiscal crisis of its own making, he turned to Washington for a bailout. This put me on a very hot political spot because I saw no constitutional or prudential justification for such a bailout. The following paper deals with the crisis and my role in it. The paper itself is something of a mystery. I had obviously put a great deal of work into it; but when I came across it in my files, I had no recollection of it. I must have written it for publication sometime in early 1977, but I don't know whether it was ever published. I believe, though, that it raises important points about state and local responsibilities and the dangers of looking to Washington for help.

One school of thought has it that a single year-old headline cost Gerald Ford the presidency. It appeared in the October 30, 1975, issue of the *New York Daily News*, and it read: "FORD TO CITY: DROP DEAD." As for my own role in the city's financial crisis, a widespread perception was summarized in a *New York Times* editorial as follows: "When this City was about to lurch into bankruptcy, he . . . bestirred himself enough to wave the City on to its apparent doom." I suggest that this was a bum rap; and so, lest the medium be the entire message, I think it useful to record some of the facts and issues as I saw them unfold in the fall of 1975, with special emphasis on the all-important distinction between what was in the best interests of New York City's people and what was in the interests of its politicians and creditors.

Now, the first part of wisdom in coming to understand the causes of New York City's desperate condition is to realize that the city was the victim not of impersonal forces, but of its own breathtaking mismanagement sustained year after year. During the preceding decade, the city had run up its overhead costs to levels impossible to sustain. Between 1966 (the beginning of John Lindsay's tenure as mayor) and 1975 (the second year of Abraham Beame's tenure), the budget had more than trebled, with labor costs alone increasing from an estimated $2.1 billion to $6.4 billion. The cost of higher education had gone from $92.5 million to $585 million. Even with sharply increased taxes, City Hall had to borrow ever-larger amounts to make ends meet, with the result that by 1976 debt-service costs had reached $1.9 billion a year, exceeding the combined cost of the police force, the fire department, and sanitation services.

Yet when the banks at long last shut their credit windows in the spring and summer of 1975, Mayor Beame presented himself and the city as very much the aggrieved parties. No further economies were possible, he warned, without jeopardy to essential services; the fears expressed by the city's bankers were wholly unjustified; the city could and would get by, if only the federal government would "lend its credit" to New York City through the device of guaranteeing its obligations.

The mayor's protestations notwithstanding, by September it was clear that the city was in deep, serious, long-term financial trouble. The state government in Albany had undertaken a series of emergency measures designed to keep the city afloat for a few more months, stretching its own credit to dangerous limits. By now, major bankers were joining city officials in pilgrimages to Washington to plead for federal loan guarantees, warning that a default by New York City would prove catastrophic for the entire U.S. economy. In time, they even enlisted the support of West Germany's Chancellor Helmut Schmidt, who solemnly suggested that a default by America's premier city would create a crisis of confidence that could plunge Western Europe into a serious economic downturn.

I spent a major portion of my time in September 1975 trying to search out the facts of the situation. This was anything but easy, given the incredibly sloppy—and misleading—condition of the city's books. I spoke to any number of informed persons, including Secretary of the Treasury William Simon, Federal Reserve Board Chairman Arthur Burns, and specialists in municipal financing, to try to assess the consequences of the dreaded default. I came to certain tentative conclusions, among them the following: First, it was inaccurate to describe the proposals for federal loan guarantees as programs for bailing out New York City. They were, more accurately, programs for bailing out New York City's creditors, because by now the city was operating under tight constraints imposed by the state. Second, the long-suffering millions who lived, worked, and paid their taxes in New York City would be best served by maintaining maximum pressure on the city and state governments to substitute managerial and fiscal prudence for the political expediency that had brought the city to its knees. Third, the financial skies would not fall if the city were simply to admit its inability to meet all its obligations as they fell due and seek the appropriate remedies under the bankruptcy law.

And so it came to pass that when a reporter asked me whether I would support Mayor Beame's and Governor Carey's efforts to secure a federal guarantee of New York City's obligations, I answered, "No," citing my aforementioned conclusions. I also said that the proposal would undercut the principle of a division of governmental responsibilities, because it was inconceivable that Congress would authorize the guarantee without imposing

guidelines and conditions—i.e., imposing federal judgments—
on the people of New York City.

The *New York Times* ran the story the next day under the
headline: "BUCKLEY OPPOSES/U.S. INTERCESSION/IN THE
CITY'S CRISIS." Members of the New York City congressional
delegation expressed shock and dismay. Editorial comments in
the *Times* and the *New York Post* were as one would expect; but
even the *Daily News*, which was usually quite sensible, raked me
over the coals for not seeking for New York the sort of special
treatment that it would have equally raked me over the coals for
supporting if the city in question had been Detroit or Philadelphia
or Boston.

No doubt about it, I was the bad guy. And so, in the ensuing
weeks, I redoubled my efforts to inform myself about and think
through every aspect of the city's rapidly deteriorating situation.
I spoke with a dozen experts on the city's finances. I met with
President Ford on two occasions and kept in close touch with his
key advisors. I even read a history of municipal defaults and reor-
ganizations during the Great Depression.

In the course of all this, I learned that the city's financial situation was far worse than the public had originally been given to
understand, even by critics of City Hall. By the end of October, it
was clear that the city would be hard put to make ends meet even
if it were to suspend all debt-service payments—on interest as well
as on principal. At the same time, I became more convinced than
ever that the nation and (Chancellor Schmidt notwithstanding)
the Western world could weather the shock of a New York City
default. Local governments would continue to be able to borrow
money at rates consistent with the historic spread between federal
and municipal paper, and it seemed to me irrational to believe
that a default by New York City would send shock waves through
the market, in the light of the now long-recognized fact that the
city was indeed insolvent.

What became a major concern for me, as I examined the
options that faced New York, was that the alternative I had come
to believe the most appropriate was one that, for purely technical

reasons, was not then available. Under existing law, a municipality's access to the remedies offered by Chapter XVI of the Bankruptcy Act required the consent of the owners of more than 50 percent of its outstanding debt. But as the great majority of New York's debt was held in bearer form, it was impossible as a practical matter to secure that consent. There were other deficiencies in the law, but this was the critical one. I found myself working in tandem with Congressman Herman Badillo of the Bronx (who shared my worries) on appropriate amendments, and I introduced them in the Senate in the latter part of October with the plea that they be considered by the Judiciary Committee on an emergency basis.

In the meantime, the Senate Banking Committee had voted, by a majority of one, to take up a proposal for a federal guarantee of $4 billion of city obligations, subject to a number of conditions. And here I had the melancholy satisfaction of finding my predictions not only realized but exceeded, as the proposed conditions were even more draconian than I had suggested thirty days earlier. They were so harsh, in fact, that just a month after I had been cast into outer darkness by various members of the New York congressional delegation, three congressmen representing districts in the city—Badillo, Benjamin Rosenthal of Queens, and Ed Koch of Manhattan's East Side—declared the Banking Committee's proposal to be totally unacceptable. In Ed Koch's words, "I could not support legislation that turned us over to those guys, or anyone else that was not elected in the State of New York." Reporter Richard Reeves summarized the case for federalism better than I could have in an article in *New York* magazine: "Can't fight City Hall? Wait until the Feds are running towns and cities and you try to get through to the White House because nobody picked up Tuesday's garbage."

On October 31, I called a press conference to present my conclusions about the most responsible way in which to approach the incontrovertible fact that, despite massive infusions of state and local loans, the City of New York was rapidly approaching the end of the line.

The best way to present the position I took is to quote extensively from the statement I issued at the press conference:

As a practical matter . . . New York faces two alternatives: to accept the conditions that Congress will impose on any substantial guarantee of city obligations or to pursue the alternative course that I would recommend.

The Senate Banking Committee proposal would require the state to increase its contributions to the city (out of new taxes) by an estimated $425 million [a year], in addition to paying a substantial fee (as much at $120 million the first year) for the federal guarantee on New York City obligations. The residents of New York State are already staggering under a state and local tax burden that is dramatically higher than that of adjoining states. The result has been to drive job-producing and tax-paying businesses out of New York. The cost of government and the resulting taxes need to be lowered, not raised.

The Senate proposal would impose the equivalent of an occupation government on the city in the form of a three-man federal board having virtually unlimited power to dictate the most fundamental policies. This alone would require a widespread abdication of state and local authority that New Yorkers ought not tolerate.

I spoke of the need to liberate New York's eight million inhabitants from the gross mismanagement that had brought the city to its knees, and to maintain pressure on City Hall to put its own house in order. I then stated:

What, then, is the best option available to the city as seen from the point of view of those who depend on its services for their essential needs and pay taxes that in the past have supported so heavy a burden of waste? I see only one answer that does not involve either placing an intolerable burden on the state government or the acceptance of intolerable terms imposed by Congress.

The city must be allowed to place its affairs in the hands of a trustee who will have the constitutional power to (a) restructure the city's huge burden of debt, (b) subordinate the claims of creditors to the paramount need of the people of the city to the uninterrupted delivery of essential services, and (c) issue new obligations (trustee certificates) with the preferential claim on future revenues required to make them acceptable investments.

I then pointed out that New York's financial situation was so bad that even with recourse to the powers of a trustee, the city simply could not in the near future generate sufficient funds to provide essential services and also pay the interest falling due on the debt. As thousands of people had invested in those bonds and notes in good faith and were dependent upon the income to make ends meet, and as they were victims of what I described as a political disaster equivalent to the natural disasters against which the federal government provided some measure of relief, I felt it would be appropriate for Washington to facilitate the placement of sufficient trustee certificates to assure the payment of interest on outstanding obligations.

Specifically, I recommended that the secretary of the Treasury be authorized to purchase, if need be, appropriately secured trustee certificates in an estimated amount of $2 billion to provide the additional funds the city would require over the next three years while it worked to achieve the balanced budget that the state had mandated for the year 1978.

Once again, my words were received with dismay. I had admitted the possibility of default and even used the unforgivable word "bankruptcy." Perhaps I should have spoken of a "Chapter XVI reorganization," thereby sanitizing the proposal. But it seemed to me then, as it does now, that the situation was far too serious to allow hysteria to be substituted for objective analysis; and as I saw it, the city would have to choose between two options: accepting the intolerable terms that would be imposed by Congress, or availing itself of the remedies offered by the Bankruptcy Act once it was amended (as in fact it was by the end of the year). Yet neither alternative was adopted, so what was wrong with my analysis?

The proposals offered by the congressional banking committees were ultimately set aside because it was clear they couldn't survive President Ford's promised veto. But under steady White House pressures, an alternative approach was worked out in high-level negotiations involving the White House, the Treasury Department, and state and city officials. These resulted in the enactment by New York State of quite extraordinary legislation that declared a moratorium on the repayment of principal on more than $1.6 billion of city notes while imposing tight supervision over the city's affairs through a specially created Emergency Financial Control Board. It was on this basis that President Ford agreed to a program for up to $2.3 billion in short-term, seasonal loans, which was enacted into law on December 9, 1975.

I plead guilty to not having thought of this third alternative. I hadn't thought of it for the simple reason that I could not conceive that such a state-legislated moratorium on debt obligations could pass the constitutional test. My judgment was subsequently vindicated by the New York State Court of Appeals, which, in December 1976, found the law to be unconstitutional.

But assuming the law had been valid, where did the arrangements arrived at by the city, state, and federal governments in December 1975 differ in substance from what I had recommended less than six weeks earlier? Instead of relying on the authority of the Bankruptcy Act for a suspension of its obligations to its note holders, the city relied on a moratorium authorized by the state legislature. Instead of being placed in the hands of a court-appointed trustee, the city's affairs were placed in the hands of the Emergency Financial Control Board. Under either program, the federal government was called upon to extend approximately $2 billion in credit. Under my proposal, however, it was quite likely that the trustee certificates could have been placed without federal help because of the superior security that a trustee under Chapter XVI of the Bankruptcy Act is authorized to provide.

The one thing as to which there is no doubt is that for over a year now, New York City has been in default on more than $1 billion of its obligations; and, as I predicted, the financial skies haven't fallen. Municipalities with decent credit ratings continue to have ready access to credit markets; and now that New York State's attempt to legislate its own substitute for the remedies provided under federal bankruptcy laws has been declared unconstitutional, solvent communities in the state should be able to borrow money at more reasonable interest rates. But the myth persists that the one course of action that New York City could not pursue was to avail itself of the constitutional procedure by which the improvident can restructure their debts so that they may reform their ways and straighten out their affairs.

At this point, I would like to comment on some of the positions and actions taken by the Ford administration. As I indicated earlier, I was in constant touch with the White House and the Treasury Department. I knew their thinking. In my judgment, the people of the City of New York owe Gerald Ford a great debt of gratitude. By maintaining a hard line, he kept pressure on the city and state that assured the adoption of measures that I believe will place the city back on its feet in the shortest time possible consistent with the ultimate best interests of its citizens, employees, and creditors. He also resisted the temptation to approve, in an emergency atmosphere, measures that would have set dangerous precedents. He understood that a responsible government must worry not only about financial costs, but about institutional costs as well; that it must think in terms of long-term consequences as well as short-term palliatives.

Many people assert that the president's ultimate acceptance of the program for seasonal financing represented a reversal of his earlier policy. I do not believe this to be the case. As early as mid-October, when the full extent of New York City's difficulties were beginning to be appreciated, I was satisfied from conversations I had with his advisors that there was an unspoken willingness to see the federal government become an accommodation lender provided the terms of the accommodation kept the heat on City Hall, did not convert federal officials into proconsuls directing the affairs of the city, and required that the loans be reasonably secured. What was clear to me was that the Ford administration was unwilling to express this willingness prematurely for all the obvious reasons.

On the other hand, I found myself somewhat in despair over the rhetoric that the president was using to describe New York's situation as he barnstormed the country in September and October of 1975. The eight million residents of the city, and the ten million residents of the rest of New York State, resented being used as whipping boys. The president was losing support so fast, even among New Yorkers who sympathized with his basic position, that I once again sought an appointment with him.

I met with President Ford and his counselor Robert Hartmann on October 28. I told the president that he was unnecessarily undercutting his New York support. I said that he should maintain his principled position with respect to the financial crisis, but at the same time he should express his personal sympathy for the millions of New Yorkers who were now having to suffer the consequences of years of gross mismanagement by public officials who had allowed the city's budget to run out of control. I told him he should urge his position on New York as the one that would most assuredly save the city and restore its vitality by forcing the necessary fiscal and managerial reforms. The president said that he understood my point, and that he hadn't intended to come on as harshly as he apparently had; he asked Mr. Hartmann to take my advice into consideration the next time he drafted a statement dealing with the city.

Just one day later, President Ford addressed the National Press Club on the New York situation. I winced as I watched him, on television, uttering the same old phrases, and using the same broad rhetorical brush in condemning the city's past extravagances. Within hours, the presses of the *Daily News* were rolling out their banner headline: "FORD TO CITY: DROP DEAD."

A year later, millions of copies of that headline would be distributed throughout New York City and the adjoining counties by the Carter campaign organization. His rhetoric notwithstanding, Gerald Ford had done New Yorkers a substantial favor. But the medium was the message. And that headline may have cost him the 144,384 votes that would have won him New York State, and hence the presidency.

For my part, even though I had correctly predicted that Congress would approve loan guarantees only on terms that would prove unacceptable to New York, had been the first to recommend the alternative approach to the city's problems that was ultimately adopted in substance if not in form, and had worked on a dozen other fronts during 1975 and 1976 to increase the city's revenues and enable it to maintain its essential services, I remained in all too many eyes the man who turned his back on the city in its hour of need.

My opposition to the proposed bailout of New York City must sound quaint in the light of recent events, where we saw the federal government borrow hundreds of billions of dollars in order to rescue a wide range of institutions from the consequences of their own mismanagement. At the outset of 2010, 43 states were projecting 2010–11 deficits totaling more than $250 billion, and governors were, predictably, turning to Washington, hats in hand, for relief—never mind the strings that would inevitably be attached. Washington obliged by distributing over $200 billion in "stimulus" funds to states and municipalities—with requirements that they maintain current levels of spending on a variety of programs they can ill afford. The question too few have asked is whether such bailouts serve anyone's long-term interests. Our wealthiest states are among those experiencing the largest per capita deficits, which suggests that they have been among the most improvidently governed. If denied help from Washington, they would be forced to weed out frills and learn to live within their considerable means. The resulting disruptions would undoubtedly be horrendous, but tough love from Washington and a return to fiscal discipline at home would surely be in the best long-term interests of their citizens. At the same time, of course, Congress would have to kick the habit of requiring the states to pay for programs mandated by Washington.

Family, Community, and Responsible Citizenship

I delivered these remarks at an Episcopal Church breakfast during my 1980 campaign for election to the Senate from Connecticut. Although it was not a political occasion, I ended with a plea for a return to federalism. As Alexis de Tocqueville once observed, "It is in the township that the strength of free peoples resides. . . . Municipal institutions are for liberty what primary schools are for science; they place it within reach of the people."

It is often observed that one of the striking features of our times is the speed with which so many traditional values and institutions are disintegrating. Increasingly, we live in an age in which anything goes. Perhaps we are just in transition as we move into a new era, with new standards suited to new realities.

Perhaps so. But in the meantime we seem in danger of losing our moorings, and I must confess to being disquieted by the statistics indicating that the three leading growth industries in America today are drugs, gambling, and pornography. That last, of course, is now beyond reach of the law, the Supreme Court having informed us that pornographers are protected by the same

First Amendment that forbids our children to join in classroom prayer in public schools.

Among the many things that disturb me about the attempt to read God out of the classroom is that it encourages a distorted view of the origins and meaning of our fundamental political institutions. One doesn't expect to receive insights about the foundations of those institutions from a foreign monarch, especially a Spanish monarch. But one of the most perceptive observations I heard about our country during our bicentennial celebrations was spoken by King Juan Carlos of Spain. In a toast delivered at the White House, he remarked on the durability of our experiment in political liberty, and he attributed our success to what he described as the "profoundly religious principles" on which our Constitution was based.

To me this is a sensitive and accurate reading of the true nature of the American Revolution. What began as a struggle to protect the colonists' rights as Englishmen ended up as one to assert their rights as human beings. And in the process, the rebellion was transmuted into something infinitely more significant than a struggle to sever the political ties between the thirteen American colonies and the British Crown.

The essential truth about America, the truth that in these secular days we are in all too great a danger of forgetting, is that our nation is, and has been from the beginning, far more than a political system. It is, rather, an affirmation of inherent rights that transcend the political order. "We hold these truths to be self-evident," that man is endowed not by government, not by a written constitution, but by our Creator with certain inalienable rights that no government, no majority, however large, has the moral authority to diminish or destroy.

It is this assertion of the primacy of the individual, this ringing affirmation of the inherent dignity of man, that was our revolutionary message to the world two hundred years ago, and that continues to be our greatest heritage. Only if we keep faith with the great insights of the American Revolution can we be assured of the survival of the freedoms we have so long enjoyed.

The Constitution was designed to help protect and preserve those freedoms; but a constitution is no more than a scrap of paper if it does not continue to draw life from the people, from the continuity of traditions that keep old truths fresh and old commitments strong in the life of the society.

What disturbs me as I think about the future is that over the past generation we seem to have systematically undercut the three vital elements by which this continuity is historically preserved: a common set of standards by which the individual and society are to be guided; the institution of the family, through which those standards are nurtured and passed on from one generation to the next; and a sense of community, which reinforces them and gives them meaning in the life of the individual.

The more I think about the future, the more convinced I am of the absolute necessity of reaffirming the basic values and reinforcing the basic units of society so that we can restore a humane perspective to our lives and protect the social and political institutions on which our liberties ultimately depend.

The Founding Fathers understood the relationship between morality and freedom. They understood that only a moral people, an independent people, a self-reliant people could successfully resist the impulse to concentrate power in a central government, which has historically been the enemy of individual freedom.

When I speak of morality in this context, I use the word to describe a consensus as to what is right, what is wrong, and what are the duties to society that endow a people with the capacity to exercise successfully the right of self-government. It is a commitment to shared values and obligations that makes possible the substitution of personal self-discipline for public discipline; that is to say, of self-government for authoritarian government.

If you will bear with me, I will read an extended passage from a recent essay that bears on what Madison, Jefferson, Lincoln, and others so often reminded us; namely, that only a virtuous people can retain their freedom. One of the most acute students of the present American scene, Irving Kristol, has described this perception in these words:

Though the phrase, "the quality of life," drips easily from so many lips these days, it tends to be one of those clichés with many trivial meanings and no large, serious one. Sometimes it merely refers to such externals as the enjoyment of cleaner air, cleaner water, and cleaner streets. At other times it refers to the merely private enjoyment of music, painting, or literature. Rarely does it have anything to do with the way the citizen in a democracy views himself—his obligations, his intentions, his ultimate self-definition. . . .

There is, however, an older idea of democracy—one which was fairly common until the beginning of this century—for which the conception of the quality of public life is absolutely crucial. This idea starts from the proposition that democracy is a form of self-government, and that if you want it to be a meritorious polity, you have to care about what kind of people govern it. Indeed, it puts the matter more strongly and declares that, if you want self-government, you are only entitled to it if that "self" is worthy of governing. . . .

And because the desirability of self-government depends on the character of the people who govern, the older idea of democracy was very solicitous of the condition of this character. It was solicitous of the individual self, and felt an obligation to educate it into what used to be called "republican virtue."

We may today complain abut the quality of morality in public life, but after all, in a democratic society, elected representatives are apt to mirror the essential values, the essential virtues, of their constituents. Our society has taken a self-centered turn. We see a growing preoccupation with "me" at the expense of "us," as voters and organized groups of voters set out to secure special advantages at the admitted expense of the public good; and if our society begins to accept cheating in private life, we ought not to be altogether surprised if some are caught cheating in public life.

When we speak of morality, we speak of the way an individual behaves as well as an individual's perception of his own responsibility to himself, and to the society within which he lives. Morality cannot be separated from the individual, and morality has its expression only through the individual.

And this brings me to a second basic ingredient in a society that is to remain free: in this case, the most fundamental of social institutions, the family. It is the family that passes on from one generation to the next the fullest understanding of morality and virtue, of the cultural values that will knit a society together and give it both meaning and continuity.

Yes, there are churches, and the churches have transcendent importance in defining and teaching the elements of virtue and the religious precepts that remain essential to our understanding of the true nature of man—the understanding that the individual has rights derived from the Creator, as well as duties owed to God and to his fellow man. But it is the family that is responsible for enlisting the aid of the teaching authority of a church; the church cannot influence the child in the face of parental indifference or opposition.

The same can be said of the traditional role of the school. Historically, the role of education has been to supplement the role of the parents in teaching the young about their own roots, their own values, their own history—all that goes to assuring that the next generation will understand and carry forward the best of its own tradition.

But unfortunately, there are forces at work in this country—economic, governmental, academic—that are eroding the role of the family in American life and undermining the fundamental values most parents continue to hold.

A startling example of this is now unfolding in connection with—of all things—the planning for this summer's White House Conference on Families. Note the plural. It was originally to have been a conference on the family, but some officials decided that this title was a little old-fashioned, given the number of alternatives to the traditional family structure that are being promoted these days. As one member of the advisory committee appointed by President Carter recently put it, "We have no intention of glorifying the bourgeois family. Foster parents, lesbians and gays, liberated families, or whatever—all can do the job" of bringing up children.

In the field of education, self-appointed experts both in and outside of government seem bent on downgrading the role of parents in the formation of the lives and values of their children. Too often, parents are made to feel inadequate to the responsibility that God and nature vested in them for the well-being and development of their own children. Too often, the mobility of American life and the substitution of impersonal public institutions for home and family have resulted in a breakdown of a sense of family responsibility that ought to extend upstream to the old as well as downstream to the young.

Finally, there is that other natural unit upon which our society has historically built, and that is the community. It is in the community, the neighborhood, that we find life being lived on a humane and manageable scale. It is in the community that we develop a sense of belonging, of roots, of the ability to reach out, to touch others, to influence decisions.

But here again, there are forces at work that tend to undermine the community, to homogenize life, to institutionalize, to dehumanize; forces that tend to destroy the sense of cohesion and belonging that develops not only individuality and self-reliance, but a sense of mutual reliance and mutual responsibility as well.

It is also in the community, or in the collection of communities that make up a town or a state, that we have our most direct impact, as self-governing citizens, on the political process. It seems self-evident that government of, by, and for the people can be exercised most effectively through those levels of government that are the closest to them. Over the past generation, however, we have seen a massive transfer to Washington of responsibilities that used to be exercised by state and local officials operating under the direct scrutiny of their constituents and sensitive to their needs. So, today, many of the governmental decisions that have the most intimate impact on individual citizens and on their communities are being made by officials who are the furthest removed from them.

I may be straying over the line into the realm of politics; but we have moved so many governmental decisions beyond the reach of the people that we are seeing an erosion of our political morale as a self-governing people. The resulting sense of powerlessness is the principal factor behind the massive absenteeism we have been seeing on election day. This is one reason why I believe so strongly in the need to rediscover and reapply the principles of federalism.

We need to reassess, in the light of today's conditions, which level of government ought to be doing what, with the objective of limiting Washington to those responsibilities that can be exercised adequately only at a national level. If we want Congress as a whole to be able to focus the time, thought, and intelligence required to tackle such important matters as inflation and energy, we will have to relieve its members of having to worry about matters that can be handled as well or better at state and local levels of government.

The impulse to centralize is strong; but when I think of the dangers that flow from a concentration of power in Washington— the growing inability of Congress to cope, the documented inefficiencies of doing things the federally mandated way, the spreading gulf between government and the governed—then I for one will opt for a concerted move towards a reinvigorated federalism. It represents, I am convinced, the surest path towards more efficient, and effective, and responsive government. Only in this way can we restore to Congress the time to consider such matters as freedom and the destiny and direction of the American Republic; and to the people, the sense of individual responsibility and self-reliance that are the essential safeguards of their liberties.

Perhaps it is not altogether romantic to hope that necessity, if not philosophy, will lead us to take stock of where we are and to recommit ourselves to the civic virtues so prized by the Founders of the Republic, and to the social and political institutions through which a humane and self-reliant people can continue to work together to ensure that this nation shall remain a beacon of liberty and hope for all the world.

THE ROLE OF A JUDGE

I served on the U.S. Court of Appeals for the D.C. Circuit from 1985 to my retirement in 2000. During those years, our country was treated to a series of acrimonious circuses as the Senate Judiciary Committee considered the nominations of Judges Robert Bork, Clarence Thomas, and others for the Supreme Court. These hearings brought into sharp focus competing understandings of the nature of our Constitution and the role of federal judges in applying it. I include in this section my rather strong views on those subjects.

The Constitution and the Courts: A Question of Legitimacy

The following article was based on a speech I delivered at the National Press Club in Washington on Constitution Day, 2000. It appeared in the Fall 2000 issue of the Harvard Journal of Law & Public Policy.

Like ill-mannered children, some issues refuse to go away. In 1992, three Supreme Court justices issued a plurality opinion in *Planned Parenthood* v. *Casey* in which they declared that even if the Court had erred in *Roe* v. *Wade*, that error must stand because to overrule its central holding would inflict "unnecessary damage to the Court's legitimacy, and to the Nation's commitment to the rule of law." That being the case, the plurality encouraged the pro-life community, in effect, to give up, to stop trying to beat a horse that the Court had already put away. But the criticisms of *Roe* and its successors have only increased, and the efforts to narrow and ultimately reverse their holdings continue unabated.

The American Bar Association has had no better luck in confining criticism of the judiciary. Three years ago, in reaction to calls for the impeachment of a controversial judge and to congressional initiatives that would have placed various limitations on federal courts, the ABA appointed a Commission on Separation of Powers and Judicial Independence to address those matters. In due course, the commission issued a report urging the critics, in and out of Congress, to cool it lest their assaults compromise the judiciary's independence and undermine public confidence in the courts. The commission was especially worried about the latter point, citing polls that recorded a significant deterioration in public support for the judiciary. To reverse that regression, the commission recommended that the courts and Congress, particularly the latter, manifest the "spirit of restraint and common purpose" required by a system based on the separation of powers; and, most particularly, it stated that there was a need to "expand the public's knowledge of our judicial systems and the fundamental importance of the principle of judicial independence in a healthy democratic republic."

Those are serious concerns, and the commission's recommendations were well taken as far as they went. For whatever reason, however, the commission largely ignored the part played by judicial overreaching in sparking the court-bashing it decried. Instead, it described charges of judicial encroachment on legislative and executive functions as old hat; and while it acknowledged that judges who failed to decide cases in accordance with the law could be "a threat to their own independence," it proclaimed that "activism" had become a "code word for a personal, political or ideological difference with a particular decision."

Thus, in the hoary tradition of too many professional associations, the ABA's response has largely been to circle the wagons in order to protect the judiciary against attacks from any quarter, however legitimate some of them might be. And this appears to be the response of the legal establishment generally, *vide* an article by the president of the Los Angeles County Bar Association, in which he notes that "our federal and state courts are under attack [for activism] on many fronts" and states that lawyers "have a professional and moral obligation to defend both the courts as institutions and our judges against these unwarranted and dangerous threats."

What these defenders of the status quo ignore is that not all of the criticism is unwarranted. Serious persons have leveled serious attacks on an approach to constitutional interpretation that has permitted American judges to carve their policy preferences into constitutional granite, and it serves no interest I know of to ignore that fact.

One of the blunter and, given its source, more sobering statements of that concern was issued, as far back as 1958, at a conference of the chief justices of the state supreme courts, in reaction to the perceived excesses of the Warren Court. Addressing themselves to the problem of federal-state relations, the attending chief justices adopted, by a vote of 36 to 8, a resolution in which they respectfully urged

> that the Supreme Court of the United States . . . exercise one of the greatest of all judicial powers—the power of judicial self-restraint—by recognizing and giving effect to the difference between that which, on the one hand, the Constitution may proscribe or permit, and that which, on the other, a majority of the Supreme Court, as from time to time constituted, may deem desirable or undesirable. . . .

Members of the Supreme Court have delivered even harsher assessments of their colleagues' work. I cite, as one example, Justice John M. Harlan's dissent from the Court's discovery, some ninety-six years after the Fourteenth Amendment was adopted, that its Equal Protection Clause required one-man-one-vote representation in each house of every state legislature. In his dissent, Justice Harlan lamented what he described as the

> current mistaken view . . . that every major social ill in this country can find its cure in some constitutional "principle" and that this Court should "take the lead" in promoting reform when other branches of government fail to act.

He then had this to say:

This Court . . . does not serve its high purpose when it exceeds its authority, even to satisfy justified impatience with the slow workings of the political process. For when, in the name of constitutional interpretation, the Court *adds* something to the Constitution that was deliberately excluded from it, the Court in reality substitutes its view of what should be so for the amending process.

That last statement places the issue of judicial activism in its constitutional context. What we are faced with, at the heart of the argument, is a question of legitimacy: whether, in issuing a particular decision, a court has acted within the scope of its constitutional authority. In addressing that question, it is useful to review some constitutional fundamentals, beginning with the source of all legitimate governmental power as it is understood in the American tradition.

The Declaration of Independence affirms that governments "deriv[e] their just Powers from the Consent of the Governed." The Framers required that the Constitution be ratified by special conventions so that "We the People," through the act of ratification, might register our consent to the Constitution's assignment of specific powers to the three branches of the federal government and to its limitations on their exercise.

In *The Federalist Papers*, Alexander Hamilton described the federal judiciary as "the least dangerous" of the three branches because it had "neither FORCE nor WILL, but merely judgment." Hamilton saw no threat in the judiciary because its role, as he and his contemporaries understood it, was to examine the language of the Constitution or of a particular statute and, having ascertained its meaning, to apply it in the resolution of a case or controversy. As John Marshall would later affirm, "the framers of the constitution contemplated that instrument as a rule for the government of *courts*, as well as of the legislature."

Unfortunately, there is a deep division today over the rules of interpretation that are to be applied to the Constitution. One school, which is exemplified by Justice Antonin Scalia's focus on original meaning, maintains, essentially, that in construing the

Constitution, a judge is bound by the meaning of its text as illuminated by contemporaneous usage and tradition; that is to say, its meaning as understood by those who ratified it. The second school, as epitomized by the late Justice William Brennan, views the Constitution as a "living" document that each generation of jurists is at liberty to adapt to the exigencies of the times. Thus, as Justice Brennan expressed it in an address at Georgetown University,

> the genius of the Constitution rests not in any static meaning it might have had in a world that is dead and gone, but in the adaptability of its great principles to cope with current problems and current needs.

Needless to say, such a view of the Constitution will allow a jurist to make rather breathtaking departures from the original understanding of what the Constitution permits.

There is, of course, an uneasy middle ground between the Brennan and Scalia positions that is occupied by shifting blocks of "swing" justices. My sense of it is that although such justices do not expressly subscribe to either camp, in difficult cases they will allow themselves to be guided by their own understanding of what is desirable. That view was reinforced by a *New York Times* obituary that reported the reasons the late Justice Lewis Powell had given, in post-retirement interviews, for his voting with the majority in *Roe* v. *Wade* and for his coming to regret his support of capital punishment. In each instance, those reasons rested entirely on considerations of policy rather than on an analysis of the Constitution.

For better or worse, an inclination among federal judges to take policy into account is hardly new. What *is* new is the profound impact that a number of the Court's more recent decisions have had on the social and political life of this country; and it is this that is directly relevant to the concerns expressed in the plurality opinion in *Casey* and by the ABA Commission over the erosion of public confidence in the judiciary.

To appreciate the full effect of these decisions, it is important to understand the social consequences that can flow from a particular Supreme Court ruling. There is a fundamental difference between a practice that society condemns and may or may not choose to forbid and one that the Court has declared to be constitutionally protected. The latter tips the psychological as well as the legal balance in favor of a newly defined right because that which society may not forbid acquires the presumption of moral legitimacy, for how can one condemn the exercise of a constitutional right?

While such widely criticized Warren Court decisions as *Mapp* v. *Ohio* and *Miranda* v. *Arizona* may have given rise to grumbling over the Court's "coddling" of criminals, they did not cause citizens to take to the streets. In recent years, however, the Supreme Court has entered the cultural arena and issued decisions based on newly defined rights that millions of Americans see as threats to their most deeply held values. Because many of these have overturned laws and practices that date back to the earliest days of the Republic, it is hardly surprising that great numbers of Americans have come to view the Court as an active player, perhaps the major player, in the ongoing culture wars as it pursues goals which they believe to be beyond its authority. Three particularly sensitive lines of cases come to mind; namely, those in which the Supreme Court has virtually banished religion from public life, has extended First Amendment protection to the most explicit pornography, and has proclaimed a virtually unrestricted right to abortion.

For most of our nation's history, the Establishment Clause was understood to do no more than forbid government preference for one faith over another. As Thomas Cooley noted in his authoritative treatise, *Constitutional Limitations*, the Framers considered it appropriate for government "to foster religious worship and religious institutions, as conservators of the public morals, and valuable, if not indispensable, assistants to the preservation of the public order." Thus early Congresses made grants of land in support of religious purposes and funded sectarian education among the Indians. Yet in its 1962 decision in *Engel* v. *Vitale*, the Supreme Court declared that the daily recitation, on a voluntary basis, of a twenty-two-word non-denominational prayer in New

York's public schools violated the Establishment Clause, notwithstanding the fact that the Congress that authored the First Amendment itself began its days with prayer.

In so holding, the Court ended a practice that had been part of the American experience since the outset of public education and that an overwhelming majority of American parents wished to have continued. *Engel* was one in a series of Establishment Clause cases that began in 1947 with the Court's embracing Jefferson's "wall of separation" between church and state and that has by now excluded religion from almost every aspect of public life. The net effect of the new dispensation has been to encourage a belief that religion is irrelevant to the public welfare. More than that, in the words of Yale professor Stephen Carter, it has led to "a discomfort and a disdain for religion in our public life that sometimes curdles into intolerance." In the meantime, we blame the manufacturers when children attending our value-free schools decide to work out their grudges with a handgun.

The Supreme Court's recent interpretations of the Speech Clause have had an equally dramatic impact on our society and culture. The Court's expansion of protected speech to include pornography has abolished any meaningful limitations on its commercial distribution. The Court did hold, in *Roth* v. *United States*, that obscenity is not protected by the First Amendment, and it described as obscene any work that, in the view of "the average person, applying contemporary community standards, [has a] dominant theme [that] . . . taken as a whole appeals to prurient interest." But such has been the erosion of community standards since the Court opened the floodgates for pornography that the Second Circuit recently had to rule that the notorious film *Deep Throat*, which contains wall-to-wall depictions of sexual intercourse, fellatio, and masturbation, was not obscene because it was not patently offensive to jaded New York City audiences. Gresham's law, it seems, is as applicable to culture as it is to currency.

The Supreme Court has ruled that although merely "indecent" pornography is protected speech, it is nonetheless subject to reasonable control in pursuit of a compelling government interest in protecting the well-being of the young. Thus peddlers of nonobscene pornography may be prohibited from selling their wares to customers under the age of eighteen. Our children, however, now have ready access to the raunchiest materials in the privacy of their own homes, thanks to cable television and the Internet; and thanks, too, to recent Supreme Court rulings that adults have a constitutional right to view indecencies during hours when well-behaved children are presumed to be at school or asleep. Thus a constitutional right to self-gratification trumps the efforts of society to protect its young. Under the circumstances, it is hard to disagree with citizens who complain that the effect of the Court's First Amendment jurisprudence has been to degrade our culture and rob our children of their innocence.

The Supreme Court's decisions in *Roe* v. *Wade* and *Doe* v. *Bolton* have had a similarly traumatic effect on traditional values. In discovering a right to abortion for any reason and, as a practical matter, at any point in a pregnancy, the Court overturned the laws of all fifty states and unleashed the most divisive political issue since *Dred Scott*, one that remains a major factor in American politics twenty-seven years after the decisions were announced. Once again, we see in action the Court's power to shape perceptions of what conduct is permissible. Even though polls confirm that the vast majority of Americans strongly disapprove of the reasons most women give for seeking an abortion, they now accept the Court's decree that women have a right to have them.

Aside from their dramatic impacts on American life, what these three lines of cases have in common is their creation of constitutional rights for which there is no historical or textual basis and which anyone with a feel for American history must know the authors of the Bill of Rights would never have condoned. As then Associate Justice Rehnquist observed in his dissent in *Wallace* v. *Jaffree*, because there is no historical basis for reading a wall of separation into the Establishment Clause,

[i]t would come as [as] much of a shock to those who drafted the Bill of Rights as it will to a large number of thoughtful Americans today to learn that the Constitution . . . prohibits the Alabama Legislature from "endorsing" prayer.

Nor could Justice Byron White find anything "in the language or history of the Constitution to support" the Court's discovery of a right to abortion, which he characterized as "an exercise of raw judicial power." Justices Rehnquist and White were writing in dissent, of course, but what they had to say does suggest that it is an oversimplification to dismiss citizens who express identical views as soreheads in need of instruction in basic civics.

Furthermore, federal courts at every level continue to issue opinions that keep the debate over judicial activism alive, especially when the proclamation of new rights or the expansion of old ones frustrates the popular will as expressed in referenda. Examples of the latter include a California district-court decision enjoining enforcement of a newly adopted provision that would bar race- and sex-based preferences in public employment, a Ninth Circuit decision holding that an Arizona initiative making English the state's official language violated the First Amendment, and the Supreme Court's latest entry in the culture wars, its decision to set aside an amendment to the Colorado constitution that would deny a favored status to homosexuals, in part because of what the Court considered to be the mean-spiritedness of the Coloradans who had voted for it.

At this point, I need to emphasize that the vast majority of the decisions issued by our federal courts fall within the bounds of the constitutional or statutory texts being applied, with the important understanding that the lower courts are required to apply the Supreme Court's interpretation of those texts. The problem lies principally with that small percentage of Supreme Court decisions in which the Court may reasonably be charged with having acted beyond its authority. It is these decisions that have sent shock waves through the body politic and raised doubts about the stability of the law.

It is because of this sense that something is seriously awry that the ABA Commission's plea to cool it has been ignored. Too much is at stake; and nothing could be more certain to undermine confidence in the rule of law than a perception that Supreme Court justices have the authority to update the Constitution to suit their own notions of what it ought to require. Yet that has become the prevailing view. How else to explain the litmus tests that presidential candidates have volunteered to apply in filling vacancies on the Court? How else to explain the passions that have turned Senate judicial-confirmation hearings into political circuses, or the argument so often heard these days that the most important reason for electing this or that presidential candidate is the next president's ability to fill the vacancies that may occur on the Court?

It is this pervasive perception that the ABA and other professional organizations should be worried about, because judges who serve as philosopher kings have no place in a polity based on the separation of powers and the rule of law. But if the legal profession is to encourage confidence in our judiciary, it must first acknowledge that, on occasion, federal courts have indeed trespassed on legislative prerogatives and then see what can be done to rein in judicial overreaching before Congress is provoked into enacting unacceptable limitations on judicial independence.

This task will require a significant change in a legal culture that too often has excused the blurring of judicial and legislative lines. It will most certainly require a repudiation of Justice Brennan's statement, in his Georgetown lecture, that the act of constitutional interpretation "must be undertaken with full consciousness that it is, in a very real sense, the community's interpretation that is sought." Among the many things wrong with that statement is that it begs the question of a tenured judge's competence to speak for the community at large.

Although I am aware of the sophisticated arguments offered in support of Justice Brennan's living Constitution, I am persuaded that a reliance on original meaning is not only sounder in principle but also better designed to narrow the occasions for the ultimate judicial sin, the abuse of power. It ought to be clear that in a polity based on the rule of law, federal judges have no license to insert their own views of what is right or appropriate into the Constitution and the laws they are sworn to apply. To put it bluntly, no federal judge, however wise, has the moral authority or political competence to write the laws for a self-governing people, and no American should wish it otherwise. The federal judiciary is recruited from a professional elite, it enjoys life tenure, and, at the appellate level at least, it is sheltered from the rough and tumble of everyday life.

But if we are to keep faith with the Constitution, we may have to do more than embrace originalism; and here, I acknowledge that the views I am about to express are based on intuition rather than scholarship. As I see it, there is a more benign explanation than judicial activism for most of the departures from constitutional bedrock that have occurred over the years. I refer to our use of the precedent-bound methodology of the common law in our application of written law. That was Thomas Jefferson's concern after having observed federal courts in action for thirty years. In 1823, he wrote that the judiciary was proving to be the most dangerous branch of the federal government because its

> decisions . . . become law by precedent, sapping, by little and little, the foundations of the Constitution, and working its change by construction, before any one has perceived that that invisible and helpless worm has been busily employed in consuming its substance.

While it is true that *stare decisis* is conducive to stability and predictability in the law, it poses an inherent hazard when a court is fleshing out the meaning of a constitutional provision. Over time, judges adding another link to a precedential chain can become so intent on exploring the implications of the last preceding case that they lose sight of the underlying text and its inherent limits. Freed of textual restraints, it took the Supreme Court only thirty-one years to transmute *Skinner* v. *Oklahoma*'s constitutional right to procreate into *Roe*'s right to abort—with an assist, admittedly, from the penumbras emanating from the First, Fourth, Fifth, Ninth, and Fourteenth Amendments that the Court had detected *ex nihilo* in *Griswold* v. *Connecticut*.

There may be another problem with the common-law methodology as now applied. Prior to the publication of Oliver Wendell Holmes's *The Common Law*, common-law judges believed that its rules were based on immutable principles of justice. They spoke of the "seamless fabric" of the common law; and when they found

92

it necessary to go beyond existing precedent in order to resolve a case, they thought of themselves as doing no more than unveiling principles that had hitherto remained hidden. Even if this notion was a legal fiction, as Holmes would later prove it to be, it nonetheless fostered a formalism that discouraged judges trained in the common-law tradition from being influenced by their own policy preferences when deciding a case.

The publication of *The Common Law*, however, changed the dynamics of the judicial process. Holmes's elegant demonstration that common-law judges had actually been engaged in creating new law necessarily transformed what had been an unconscious, evolutionary process into one in which those judges were aware of their occasional role as lawmakers. With that awareness has come a shift from formalism to subjectivism that must encourage at least some post-Holmesian judges to shape the law more aggressively, whether they are dealing with common-law principles or the Constitution and statutes of the United States.

If these thoughts have any merit, the task of changing our common-law–based legal culture will prove a formidable one. Professor Mary Ann Glendon of the Harvard Law School, however, has given considerable thought to this matter. She notes that European jurists raised in the tradition of the civil code have developed approaches to the interpretation and application of written law that American judges could well adopt. At the same time, she believes that the Europeans would benefit from the stability provided by an appropriate respect for precedent.

Whether such a synthesis is feasible, I leave to others. At the very least, however, we must go beyond the ABA's desire to instruct the public on the importance of judicial independence. We must recognize that if it is at risk, it is in substantial part because our courts have led so many Americans to believe that judges have the authority to write policy into law. It is for this reason that we hear so few objections when the political branches establish issue-based tests for the selection or confirmation of candidates for the judiciary, or when congressmen introduce bills that would impose ill-advised restrictions on our courts.

This is the reality with which we have to deal. Therefore, if we are to protect the independence of judges, we must do far more than remind Americans of the imperative need to shield the judiciary from political interference. We will have to disabuse them of the notion that judges are entitled to act as philosopher kings and at the same time dissuade our more venturesome judges from acting as if they were. In the meantime, pending that happy day when originalism is generally accepted, there can be no surer way to enhance public confidence in our courts than for all judges to practice the virtue that our state chief justices urged on the Warren Court a generation ago, the virtue of judicial self-restraint.

On Balancing Courts

In 2000, I was asked to submit a statement to a subcommittee of the Senate Committee on the Judiciary that was examining the following subject: "The D.C. Circuit: The Importance of Balance on the Nation's Second Highest Court." The following is relevant to recent suggestions that nominees for the Supreme Court should have empathy for underdogs and the dispossessed.

Mr. Chairman, members of the subcommittee. By way of background, I was appointed to the Court of Appeals in 1985 and became a senior judge in 1996. I continued to hear cases on a part-time basis for four additional years, after which I hung up my robe and retired to Connecticut. In an earlier incarnation, I was privileged to serve in this body for six years as the junior senator from New York.

I appreciate the opportunity to comment on the proposal that the balance of ideologies on the Court of Appeals for the D.C. Circuit be taken into account when considering candidates for that court. To be candid, I can think of nothing more subversive of the rule of law, which is based on the understanding that the laws of the United States are capable of objective application and that the function of the federal judiciary is to do precisely that: to apply the laws of the land objectively. That is the duty of a federal judge; and any candidate for the judiciary who is incapable of distinguishing between the legislative function of formulating public policy and the judicial one of implementing it is by definition unqualified for the job. If the proposal under consideration were to be adopted, it would feed the cynical view of the judiciary as merely the third political branch of our federal government and encourage future appointees to act as if it were.

I respectfully submit that in assessing the merits of a judicial nominee, the Judiciary Committee's exclusive concern should be with his or her professional competence, personal integrity, understanding of a federal judge's constitutional role, and, most importantly, judicial temperament. If those criteria are met, the strength and nature of a candidate's political views are irrelevant because, if confirmed, the candidate can be counted upon to make an objective assessment of the relevant law's meaning and apply it fairly to the facts of the case at hand.

The notion that the judges on the D.C. Circuit (or on any other circuit) must reflect some sort of ideological balance flies in the face of experience. I say this on the basis of my fifteen years of hearing cases as a member of that court. During those years, I served with men and women of great professional competence and strong views on questions of public policy that span the ideological spectrum. Yet, as our former Chief Judge Harry Edwards has documented, our decisions have been unanimous the vast majority of the time despite the complexity of much of the court's workload. This reflects the fact that, regardless of our personal views as to the merits of the laws we were called upon to apply in a particular case, we employed the same legal principles in construing the controlling statutes and came to the same conclusion as to how the case should be decided. We also understood that whether or not we agreed with a particular Supreme Court construction of the Constitution, it was our duty to apply it—and we did.

I recognize that a small category of cases does exist where standards established by the Supreme Court invite the application of an essentially subjective judgment, such as a determination of when a government interest is sufficiently compelling to justify a restraint on speech. Honest judges can and do differ on such judgment calls; and while this may say something about the criteria to be applied, it does not constitute a rampant problem that would justify the use of ideological litmus tests in the confirmation process. I also recognize that judicial wild cards have given rise here and there to what may be legitimate claims that laws are being bent in pursuit of political goals, whether they be of the Right or the Left. The solution, however, does not lie in seeming to condone any such practice by seeking ideological balance on a court; it lies in the careful screening of candidates for the judiciary to ensure that those confirmed understand the nature of the duties they are about to assume and are capable of putting their own views of sound policy aside, however strongly held.

That, by the way, is not all that difficult to do. While in the Senate, I had strong views on questions of public policy and tried my best to persuade my colleagues of their merit. But I have had no trouble, as a judge, in faithfully applying laws that I had fought on the Senate floor and still believe to be wrong-headed, because I know the huge difference that exists between Congress's authority to fashion laws and a court's duty to apply them. There is nothing unusual or heroic about this. It represents nothing more than an elementary understanding of the responsibilities that the Constitution has assigned to each branch of our government, together with a willingness to take seriously the obligations that a judge assumes on taking the oath of office.

RELIGION AND PUBLIC SERVICE

The past half-century has been marked by a sustained and largely successful effort to remove religion from every nook and cranny of public life. I have had the temerity to suggest that the authors of the First Amendment would have been astounded by current claims that religion has no place in the public square; that it must be regarded as a purely private concern.

The Place of Religion in American Public Life

In his book The Culture of Disbelief, *Yale Professor Stephen L. Carter wrote that "In our sensible zeal to keep religion from dominating our politics, we have created a political and legal culture that presses the religiously faithful to be other than themselves, to act publicly . . . as though their faith does not matter to them." The following talk, which I gave, with variations, on many different occasions, is my attempt to place the issue of religion and public service in its proper constitutional perspective. This version of the talk was delivered at the annual luncheon of New York City's Riot Relief Fund in October 2006.*

Some odd notions have been floating around in recent times regarding religion and public service. I cite, as one example, the statement made a few years ago by then Governor Wilder of Virginia on hearing that my then colleague on the Court of Appeals, Clarence Thomas, had been nominated for the Supreme Court. Governor Wilder announced that he opposed the nomination because Judge Thomas was a Catholic, and Catholics opposed abortion. It is hard to pack, into a single sentence, so large a misunderstanding of the roles of both religion and the judiciary under the Constitution.

By way of full disclosure, I should state that I am a Catholic who takes his religion seriously. I am also an American who, over the past thirty-odd years, has been privileged to serve in all three branches of our federal government. As might be expected, I have developed my own views concerning my responsibilities and obligations with respect to each. So today I propose to touch on those responsibilities, with particular emphasis on those of a judge, because the guerrilla warfare in recent years over judicial appointments reflects so distorted a view of the role of the judiciary.

As we are all aware, the Constitution assigns the respective duties of the three branches of our federal government, and its system of checks and balances was designed to keep the members of each of these branches within their proper bounds. But few people today seem to appreciate that the Constitution contains an additional safeguard. It is to be found in the first part of the third clause of Article VI, which reads as follows:

> The Senators and Representatives . . . and the Members of the several State Legislatures, and all executive and judicial Officers, both of the United States and of the several States, shall be bound by Oath or Affirmation, to support this Constitution.

The balance of that clause provides that "no religious Test shall ever be required as a Qualification to any Office or public Trust under the United States."

It should be noted that this clause is the only provision of the original Constitution that applies to all three branches of government, and the only one that applies to state as well as federal officials. So it should be obvious that the Founders intended the oath to serve more than a ceremonial purpose. They were launching an extraordinary experiment in governance, and they knew that it could succeed only if every public officer in their fledgling nation were to bind himself to make it work. To this end, they consciously enlisted the power of religion to ensure fidelity to the Constitution. James Madison, in fact, would comment on the seeming paradox that such a requirement should appear in the same clause as the provision abolishing religious qualifications for office. As he wrote in October of 1787, "Is not a religious test . . . involved in the oath itself?"

It doesn't speak well of our age that we must remind ourselves that in taking an oath, we call on God to bear witness to the promises we make with the implicit expectation that He will hold us accountable for the manner in which we live up to them. This understanding of the meaning of an oath is as ancient as our civilization. Edward Gibbon made the point in a wry passage on the role of religion in the Roman Empire:

> The various modes of worship, which prevailed in the Roman world, were all considered by the people, as equally true; by the philosopher, as equally false; and by the magistrate, as equally useful. . . . The magistrates could not be actuated by a blind, though honest bigotry, since the magistrates were themselves philosophers. . . . [But t]hey knew and valued the advantages of religion, as it is connected with civil government. . . . [A]nd they respected as the firmest bond of society, the useful persuasion that, either in this or in a future life, the crime of perjury is most assuredly punished by the avenging gods.

Like the Roman magistrates, the Founders of the American Republic took full advantage of this "useful persuasion" to further the interests of their new nation; but unlike those magistrates, they were believers in both the religious nature of an oath and its implications. In his Farewell Address, George Washington would ask, "Where is the security for property, for reputation, for life, if the sense of religious obligation desert the oaths . . . ?" And in an opinion quoting the judicial oath of office, Justice Samuel Chase would write, "No position can be more clear than that all the federal judges are bound by the solemn obligation of religion, to regulate their decisions agreeably to the Constitution of the United States."

The second provision of the third clause, the one forbidding religious qualifications for public office, did not banish religion from public life; rather, it protected freedom of conscience and ensured that government would be open to persons, and therefore to influences, of every faith and of none. The Founders were not afraid of religion. To the contrary, they thought it essential to the success of their great experiment. A common theme that ran through their writings was that the survival of the Republic, and the liberties it was intended to protect, ultimately depended on the morality of its citizens as formed and reinforced by their religious beliefs. Thomas Jefferson, hardly a "churched" man, referred to religion as the "alpha and omega of the moral law"; John Adams asserted that "Our Constitution was made only for a moral and religious people"; and Washington warned that "reason and experience both forbid us to expect that national morality can prevail in exclusion of religious principle."

I think it useful, at this point, to note that the idea that religion is a purely private matter is of recent vintage. For most of our history, the First Amendment's provision prohibiting the "establishment of religion" was understood to do no more than forbid the federal government to give preferential treatment to a particular faith. But while the First Amendment's purpose was to protect religion and the freedom of conscience from governmental interference, as Thomas Cooley noted in his 1868 treatise, *Constitutional Limitations*, the Framers considered it entirely appropriate for government "to foster religious worship and religious institutions, as conservators of the public morals, and valuable, if not indispensable, assistants to the preservation of the public order." As that perceptive observer of the American scene, Alexis de Tocqueville, put it, "while the law allows the American people to do everything, there are things which religion prevents them from imagining and forbids them to dare."

And so it is not surprising that the Congress that adopted the First Amendment also re-enacted the provision of the Northwest

Ordinance which declares that "Religion, morality, and knowledge being necessary to good government and the happiness of mankind, schools and the means of education shall forever be encouraged"; and early Congresses proceeded to make grants of land to serve religious purposes and to fund sectarian education among the Indians.

In sum, the First Amendment, as understood by those who wrote it, did not forbid the government to be biased in favor of religion *as such*, so long as it championed no particular denomination. Nor did it require that the state be insulated from religious principles and influences. The men at Philadelphia who outlawed religious tests for public service surely had the practical common sense to know, if some of our present-day ideologues do not, that in those roles in which public servants are expected to bring their personal judgments to bear, the views of religious individuals will inevitably reflect their religious beliefs. It is, quite simply, fatuous to suppose that a public official can check the religious components of his convictions at the door before entering the council chambers of government

It follows, then, that under our constitutional arrangements, a president and members of Congress of whatever faith need never apologize for the fact that their recommendations or votes may reflect their religious beliefs. As members of the elected branches of government, they are expected to bring their best judgments to bear in the formulation of public policy. Inevitably, that policy will reflect the values and moral judgments of its makers—values and judgments that are presumably known to those who elect them.

The role of federal judges, however, is of a significantly different kind. As non-elected officials, they can claim no mandate to reconstruct public policy. Rather, their constitutional duties are exclusively judicial. It is their job to give force and effect to the law, whether they agree with it or not; and that is responsibility enough. A judge, of course, is no more relieved of moral responsibility for his work than anyone else in either private or public life. The duty of a judge, however, is to be measured by the requirements of his office. A person cannot act as the impartial arbiter of the law unless he is willing to apply it. That, in part, is what is meant by judicial temperament—the ability to subordinate personal feelings and beliefs to the constitutional duties assumed—what Robert Bork has described as the principled jurist's "continuing self-conscious renunciation of power."

Unfortunately, over the years judges have developed diverging views as to the standards to be applied in interpreting the Constitution. One school, which is exemplified by Justice Antonin Scalia's focus on original meaning, maintains, essentially, that in identifying and applying the Constitution's enduring principles, a judge is bound by the meaning of its text as illuminated by contemporaneous usage and tradition; that is to say, its meaning as understood by those who ratified it.

The second school, as epitomized by the late Justice William Brennan, views the Constitution as a "living" document that each generation of jurists is at liberty to adapt to the exigencies of the times. Thus, as Justice Brennan expressed it in an address at Georgetown University in 1985, "The genius of the Constitution rests not in any static meaning it might have had in a world that is dead and gone, but in the adaptability of its great principles to cope with current problems and current needs." Needless to say, such a view of the Constitution will allow a jurist to make rather breathtaking departures from the original understanding of what the Constitution requires.

I recognize that a body of respected thought supports the premise behind Justice Brennan's remarks; namely, that, its nuts-and-bolts provisions aside, the Constitution is essentially a depository of principles that jurists are entitled to update from time to time as conditions change. I believe, however, that a reliance on original meaning in constitutional interpretation is not only sounder in principle, but better designed to narrow the occasions for the ultimate judicial sin: the abuse of power. Over recent decades, the Brennan school has held the edge in a series of sensitive cases that have had a profound effect on the social and political life of this country.

Because millions of Americans see some of the Court's newly defined rights as threats to their most deeply held values, and because its decisions have overturned laws and practices that date back to the earliest days of the Republic, it is hardly surprising that great numbers of our citizens have come to view the Court as an active player, perhaps the major player, in the culture wars as it pursues goals they believe to be beyond its authority.

Three particularly sensitive lines of cases come to mind; namely, those in which, by narrow margins, the Supreme Court has virtually banished religion from public life, extended First Amendment protection to the most explicit pornography, and proclaimed what amounts to an unrestricted right to abortion. To appreciate their full effect, it is important to understand the social consequences that can flow from a particular Supreme Court ruling. There is a fundamental difference between a practice that society condemns and may or may not choose to forbid and one that the Court has declared to be constitutionally protected. The latter tips the psychological as well as the legal balance in favor of a newly defined right because that which society may not forbid acquires the presumption of moral legitimacy, for how can one condemn the exercise of a constitutional right?

It is because of the pivotal role the Supreme Court has come to play in the ongoing culture wars that Senate judicial confirmation hearings have become the scenes of such destructive acrimony. And the ferocity of the attacks by such organizations as People for the American Way on candidates with the most impeccable qualifications confirms that the acolytes of today's secular religions can be as driven as any of those fighting in the name of the Lord.

Qualitatively, in fact, I can see little to distinguish radical evangelicals from, say, the radical feminists who have spearheaded so many of the attacks on recent judicial nominees. Each group has political axes to grind, each is profoundly convinced that reason and virtue are on its side, each has become sophisticated in the arts of political warfare, each has important constituencies both in the electorate at large and in Congress, and each has an equal right to pursue its goals in the political marketplace. What does distinguish the evangelicals is that the values they champion have fallen into disrepute with both the establishment media and the Atlantic and Pacific Coast elites, even though they seek no more than to protect institutions and standards that were almost universally accepted as recently as a generation ago. Call it a question of style, if you will.

Whatever its cause, the undeniable fact is that we have witnessed an astonishing sea change in American practices and attitudes over the past forty years or so. Such words as "sin" and "honor" and "virtue" sound quaint as we discard moral precepts and codes of behavior that had been rooted in our society since the founding of the Republic. Moreover, we have shown a dismaying tendency to recast God in man's image. If enough people engage in conduct that society once condemned, we rewrite the rule book and assume that God, as a good democrat, will go along.

As a result, since the 1960s, we have witnessed an erosion of moral standards and self-discipline that has given us among the civilized world's highest incidences of crime, abortion, pornography, drug abuse, and illegitimacy, as well as some corporate scandals of Olympian proportions. To cite just one striking statistic, in 1960, one out of twenty births in the United States was illegitimate; today, the figure is one out of three. And over the same period, we have also managed to create what Professor Carter called a "culture of disbelief."

It is hardly surprising, then, that there should have been a reaction to this culture of disbelief and to the loss of moral moorings that many attribute to it. That reaction is embodied in the so-called "Religious Right," which consists of a loose coalition of men and woman of all faiths who, taking religion and their civic responsibilities to heart, have decided to become politically engaged. And they are not alone in their concerns. According to the exit polls conducted on behalf of the *Los Angeles Times*, in each of the last three elections the issue of moral and ethical values was uppermost in the voters' minds. In 2004, that issue outweighed concerns over the economy, homeland security, and Iraq by substantial margins.

As one would expect in a functioning democracy, this phenomenon has helped frame the issues for public debate, and it has had its impact on both the choice of political candidates and their election to office. The caterwauling of the establishment media notwithstanding, however, I can see nothing more sinister in the activities of the Religious Right than an attempt to elect officials who share their convictions on certain matters of public policy. That is their right, and it does not offend the Constitution that their views should fail to accord with those of the *New York Times* or the *Washington Post*.

The Constitution is quite capable of protecting our liberties so long as those in office feel bound by its terms. For this reason, it seems to me that the American people have little to fear from public servants who take their religion seriously. In fact, I can't help wondering what changes there might be in the quality of public life today if more of our officeholders could be persuaded to take a truly scrupulous view of the responsibilities they assume when, with hand placed on Bible, they swear to faithfully discharge all the duties of their offices, according to the best of their abilities and understanding, so help them God.

A Catholic Judge in Caesar's Service

In April 1991, I was invited to participate in a symposium on "The Catholic Public Servant" sponsored by the Connecticut Catholic Forum and Sacred Heart University. As the other participants were Congressman Henry Hyde and former New York Governor Hugh Carey, I addressed the subject from the perspective of a judge.

We meet today to examine an important subject, the role of the Catholic public servant in each of the three branches of American government. Although I have served in all three, because I am joined in this symposium by a former governor and a current member of Congress, I will focus on what I perceive to be my own responsibilities as a Catholic serving in the federal judiciary.

I should note at the outset that I am not a constitutional scholar; nor do I claim any expertise in the field of Catholic moral theology. My remarks present this Catholic's understanding of the nature and limitations of his authority as a United States circuit judge, keeping in mind our Lord's admonition that we must "[r]ender unto Caesar the things that are Caesar's; and unto God the things that are God's." I suspect, nevertheless, that my views will be shared by other Catholic jurists who, like me, are tied by bonds of loyalty and conviction to both their Church and their country's Constitution.

I do claim one credential that distinguishes me from other Catholics now serving in the federal judiciary. Over the past twenty years, I have had the opportunity to serve in each of the three branches of our federal government: as a United States senator, as an under secretary of state, and, now, as a circuit judge. Having in times past jealously protested attempts by other branches to trespass on the responsibilities assigned by the Constitution to the one in which I then served, I may be more sensitive than most to the division of governmental labors that is mandated by the Constitution. As the principle of the separation of powers is an essential safeguard of our liberties, I believe it imperative that each branch of our federal government respect the prerogatives of the others, and that it understand the limits of its own.

The Constitution defines the responsibilities of each of those branches. Article I vests "all legislative Powers" in an elected Congress whose members are directly accountable to the people. Theirs is the responsibility for formulating public policy and enacting it into law. Inevitably, that policy will reflect the values and moral judgments of its makers; and as they act on behalf of the people, the principles they write into law must be regarded as statements of public morality.

Those who are heard to cry that one should not try to "legislate morality," or "impose" one's own morality upon others through the law, are ignorant of both history and the law. Whatever else might be said about such arguments, this much, I think, is clear: it would have struck previous generations of Americans as only slightly less than absurd to say that morality cannot or should not be legislated. Americans have always debated and will, I hope, continue to debate the propriety or prudence of incorporating certain moral propositions into the law; but to say that morality and law do not or should not mix flies in the face of everything we know about American history—or, for that matter, about the history of every system of law since at least the Code of Hammurabi.

Nor have we, in this "enlightened" age, ceased to legislate morality. How, for example, are we to describe the civil-rights laws

of the past generation except as the codification of a moral imperative? How do we justify our imposition of sanctions against South
Africa except in moral terms? And what about our various social-
welfare laws? Are they not expressions of a moral responsibility
for the old, the sick, and the poor among us?

Article II assigns the "executive Power" to an elected president who is also accountable to the people. While it is his primary
responsibility to execute the policies enacted by Congress, there
are broad areas in which he can properly define and implement
public policy on his own initiative. His authority in the area of
foreign affairs is just one example.

Article III vests the "judicial Power" of the United States in
the Supreme Court and in such "inferior Courts as the Congress
may from time to time ordain and establish." The Constitution
provides that the members of these courts "shall hold their Offices
during good Behavior." This means that so long as he commits no
impeachable offense, a federal judge is accountable only to his
conscience and, ultimately, to God.

The grant of life tenure is justified as the best guarantee of
the judiciary's independence and, in Alexander Hamilton's words
in *Federalist* No. 78, "the best expedient which can be devised in
any government to secure a steady, upright, and impartial administration of the laws." Candor, however, requires me to note
that Thomas Jefferson would later file a minority opinion. After
observing the judiciary in action over more than a quarter of a
century, Jefferson confided to various correspondents that because
the threat of impeachment was "scarcely a scare-crow," the judiciary was at liberty to be "irresponsible in office" and to act as a
"subtle corps of sappers and miners" whose decisions "become
law by precedent, sapping, by little and little, the foundations of
the Constitution, and working its change by construction." Jefferson at least agreed with Hamilton that the proper function of
the judiciary was to administer the law, and not to subvert it.

A fourth provision of the Constitution applies to every officer
in every branch of the federal government and of every state government. The third clause of Article VI requires that they "shall
be bound by Oath or Affirmation" to support the Constitution.

That clause also provides that "no religious Test shall ever be required as a Qualification to any Office or public Trust under the United States." These provisions are of particular relevance to this symposium.

That the Founders should have felt it important to require that all government officers be bound by oath reminds us of the seriousness with which the taking of an oath was viewed in eighteenth-century America and in the larger Christian tradition. Sir Thomas More, the patron saint of judges and the man described by Samuel Johnson as "the person of greatest virtue these islands ever produced," quite literally lost his head rather than swear to Henry VIII's Act of Succession. Who, having seen *A Man for All Seasons,* can forget More's rebuke to his daughter Margaret when she urged him to "say the words of the oath and in your heart think otherwise." More replied: "What is an oath but words we say to God?"

The second provision of the third clause is profoundly significant. It forbade religious qualifications for federal office at a time when twelve of the thirteen states imposed religious restrictions of one kind or another on public service. This prohibition ensured that positions of authority in the federal government would be open to persons, and therefore to influences, of every faith, or of none. This provision tends to be overlooked in the political furor that now attends certain nominations to the federal judiciary. One newspaper, for example, recently urged that a circuit-court nominee be rejected because he was active in the Presbyterian Church in America, which the paper described as "a conservative Presbyterian body . . . [that] has taken a strong anti-abortion position, does not accept the ordination of women into the ministry and views homosexuality as a sin." As one columnist observed, that journal was saying, in effect, that "If you subscribe to a religion that takes these positions, you are not qualified to serve as a federal judge. That means: No Catholic can serve. No Orthodox Jew. No High Church Anglican. And no conservative Presbyterian." So much for Article VI, clause 3, of the United States Constitution as it is read by fashionable present-day opinion.

While the First Amendment forbids Congress to make laws "respecting an establishment of religion," it has never required that the state be isolated from exposure to religious principles. To read the Constitution in that way would be to rob religious liberty of meaning. Thus, a president and members of Congress need never apologize for the fact that their views or votes reflect their religious convictions. As members of the elected branches of our government, they are expected to engage in the formulation of public policy, subject only to the restraints imposed by the Constitution. The role of a federal judge, however, is of a significantly different kind. As an unelected official, he can claim no mandate to construct public policy. Rather, his constitutional duties are exclusively judicial: it is his job to give force and effect to the law, whether he agrees with it or not.

When I took my oath of office as a federal judge, I solemnly swore that I would "administer justice without respect to persons, and . . . faithfully and impartially discharge all the duties incumbent upon me as a United States Circuit Judge, according to the best of my abilities and understanding, agreeably to the Constitution and laws of the United States." The authority that was vested in me on taking that oath is derived exclusively from the Constitution. Thus the justice I am sworn to administer is not justice as I might see it in a particular case but justice as it is understood by the authors of the laws I am sworn to apply. And if I consciously deviate from that body of law to do justice as I see it, I violate my oath of office and undermine the safeguards embodied in the separation of powers. Should I ever be asked to hear a case in which the application of the law might result in my material complicity in an immoral act, I would have to examine my conscience and, if it so dictated, recuse myself. What I may not do is bend the law to suit my conscience.

I recognize that the commands of the positive law are not always self-evident; if they were, the work of my court would be far lighter than it is. Nevertheless, whether they are clear or opaque, the same underlying principle applies. When faced with ambiguities, or with problems that fall into the interstices that inevitably exist within and between laws, a judge is necessarily called upon to exercise a large measure of discretion. In doing so, he will inevitably bring to that task everything that he is—the books he has read; his experience as spouse, parent, and public official; his beliefs about the nature of man and the responsibilities of citizenship; his sense of justice. A judge is not a machine, and the judicial function cannot be displaced by a formula or measured by an equation. But while his own experience will necessarily affect how he reads the law, it is a judge's task to discern the governing legal principles as objectively as he can, and then to apply them.

Finally, there are numerous occasions on which a judge is called upon to apply such elusive concepts as "fairness" and "reasonableness." These will typically involve a question of due process, and will draw on a judge's general experience and judgment. But even in such instances, judges are enjoined to seek out objective criteria. Thus the Supreme Court has cautioned that "Judges are not free, in defining 'due process,' to impose . . . [their] 'personal and private notions' of fairness and to 'disregard the limits that bind judges in their judicial function.' [Their] task is more circumscribed. [They] are to determine only whether the action complained of . . . violates those 'fundamental conceptions of justice which lie at the base of our civil and political institutions,' and which define 'the community's sense of fair play and decency.'" I confess that it is hard to find any "bright lines" in this instruction, but I believe the sense of it is clear.

What should also be clear is that in a governmental system based on the rule of law, federal judges have no license to insert their own views of what is right or just into constitutional or statutory law. To put it bluntly, no federal judge, however wise, has the moral or political competence to write the laws for a self-governing people; and no American, Catholic or not, should wish it otherwise. The federal judiciary is recruited from the ranks of an elite, and at the appellate level, it is isolated from the rough and tumble of ordinary life.

But while it is improper for any judge to use his position to smuggle religious doctrines into the law, the law may well benefit from a religious judge's approach to his work. To the degree that there is such a thing as a Catholic ethos, and I believe there is, it nurtures a respect for and acceptance of lawful authority and tradition; it cultivates a sense of work as vocation. Catholics understand that fidelity in service will be rewarded, and a betrayal of trust punished, in the next world if not in this. This will no doubt tag me as one of those unemancipated Catholics who still believe in Purgatory and Hell. Be that as it may, experience suggests that a healthy concern for the Last Judgment is a wonderful inducement to good behavior. This, after all, is precisely what the Founders were banking on when they wrote the third clause of Article VI into our Constitution.

In sum, the Constitution's requirement of an oath of office is the public's best assurance that a scrupulous Catholic who understands his constitutional responsibilities will apply the law faithfully, whether he agrees with it or not.

THE ENVIRONMENT

I have had a fascination with nature for as long as I can remember; and thanks to Rachel Carson's *Silent Spring*, in the early 1960s I became aware of the dangers posed by the introduction into the environment of massive quantities of newly created industrial chemicals. As a result, from the outset of my public life, I have had an active interest in protecting the environment and played a modest role in the design and application of environmental laws.

Three Cheers for the Snail Darter

This defense of the then very controversial Endangered Species Act appeared in the September 14, 1979, issue of National Review. *(The ESA remains controversial, largely for reasons that have arisen since this article was written.)*

Few laws in recent years have caused such apoplexy among so-called practical men of affairs as the Endangered Species Act of 1973. It burst upon the public consciousness two years ago when it was invoked to scuttle projected dams in Tennessee and Maine; the first time, to save a nondescript little fish called the snail darter, and the second, an inconspicuous flower called the furbish lousewort.

It is idiotic, cry Practical Men of Affairs, to allow sentimentality over a few hundred weeds or minnows to stand in the way of progress. It is irresponsible, reply the conservationists, to destroy forever a unique pool of genetic material; and the conservationists can marshal a host of non-sentimental arguments in support of what many consider to be the most important environmental legislation of this decade.

Having said that, I can hear the PMOAs swallow in disbelief as they ask, "Of what possible dollars-and-cents value is the snail darter?" To which conservationists will have to reply, "None that we know of." And that, paradoxically, is one of the major scientific justifications for the Endangered Species Act.

Our biological knowledge is still so pitifully small that it is less than likely that science can identify the immediate worth of any given species. The roster of species directly useful to man, however, is far greater than most of us would suspect; and we know just enough about the extent of our ignorance to understand how huge our untapped biological resources must be. It is therefore imprudent to allow an estimate of immediate worth, as perceived by men trained to think in terms only of near-term goals, to be the basis for deciding whether a given species is to be preserved.

What good is a snail darter? As practical men measure "good," probably none; but we simply don't know. What value would have been placed on the cowpox virus before Jenner, or on penicillium molds (other than those inhabiting blue cheese) before Fleming, or on wild rubber trees before Goodyear learned to vulcanize their sap? Yet the life of almost every American is profoundly different because of these species. The list goes on. As we squash the fruit fly on our kitchen counter, are we aware of its importance to medical research? And who would have thought the armadillo would prove of critical importance in the study of leprosy?

Fully 40 percent of modern drugs have been derived from nature. The bulk of the food man eats comes from less than a few dozen out of the thousands of plants known to be edible. And even those currently being cultivated require the preservation of large pools of genetic material on which plant scientists can draw in order to produce more useful strains or to restore the vigor of the highly inbred varieties that have revolutionized agriculture in recent years.

Just a few months ago a front-page story in the *New York Times* announced: "In a remote mountain region in Mexico, a perennial plant that cross-breeds with corn has been discovered, awakening hopes for producing a perennial variety of that food crop, with revolutionary implications for agriculture." This wild grass offers the prospect of a dramatic reduction in the cost of producing one of the world's most important foods. Had Practical Men of Affairs been in charge of building dams in the Mexican sierras, however, it might have been lost—forever.

I say "forever," because extinction is one of the few processes that man cannot reverse. In the course of time the dams in Tennessee and Maine would have silted up and outlived their usefulness; but it would be too late then to decide that we would like to have the snail darter and the furbish lousewort back. Man cannot restore a species, but he is fully capable of destroying it; which he is now doing at an astonishing rate. This century has witnessed over half the extinctions of animal species known to have occurred during recorded history; and, largely because of the vast scale on which tropical rain forests are now being cut around the world, it is estimated that by the year 2000 upwards of a million additional species—about 20 percent of those now in existence—may become extinct.

The Endangered Species Act was passed in order to slow down this accelerating rate of man-caused extinctions. Its purpose is not only to help save species that might prove of direct value to man, but to help preserve the biological diversity that, in America and on the rest of our planet, provides the fundamental support system for men and other living things.

As living creatures, the more we understand of biological processes, the more wisely we will be able to manage ourselves. Thus the deliberate extermination of a species can be an act of recklessness. By permitting high rates of extinction to continue, we are limiting the potential growth of biological knowledge. In essence, the process is tantamount to book-burning; but it is even worse, in that it involves books yet to be deciphered and read.

As originally enacted, the legislation was defective, but not for the reasons given by those for whom the snail darter has become the symbol of environmental extremism. As correctly interpreted by the Supreme Court, the act prohibits *any* federally financed activity that might lead to the extermination of *any* species. Critics were quick to point out that the legislation rendered unlawful America's contribution to the successful effort to exterminate smallpox. Man cannot escape the need to make difficult choices, and such choices will necessarily be made in the context of man's

perception of his own best interests. All one can hope for, therefore, is to establish safeguards that will tend to ensure that those
unavoidable choices will reflect a truly enlightened view of where
those best interests lie.

This need to provide for some exceptions to the operation of
the act was the focus of a sometimes bitter debate leading to the
adoption of a series of amendments on the last day of the 95th
Congress. Those amendments have been damned with equal
vehemence by total protectionists and by the bulldozer set—which
suggests that Congress may, on the whole, have worked out as reasonable a compromise as can be expected in any area giving rise
to such strong emotions. Conservationists, for example, are concerned that the criteria for exemptions are too loosely drawn, but
they can take heart from the fact that in the first two tests under
the amended act, the cabinet-level committee appointed under
its terms unanimously voted to forbid the completion of the Tel-
lico Dam in Tennessee, and to require the safeguarding of vital
whooping-crane feeding grounds as a condition for approving the
completion of the Grayrocks Dam in Wyoming. The Grayrocks
decision suggests that progress and protection are not mutually
exclusive objectives.

One might contend, of course, that our country's biological
diversity is still so great and the land is so developed—so criss-
crossed with the works of man—that it will soon be hard to
locate a dam anywhere without endangering some species. But
as we develop a national inventory of endangered species, we
certainly can plan our *necessary* developments so as to exterminate the smallest number possible, if not to preclude man-caused
extinction altogether. This, of course, is what the legislation, as
amended, aims to accomplish.

This objective represents a quantum jump in man's acknowl-
edgment of his *moral* responsibility for the integrity of the natural
world he passes on to future generations. It is this which lends
the Endangered Species Act its special significance. It recognizes
values, be they ethical or aesthetic, that transcend the purely practical and admit to awe in the face of the diversity of creation. Not
everyone will be moved by them, and they no more lend them-

selves to a cost-benefit calculus than does a Bach chorale. But surely it is an act of unseemly arrogance to decree the extinction of a unique form of life without compelling justification. Such an act is irreversible, and it diminishes by however small a fraction the biological diversity that has come down to us from aeons past.

That, in sum, is the purpose of the Endangered Species Act and its ultimate justification: to protect our natural inheritance against the awesome waste that this generation has proven itself so prone to commit.

At the time I wrote this article it was generally understood that the ESA applied only to species that might be endangered by a prospective federal program or project; hence the requirement for an "environmental-impact statement" to determine whether it would adversely affect a protected plant or animal. Since then, the ESA has morphed into a vastly more comprehensive law requiring the government to take affirmative action to protect any species found to be endangered, and imposing often formidable restrictions on private landowners. I can no longer claim detailed knowledge of the operation of the law, and I have some questions as to its current applications. The legislation's core purpose, however, remains essential to a responsible stewardship of our natural resources.

Economics and the Environment: The Problems of Coexistence

From the outset of my work on the Senate Subcommittee on the Environment, I was concerned with the need for cost-benefit analyses in the design of environmental laws. As would be confirmed when, as a judge, I later reviewed appeals from EPA regulations, the attempt to eliminate the last particle of a pollutant can impose huge costs in order to achieve benefits that are marginal at best. These remarks were delivered at Hillsdale College in 1979.

I come before you as a conservationist who is also a political conservative. I try to make up for this apparent anomaly by being at the same time what might be styled a conservative conservationist; by which I mean that I see no particular virtue in turning the American environmental clock back to the year 1491. I am among those who view man as part of nature, with natural imperatives of his own, which are not necessarily at odds with those of the rest of creation.

The distinguished environmental philosopher René Dubos has written with great eloquence of the degree to which man, when living in harmony with the natural world, has enriched his physical surroundings. He speaks of the area in which he grew up, the Isle-de-France, with its ancient towns and villages, its checkered fields and orchards and woodlands, and he contrasts the marvelous richness and variety of the resulting landscape with the monotony of the forests that existed there before man first began to cultivate the land.

Over the centuries, in most parts of the world, man managed to live in a state of essential balance with nature, adjusting his agricultural practices by trial and error to meet the natural requirements of the land he tilled. Such pollution as his industries produced could usually be dissipated or reabsorbed into the environment without lasting harm. What too many of my conservative brethren still fail to understand, however, is that over the past few decades, we have seen a dramatic change in the qualitative nature of man's impact on the world he lives in, and on which he depends for his biological survival.

We are now producing vast varieties and volumes of exotic chemicals which, when released in the air and water as industrial wastes, or spread on the land as insecticides and pesticides, can inflict damage on a scale no one could have anticipated a generation or so ago. Unlike man's earlier wastes, which were mostly derived from nature and in due course would be broken down by natural processes and recycled back into the soil, water, or atmosphere, many of today's synthetics are proving virtually indigestible. We have learned that when such substances are used on any scale, there may be no such thing as "safe" concentrations. Radioactive materials and PCBs, for example, are subject to biological concentration as they move up the food chain, and once injected into the environment, they cannot be reclaimed.

In sum, our technology has propelled us into a new era where we have achieved an awesome power to disrupt the very rhythms of life and to inflict costs on society whose full extent we have not yet learned to assess; costs that are no less real for having so long been either unsuspected or ignored.

It was a perception of the accelerating scale of the damage we were inflicting on the environment, and hence on ourselves, that sparked the environmental revolution of the past decade. One can question the appropriateness of the regulatory mechanisms we have set in place; one can question whether the costs exacted by them bear a rational relationship to the benefits gained; one can argue over the relative priority to be placed on certain environmental values whose importance few deny, but which no one has yet determined how to quantify; but no dispassionate person in possession of the facts, no one with an elementary grasp of biological cause and effect, can any longer deny that man has achieved the power to abuse his environment on a massive scale, or that there are formidable economic costs that flow from that abuse.

The challenge facing mankind, then, is not one of having to make a choice between economic welfare and ecological preservation, because our economic well-being ultimately depends on the health of our environment. It is, rather, to develop more effective techniques for bringing man's economic activities into equilibrium with the natural world of which he is an inescapable part.

This is easier said than done. There is almost universal agreement on the need to do something about pollution. It is when one tries to suggest what should be done that the discussion tends to degenerate into a brawl. Part of the problem is that the costs of implementing our existing anti-pollution laws are huge, and they fall on relatively few backs. On the other hand, while the undeniable but infinitely harder to document costs imposed on society by pollution are also huge, their impact is diffused over large populations who are unaware of the true extent of the burdens they bear.

Until relatively recently, public waters and the atmosphere were routinely considered to be available to all comers—industry, municipalities, individual households—as cost-free "dispose-alls." Thus, the disposition of waste did not constitute a cost of production and was not reflected in the price of goods. But the wastes discharged into the environment nevertheless gave rise to very real costs—costs as measured in terms of corrosion, crop losses, doctors' bills, declines in fisheries, loss of recreational values, industrial absenteeism, and the like—which society as a whole has had to absorb.

Properly designed anti-pollution strategies will result not so much in added burdens on society as in what economists call the "internalizing" of external costs. This comes about as manufacturers incorporate the expense of cleaning up their wastes into the prices they charge for their products. Thus the ultimate consumer is required to pay the full cost of what he elects to use. Viewed from another perspective, if polluting is recognized as a form of public nuisance in which environmental freeloaders impose real costs on their downwind or downstream neighbors, then it is not unreasonable for the neighbors to ask that the polluters be required to absorb those costs.

Therefore, what we ought to be asking ourselves is not whether we can afford a cleaner environment, but how we can best go about achieving one. Specifically, we need to determine whether the costs associated with our current pollution-abatement strategies bear a reasonable relationship to the benefits to be derived from them. In saying this, I fully admit how exquisitely difficult it can be to identify all the adverse effects of pollution in the first place, and to quantify many of them in the second. Nevertheless, this is the rational context within which the current debate over our environmental laws ought to proceed; and the weight of the evidence seems to be on the side of those who argue that the real economic costs that result from the indiscriminate discharge of man-made wastes are far larger than most people suspect. Too many examples are now surfacing where an ounce of pollution prevention could have saved a ton of environmental headaches.

Our experience with the notorious Love Canal in Niagara Falls, New York, is a case very much in point. Over the years, dozens of chemicals—eleven suspected of producing cancer—were discovered to have oozed from their containers in the canal and percolated through the soil into the basements of nearby houses, with a disastrous impact on the health of their residents, including unusually high rates of miscarriages, abnormal births, and chronic illnesses.

This toxic disaster has thus far cost the state of New York approximately $23 million, and I understand that some $2 billion in legal claims are pending against the state, the city, and the chemical company involved. Yet all of this could have been avoided through safeguards that over the years would have cost $4 million or less.

We still have an enormous amount to learn about the full implications of man's newly developed ability to disrupt the natural order. When Congress began to work on the Clean Air Act of 1970, relatively little was known about the exact nature and extent of the harm done to human health by air pollution, although the fact of such harm was apparent to anyone who had coughed and wheezed his way through a Los Angeles smog. Nor was much known about the probable cost of doing something about it. All that was known was that the situation was rapidly deteriorating, the costs in terms of health were undoubtedly soaring, and something had to be done. But what?

Under Senator Edmund Muskie's leadership, Congress came up with a strategy and a standard which at the time were entirely reasonable, especially as no one could have anticipated that they would take on something of the aura of the tablets handed down by a Higher Authority some millennia ago on Mount Sinai. The standard was human health. Congress would mandate the achievement of ambient-air-quality standards that would take us a long way towards the achievement of ultimate goals. What is more important, increasingly reliable studies, including one correlating the relationship between air-pollution levels and days lost from work as a result of chronic respiratory illnesses, are demonstrating that, taken as a whole, current ambient-air-quality standards make good economic sense.

Research conducted by the Council on Environmental Quality and others suggests that the achievement of current ambient-air-quality standards would result in savings of between $20 billion and $25 billion a year. This compares with a cost (as estimated by the EPA in 1978) of $12 billion per year for the air-pollution controls required to achieve those standards. And these studies have not taken into full account some of the unsuspected consequences of air pollution that are just now beginning to be perceived.

A few years ago, a popular way of handling emissions of sulfur dioxide was to build very tall smokestacks that would protect surrounding areas by dissipating the gas into the atmosphere. The strategy was first tested in England, where it achieved local miracles. Shortly thereafter, however, German and Swedish scientists hundreds of miles to leeward began to notice a sharp increase in the sulfuric-acid content of their rainwater. Thus did the phrase "acid rain" enter our vocabulary.

Foresters working in our Northeastern states subsequently noticed the same phenomenon and began to speculate as to the possible impact of changes in soil acidity on the growth rate of timber. But hard evidence of the adverse environmental impact of acid rain is now coming to the fore. Just a few months ago, Canadian biologists found that more than two hundred lakes in the province of Ontario have been rendered sterile; and the EPA has now identified between ninety and a hundred lakes in the Adirondacks that no longer support fish life. Apparently the acidity of their waters has reached levels where the fish are unable to reproduce. In short, we have not yet reached the end of the catalogue of damage attributable to air pollution.

By the same token, when Congress decreed health safety as the criterion to be applied in determining ambient-air-quality standards, it was assumed that human beings had certain threshold tolerances somewhere short of the atmospheric equivalent of distilled water. What has since been learned, however, is that the existence of even the most minute quantities of pollutants can affect the health of some human beings. This suggests that the EPA's current ambient-air-quality standards are far less strict than a literal application of the Clean Air Act would require—a development that creates enormous political difficulties for our policy-makers, and especially for members of Congress who find it virtually impossible to exclude a single individual from the protection of health-oriented laws.

There is something else that we have learned since our original landmark environmental laws were enacted. Whereas the great majority of our air and water pollutants can be brought under control at costs that most people will consider reasonable, it can become incredibly expensive to remove the last few increments that existing legislation requires to be removed within stated periods. Furthermore, the cost of such removal will vary by enormous margins depending on the particular industrial processes involved. Finally, there is increasing doubt as to whether the achievement of our environmental goals really requires the uniform application of statutory standards irrespective of cost in specific and localized instances; or, for that matter, whether it is prudent or even possible to impose programs that will disrupt entire communities.

Let me illustrate by taking the celebrated case of Los Angeles and the ambient-air-quality goals legislated by Congress in 1970. Given Los Angeles's location and its dependence on the automobile, given the state of emission-control technology, given the lack of adequate public-transportation systems and the impossibility of conjuring them up overnight, it had become apparent by 1973 that there was no way of meeting the statutory deadlines without closing down the city.

When the EPA decided to handle this dilemma by simply ignoring the explicit requirements of the law, environmentalists took the agency to court, and a judge issued a decision that required the agency to promulgate a plan for the city that would in effect have declared a moratorium on the use of private automobiles during much of the year. This in turn left Congress with little choice but to enact legislation extending the deadlines.

What becomes increasingly clear is the need for greater flexibility in the application of our environmental laws in order to enable us to cope with the exceptional situations. For example, if it should prove impossible, except at exorbitant cost, to achieve the incremental improvements in air-pollution controls required to keep pollutants in the Los Angeles basin at the national ambient standards during periods of atmospheric inversion, then perhaps we ought to allow Angelenos the option of suffering under less than optimum conditions, perhaps requiring them to post signs along highways leading into the city warning travelers that "Breathing Los Angeles air may be dangerous to your health."

None of this suggests that we should back away from our broadly defined environmental objectives; rather, we should recognize that the time has come to take advantage of the substantial experience we have accumulated over the past decade and see how we can better achieve those objectives with a special eye to cost efficiency. Without pretending to cover the universe, let me suggest a few modifications in our present approach that I believe would go a long way towards dispelling the idea that there is a necessary conflict between environmental and economic goals.

The first and foremost problem posed by our environmental laws is the way they are structured—their almost total reliance on regulation for the achievement of stated objectives. The regulatory approach to the implementation of public policy in any complex area requires the drafting of hundreds of detailed rules, and these rules in turn require the exercise of thousands of individual judgments by those charged with enforcing them. Furthermore, our anti-pollution laws have tended to describe their policy objectives in the broadest terms. Because of all these factors, the regulations drawn up and administered by the EPA have proven in case after case to be inordinately complicated, their implementation needlessly costly, and the decisions made by individual EPA administrators subject to infinite challenge.

The answer to this regulatory morass is not to create an energy-mobilization board with the power to override the most important environmental safeguards by simple fiat, as Congress is now in the process of doing. Not only is such an approach irresponsible, it is apt to delay the kinds of revisions in our environmental laws and procedures that are so clearly needed.

We need, for example, to enact procedural reforms that will allow specific proposals to be submitted, considered, and ruled upon, the rulings challenged, and the challenges adjudicated with an eye to achieving as expeditious a final determination of a particular matter as prudence will allow. We cannot continue to permit the endless second-guessing that creates unconscionable delays and gives rise to confrontations and public frustrations which in the end can only harm the environmental cause.

We should also move, where possible, from a reliance on regulations towards a strategy of economic incentives. The fact is that no mechanism has yet been discovered that is as effective as the marketplace in harnessing human energy and ingenuity. Such a strategy offers the surest way to make pollution control less arbitrary, lest costly, and less bureaucratic.

Before I left the Senate, I introduced an amendment to a revision of the Clean Air Act that would require the EPA to study various ways of harnessing economic incentives for the abatement of nitrogen-oxide emissions from stationary sources as a test of this approach to pollution control. Nitrogen oxides are produced in all combustion processes; but up to that time, efforts to control this particular pollutant had been limited to automobile emissions. My amendment survived my own tenure in the Senate, and became law in 1977.

The EPA report mandated by the amendment is now close to completion, and its conclusions are more favorable than even I had anticipated. They show that economic alternatives to regulation—such as a system of emission charges or pollution permits—are likely to produce the same degree of nitrogen-oxide control at anywhere from one-fourth to one-tenth the cost of the present system of regulation. In the words of the study: "Perhaps the greatest strength of economic approaches relative to regulatory approaches is that they tend to locate decision-making responsibility with those who possess the information needed to make the best decisions."

Another concept that I believe holds merit is what the EPA terms its "offset" policy. Under this approach, a corporation wishing to locate or expand its operations in a polluted area may buy and retire the existing source of pollution from another company. An oil refinery, for example might buy out a local dry-cleaning plant and close it down rather than install a highly expensive, stringent pollution-control system of its own. The refinery would thus obtain the degree of pollution reduction required to offset the pollution that its proposed facility would generate.

Obviously, an offset purchase would occur only when it would be less costly than the alternative. Furthermore, this approach does not necessarily mean that the dry-cleaning establishment would vanish from the area. If dry cleaners can handle their own pollution at a significantly lower cost per unit of pollution than a refinery, then they can utilize the funds received from the refiner to install the necessary hardware and continue in operation at no net increase of pollution in the area. Thus flexibility replaces rigidity, and pollution-abatement dollars are focused where they can achieve the greatest good.

Perhaps most important, such economic incentives are more likely to encourage the development of new pollution-control technology. Under the present regulatory strategy, industry often balks at investing large sums in developing technological breakthroughs that would achieve a greater degree of pollution control because success is likely to mean that the industry will have to install the new technology even when to do so will significantly raise the overall costs of its operations. Under a system of economic incentives, however, the development of more effective technology becomes a logical goal. In short, a move towards market incentives seems a far surer way of marrying economic and environmental objectives than the existing strategy of forcing industries to achieve fixed statutory goals.

Which brings me to another area for reform, which deals with what might be called the problem of environmental holy writ. The decision nine years ago to decrease each component of automotive pollution by 90 percent over a five-to-six-year period was acknowledged at the time to be wholly arbitrary. Yet it has fixed some totemic numbers in the statute books. Nitrogen oxide must be reduced to 0.4 part per million because that was what was decreed in 1970, irrespective of what later studies may tell us as to the merits of such an objective.

If the necessary coexistence between economics and the environment is to be achieved, it is essential that specific goals be reviewed periodically in the light of developing knowledge so that we may always be sure that the costs imposed by the goals can be justified. Such reviews, of course, will try to apply the disciplines of cost-benefit analysis to the evaluation of pollution-abatement strategies. But here I think we should keep in mind certain inherent limitations of this kind of exercise when applied to environmental problems. Reasonably reliable values can be assigned to the more obvious kinds of damage done by specific pollutants; and, as I have suggested, I believe the case can be made that, once in place, properly structured pollution controls will more than pay for themselves in savings of a kind that the least imaginative cost accountant can recognize.

But inevitably there will be cases at the margin, some of them involving substantial sums or important economic objectives, where the value to be placed on specific environmental benefits becomes more difficult or even impossible to quantify; and these are the cases that tend to become the focus of the most heated controversies. I do not suggest that the case for environmental protection is necessarily the weaker for having to deal at times with intangible values; only that at times the case may be more difficult to present and understand. What value, for example, does one place on the Parthenon, whose façade is being eaten away by the pollutants generated in modern Greece? What value on a pristine Grand Canyon, given its hydroelectric potential? And in weighing the cost of protecting migratory birds, what value does one place on a wood thrush's haunting song?

Here I would plead for a better public understanding of fundamental environmental values and for fair debate, especially where irrevocable decisions are to be made which could by whatever margin impoverish our natural heritage, and therefore the lives of future generations.

As Edmund Burke reminded us years ago, the men and women of each generation are but "temporary possessors and life-renters" who "should not think it among their rights to cut off the entail or commit waste on the inheritance," lest they "leave to those who come after them a ruin instead of a habitation."

I can think of no more appropriate perspective than Burke's as we work to establish a new harmony between man and the natural world he lives in.

Debates about environmental policy have only grown more politicized and polarizing in the decades since I left the

Senate. This is attributable in substantial part both to the excesses of "greens" who have converted environmentalism into a secular religion and to the continuing blindness of too many conservatives to legitimate environmental concerns.

ENERGY AND ITS
REGULATION

For seventeen years prior to my election to the Senate, I had worked with a group of small companies engaged in the high-risk business of exploring for oil and gas outside the United States. There is nothing like this kind of hands-on experience to give one an understanding of some basic rules of economics—rules that, alas, appear to be foreign to too many of those who gravitate to elective office. Which may explain why, after forty years of wrestling with such problems, Congress has so little to show for it. Government has a proper and necessary duty to ensure the safety and environmental responsibility of mining and oil and gas operations. It creates problems, however, often enormously costly ones, when it tries to tell us how to produce, market, and price the energy that is essential to our economic survival. As Thomas Jefferson once observed, "Were we directed from Washington when to sow, & when to reap, we would soon want bread."

The Economics and
Politics of Energy

*From my first days in the Senate, I devoted a great deal of
attention to energy problems; and when I became a member
of the Interior Committee, energy became an important part
of my official responsibilities. As a result, the Economic Club
of New York invited me to address the issue in March 1973, a
few months before the Arab oil embargo made our reliance on
imported sources headline news.*

As today's clergy show little reluctance to involve themselves
in politics, I think it fair to open this sermon on the economics and politics of energy with a reference to Scripture. In
the Sermon on the Mount, the Lord speaks of the "foolish man"
who, ignoring His words, "built his house upon the sand: and the
rain descended, and the floods came, and the winds blew, and
beat upon that house; and it fell: and great was the fall of it." In
contrast, the wise man who acted on those words "built his house
upon a rock; and the rain descended, and the floods came, and the
winds blew, and beat upon that house; and it fell not: for it was
founded upon a rock."

In applying this text to the construction of an energy policy
appropriate for our times, the sand is the pervasive conviction in

Washington that any problem can be solved, and economic laws amended, by government fiat; the rock is a national energy policy constructed upon a conceptually solid foundation. Any policy that isn't based on tested economic principles will prove to be a costly failure.

Since January of last year, I have been a participant in the Senate Interior Committee's National Fuels and Energy Study, which has held nearly forty days of hearings and accumulated a record of many thousand pages. Other energy studies have been and are being done. These include the massive three-year study completed by the National Petroleum Council, which has involved an estimated four hundred man-years of work, with full cooperation from representatives of the coal, nuclear, and electrical-utility industries. From all this material, and from all the comments, recommendations, and questions made and asked by those who have a hand in formulating policy, we can begin to see the full dimensions of what has come to be called the "energy crisis," as well as the principal options that will be available to us in coming to grips with it.

I find the word "crisis" less than satisfactory, as it implies an unstable state of affairs of short duration which will be resolved, for good or ill, in the not-too-distant future. What we are faced with, instead, is a protracted period of chronic and growing deficiencies in the supply of indigenous fuels, which will make our nation uncomfortably and some believe dangerously vulnerable to external economic and political pressures. This period of vulnerability will be of at least a dozen years' duration, probably more, depending on the wisdom we exhibit in establishing our energy goals and in adopting policies designed to achieve them.

Fortunately, the situation we face is not insoluble. We have options, because the United States and its territorial waters still contain enormous reserves of fossil fuels waiting to be defined and developed. Coal, of course, is a resource that can be liquefied and gasified, and thus is a source of supplementary supplies of oil and natural gas. Our known and probable reserves of uranium could support a faster development of nuclear energy than that now projected, and the oil shales of the West contain an estimated 1.8

trillion barrels of oil, of which 54 billion barrels are contained in zones considered to be economically recoverable. [*Today we would add wind, solar, and biomass to this list of potential alternatives.*]

It is clear, in short, that we are not shy of the basic sources of energy. We are, however, falling increasingly short of self-sufficiency for a variety of reasons. We are running into short-ages of natural gas for the clinically demonstrable reason that the artificial wellhead prices imposed on producers by the Federal Power Commission long ago destroyed any incentive to search for gas for commitment to interstate pipelines. Prevailing prices for crude oil do not justify the high cost and risk involved in seeking out the deeper or more marginal fields still to be found in the contiguous forty-eight states. [*While that was true in 1973, when this talk was delivered, the sharp rise in the price of oil since then has opened up new prospects today, especially off our coasts.*] A new—and, I believe, long overdue—environmental conscious-ness has resulted in a number of delays now in the process of being resolved on the basis of a more careful balancing of social and economic benefits and costs. I speak of the temporary delay in the issuance of offshore leases in the Gulf of Mexico, of the controversy still surrounding the Alaska Pipeline, and of the restrictions imposed on the burning of high-sulfur coal. On the technological front, we are still seeking reliable and economical methods to remove the sulfur dioxide created in the combustion of that coal, and we have yet to learn how to liquefy or gasify our coal, or extract oil from our shales, at costs competitive with the prices at which primary fuels are currently available.

There is no question about it: The primary fuel resources are there to be found and produced—at a price. And the technology required to supplement those traditional sources of energy is also there waiting to be developed, also at a price. No one now questions that a substantial price must be paid if we are to bring domestic energy demand and supply within prudent reach of each other. The developing debate will focus not so much on cost as on method. My own fear is that a growing demand for action will translate itself, through the political process, into demands for public activism. Yet I am convinced that no course could prove so unnecessarily costly or uncertain of success as for the federal government to attempt an active or pre-emptive role in those areas that are clearly within the competence of the private sector. Rather, where that competence does exist, the appropriate role of government should be to foster an economic environment that will provide the incentives required to stimulate the greatest intensity and diversity of private initiatives.

Such a role is proposed by the National Petroleum Council in the first of four hypothetical cases it developed in order to determine the degree to which our need for primary energy fuels could be satisfied from our own resources. Case I presupposes, among other things, the complete deregulation of natural gas, the retention or improvement of existing tax incentives, the relaxation of some environmental constraints, and the adoption of policies that would allow a rise in the price of crude oil. The NPC estimates that under such conditions, we would witness a cumulative capital investment, between 1971 and 1985, in the neighborhood of $547 billion in the expansion of our production of indigenous fuels, including oil and shale oil, natural gas, coal, synthetic oil and gas derived from coal, and nuclear fuels. The study concludes that this investment would generate such a dramatic step-up in the production of domestic fuels that by 1985 our dependency on foreign imports would be reduced to 11 percent of our total projected energy needs, with a peak dependency of about 20 percent in 1975. [*The deregulation of natural gas begun in the Carter years and completed under Reagan more than met the expectations of Case I as far as that fuel is concerned. Other obstacles, however, including some necessary environmental ones, have largely remained in place.*] By way of contrast, Case IV [*which essentially assumed no new initiatives*] projects a dependency reaching 38 percent by 1980.

This summary of the NPC's Case I is not intended as a brief in favor of every element of policy that went into its construction. It is instructive, however, in indicating the extent to which the economics of the marketplace can be relied upon to achieve our national policy objectives in the energy field. Under conditions of rising costs and increasing difficulties in finding domestic oil and gas, and given environmental constraints on mining and burning

coal, private capital will flow out of this country to produce or purchase fuels abroad so long as they can be secured there at a lower
cost than in the United States. Thus, if we should determine, as
I think we must, that our dependence on foreign fuel may be
exceeding the levels dictated by prudence, economic experience
and economic common sense suggest that the most effective way
to increase domestic supply is to assure those investing in the
development of our domestic resources an adequate opportunity
to realize profits commensurate with the risks to be undertaken.
[*At the time I gave this talk, the worry over our growing dependence
on foreign oil was focused on our vulnerability to an Arab embargo.
That hazard no longer exists, because of subsequent discoveries outside
the Middle East; but the problems posed by massive transfers of dollars
abroad remain a continuing concern.*]

It is at this juncture that we run headlong into the tangled
world of energy politics. We live in a time when the general public
and our elected and appointed officials are remarkably innocent of
the dynamics of a free economy. Too few today really understand
how capital is mobilized, and what motivates its investment. Too
few sufficiently appreciate the enormous size and diversity of the
resources that the private sector can focus on any given problem,
often at very high risk, if appropriate incentives are present. In
this day of consumerism, too few stop to calculate the real cost
to consumers of ill-conceived attempts to protect them from the
operations of the marketplace.

Nowhere is this stubborn refusal to face the economic facts of
life more evident than in the current resistance to the proposal that
the wellhead price of natural gas be decontrolled. The evidence is
irrefutable that the decision of the Federal Power Commission a
decade or so ago to regulate the price of gas delivered to interstate
pipelines set in motion a series of economic causes and effects—
just about all of them bad—that now threaten to leave hundreds
of thousands of consumers across this country stranded without
gas at any price. Yet too many regulators—and consumerists—
refuse to bite the bullet. Instead of deregulation, they ask for still
greater regulation—over intrastate sales and over the selection of
ultimate consumers. I for one, both as a consumer and as a rep-

resentative of a consumer state, have greater confidence in the ability of market forces to assure me and my constituents of an uninterrupted supply of natural gas at reasonable prices, and to see that natural gas finds its way to its highest economic uses, than I have in the ability of the most exquisitely informed and motivated regulators to achieve these ends.

Quite predictably, we will find greater pressures for federal action than for federal restraint as we begin formulating the specifics of a national energy policy. I suspect we will even hear proposals that a government corporation be organized to explore for the people's resources on the people's lands. We will hear such proposals despite the fact that no government elsewhere in the world has ever been able to find and produce the people's oil at a lower net cost to the people than have private companies working in a competitive environment in search of profits.

One of the major obstacles to a rational and truly effective energy policy may result from the impulse these days, whenever a problem arises that requires a technological solution, to seek a massive federal program to find the answer. And of course, almost every aspect of the energy problem depends to one degree or another on technological advances. It is a failure to make an appropriate distinction between the natures of the contemplated developments that can so distort our thinking.

The impulse I speak of will attempt to solve the variety of technological challenges on a "crash" basis through massive infusions of research-and-development funding analogous to the Manhattan Project, which developed the atomic bomb during World War II. This impulse is understandable, as very clearly delineated R&D objectives, such as placing a man on the moon, have often been achieved on a crash-funding basis. There are, however, sufficiently significant differences among the technological objectives within a comprehensive energy policy to cause us to be wary of government panaceas.

Over the years, our industries have achieved a series of spectacular technological triumphs without help or encouragement from government. In most cases, these have involved the pursuit of tangible goals having a meaningful prospect for profit. When

there is a chance for private enterprise to solve a given technological problem within a time frame that justifies the present risk
of important funds, experience confirms that innumerable firms,
large and small, will concentrate a vast variety of efforts on finding
appropriate solutions, a variety which a centrally directed federal
program cannot hope to duplicate and whose quality and scope it
cannot expect to improve upon. On the other hand, other technological objectives, especially those requiring extensive pioneering
research before their technical feasibility can even be assessed,
involve lead times so prolonged that no private firm can justify
the necessary investment. It is on these that government-funded
research can prove indispensable.

The problem of discriminating between areas appropriate
to government and those best left to private initiative is well
illustrated by a major legislative proposal introduced last week
by Senator Henry M. Jackson. He proposes that we undertake a
Manhattan Project–like effort "to move quickly and efficiently in
research and development in the areas of liquefying and gasifying
coal, converting oil shale to synthetic liquid fuels, developing geothermal energy, demonstrating advance power cycle technology,
and finding economical means for improving the environmental
technology associated with the production of energy." To this
end, his bill would establish a complex including four mission-
oriented federal corporations having a ten-year budget of $2
billion per annum to work in partnership with private industry
towards the achievement of the stipulated objectives.

I do not quarrel with the objectives, but I do question whether
the vast majority of them could not more readily be achieved
through the adoption of federal policies that would do no more
than harness the dynamics of the marketplace. When it comes
to the liquefaction and gasification of coal, there are no quantum
jumps to be made. The basic technology is known, and it is only
the refinements that need to be worked out. In this connection,
the National Petroleum Council's hypothetical Case I is instructive. The policies on which it is predicated would result in the
development of synthetic fuels from coal which by 1985 would
contribute 4 percent of our total oil supply and 6 percent of our

total gas supply. Given the abundance of the basic raw material, this contribution to our fuel supply twelve years hence is small. But the reason for this is simple. The cost of producing these products will remain for some time into the future considerably higher than the cost of conventionally produced crude oil and natural gas. The marketplace, if left to its own devices, will simply not hasten the production of the supplementary fuels until they can compete with conventional oil and gas.

Under the circumstances, it seems to me that the precedent to be followed, if we want to accelerate the availability of such fuels, is not the massive crash-funding approach of a Manhattan Project but the approach adopted in the years following the Second World War to stimulate the discovery of adequate domestic reserves of uranium. In that case, the federal government created the necessary market incentive by guaranteeing, under the appropriate circumstances, the purchase of uranium ore at a price of $3.50 to $4.50 per pound.

This assured market for the product sparked an exploratory effort that sent thousands of individual prospectors and corporate geologists into the field, and in very short order we were able to establish the indigenous base of uranium that national policy demanded. The same approach could be utilized to stimulate a comparable expansion of private investment in bringing shale oil into substantial production well ahead of the time projected by the NPC's Case I.

It is my judgment, in short, that the federal government ought not to attempt to involve itself directly in those areas of technology in which market incentives, whether natural or induced by special legislation, can be relied upon to achieve the desired ends with maximum effectiveness and minimum cost to the taxpayers. To attempt to deploy federal resources over too broad a front will not only squander them but may actually restrict the overall national effort by discouraging private initiatives. Rather, I would like to see the federal government concentrate its own research and development on such areas as fusion, hydrogen, and other exotic but promising energy alternatives which lie beyond the reach of the private sector.

If I may summarize my own concept of the appropriate role of government in any comprehensive energy policy, it would include the following:

1. Abolition of current artificial disincentives to the discovery of new energy resources. I speak specifically of the deregulation of natural gas.
2. Encouragement of conservation measures, so that by reducing waste we may keep the projected increase in the demand for energy at a minimum consistent with the needs of our economy. Government policies, for example, can encourage large savings of energy by requiring appropriate insulation in new buildings and by discouraging the purchase of inefficient automobile engines and household appliances.
3. Development of strategic stand-by reserves consisting of greatly expanded storage facilities and a stand-by capacity of producible conventional and synthetic fuels that can be put on stream in relatively short order in times of national emergency.
4. Establishment of an economic and political climate that encourages the development of indigenous sources of energy to the levels required by considerations of national security—the cost of the necessary subsidies and other measures to be chargeable to defense. [*This recommendation was based on the then legitimate fear of the consequences of a prolonged Arab oil embargo.*]
5. Planning for major federal investments in those areas of research and development that lie beyond the reach of the private sector, to the end that we may develop and have on hand sufficient energy alternatives to supply us with the options we will need as we approach the end of this century.

These and other measures must and can be initiated by the federal government. The effectiveness of the policy ultimately adopted, however, will depend on the extent to which we are willing to rely upon and utilize the extraordinary creative energy that exists within our system of private, free, competitive enterprise; the energy that exists—if you will pardon my use of a phrase not frequently heard these days—within the capitalistic system.

Only in this way can we build a truly firm foundation on which to construct a national energy policy. If built upon such a foundation, the house will fall not. If, on the other hand, we attempt to build the house on a foundation of costly bureaucratic sand, it will fall and great will be the fall of it.

Thirty-seven years have gone by since I gave this talk. At that time, we were importing 28 percent of our oil requirements. Today we import 58 percent, and we have yet to develop a coherent policy on energy. Thanks to global-warming fears, what passes for one today has focused on achieving sharp reductions in the carbon dioxide produced by the combustion of fossil fuels. Hence the emphases on developing biofuels and harnessing wind and sun as alternative sources of energy. If climatic imperatives indeed require a severe cutback in our generation of CO_2 (I am an agnostic on the subject: too many qualified scientists have raised too many questions about the reliability of the computer models on which the Gore alarums depend), we are going about it in extraordinarily costly and ineffective ways.

Let's begin with ethanol, which is our only commercially available biofuel. To reduce the use of petroleum to power our cars, Congress has ordered the blending of increasing amounts of biofuels, i.e., ethanol, into our gasoline. Thanks to politics, instead of allowing refiners to use the cheaper ethanol produced in Brazil from sugar cane, Congress priced it out of the U.S. market by imposing a 54-cent-per-gallon tariff on imported ethanol while providing a 51-cent-per-gallon subsidy for the production of corn-based ethanol here at home. A windfall for American farmers; but as a result, a vast amount of land has been diverted from the production of food, the price of corn has skyrocketed, the efficiency of gasoline has decreased, and little has been added to our store of energy, because ethanol takes almost as much energy to produce as it contributes to the gasoline we place in our tanks. (This calculation takes into consideration the fuel and oil-derived fertilizers that are required to produce the corn from which the ethanol is derived.)

With respect to electricity, instead of working to expand our production of carbon-free nuclear power, which currently supplies over 20 percent of our needs (and over 80 percent of France's), our planners have focused on the costly alternatives of wind and solar power. To place these in perspective, the Department of Energy's Energy Information Administration tells us that renewable energy sources other than biomass (namely geothermal, wind, and sun) supplied 1.2 percent of our energy needs in 2008 and are projected to provide just 2.8 percent in 2028. While wind and sun will prove important in the longer run, they are not near-term solutions; and because they are interruptible and require large areas of land, they will never be panaceas.

If saving the planet indeed requires a severe cutback in our release of CO_2, the answer doesn't lie with these initiatives or with complex "cap-and-trade" proposals with their inevitable politically driven exemptions. The simplest and most direct approach to the problem would be to tax CO_2 emissions. By raising the price of fossil fuels across the board, this would simultaneously encourage conservation and provide incentives for the private development of the widest spectrum of cost-effective carbon-free alternatives.

But regardless of what we do with respect to carbon, the unavoidable fact is that we will continue to be dependent on petroleum for a long time to come, and it is important that we produce as much of it at home as we can. The disastrous BP oil spill in the Gulf of Mexico could prove a significant setback in this regard. Government has the responsibility for ensuring the safety of offshore drilling. That is its proper job. But environmentally responsible drilling is in fact possible today, and the sooner we resume exploration off all our coasts, the better off we will be.

Ol' Debbil Oil

The Arab oil embargo of 1973–74 triggered major dislocations in American markets. The result was shortages, long lines at gasoline stations, skyrocketing prices, and a smoldering anger at the villains at hand. It also sparked an astonishing anti-oil hysteria in Congress. I describe its manifestations—and implications for American business at large—in these remarks at a meeting of the American Association of Petroleum Geologists in Dallas, Texas, in April 1975. Fortunately, none of the legislative proposals I describe below were ever enacted, because the oil markets settled down in time and cooler heads prevailed. But the initiatives I describe serve as a reminder of what kinds of laws Congress might be capable of passing during a future legislative feeding frenzy.

I am delighted to be here today for several reasons. First, it is refreshing to find myself in the company of professionals who understand there really is such a thing as a bottom line. You are scientists who know that in the real world large financial risks and commitments can be justified only on the basis of a hard-headed assessment of potential returns—*after* taxes. I say "refreshing" because I now work in a town where the ruling gentry are insulated from the need to think about making profits, let alone balancing books. In a pinch, all they have to do is print some more money and then blame the resulting inflation on the obscene windfall profits of Ol' Debbil Oil.

I am also delighted to be here as the special guest of the organization's vice president, Duncan McNaughton. I have known Duncan many years. He is a hard man to keep up with, having, among other things, won an Olympic gold medal in hurdling; but I have, quite literally, circled the globe with him, spending many instructive hours at his feet in such exotic ports of call as Manila, Alice Springs, Pretoria, Amsterdam, and, of course, the oil capital of the world, New York City.

Or didn't you realize that I am an oil-state senator? I didn't either until last year, when I read that I was one in the *New York Times*. It happens that in January 1974 I joined three senators from Western states in arguing the economic idiocy of an emergency bill that would roll back the price of new and stripper oil to $5.25 a barrel—"economic idiocy," that is, unless its purpose was to guarantee our perpetual servitude to the OPEC cartel. [*At the time, the Organization of Petroleum Exporting Countries (most of them in the Middle East) had the power to set international oil prices.*] Having helped inject what I thought to be large doses of common sense into the debate, I rushed to my *New York Times* the next day to see how our pearls of wisdom had been reported. I found that all our well-honed arguments had been dismissed with a single sentence: "Several oil-state senators spoke in opposition."

I had never thought of New York as an oil state, but knowing the *Times*'s reputation for accuracy, I decided to check the facts. I called the New York State Department of Mines—yes, we are a mining state as well—and discovered that New York had more than 5,200 oil wells, which in 1973 had produced, in the aggregate, 949,000 barrels of high-quality crude, or about half a barrel per well per day. I also found that we had 725 gas wells producing almost 12 million cubic feet per day, or something less than 1 percent of New York's consumption. Clearly, we were an oil-and-gas-producing state. It was equally clear that we had a ways to go before New York achieved its goal of independence from insecure

sources of supply in Texas, Louisiana, and Oklahoma; but the prospects are encouraging. Because our gas is sold intrastate and our
oil is exempt from price restraints, the incentives created in 1973
by sharply rising prices were working their old-time magic. In
less than a year, land-leasing activity has tripled, while exploratory
drilling has almost doubled—from eight wildcat wells in 1972 to
fourteen in 1973. Depleted fields are being reworked, and deeper
targets, previously considered uneconomic, are now being tested.

I found, in short, that in New York—one of the consumingest
of consumer states—we had a mini petroleum boom in full progress, an example in microcosm of how the oil and gas industry
will respond when market forces are allowed to mobilize the necessary risk capital.

Unfortunately, there is little evidence that this and other
examples of economic cause and effect in the field of energy have
pierced the consciousness of the majority in Congress, in whose
hands lies the future of the oil and gas industry. The implications
of this are far more serious than what it portends for your industry
alone. They go to the heart of the current understanding of how
our economic system of private competitive enterprise works, and
why.

Have no doubt about it. The free-enterprise philosophy
is being attacked on a wider scale than ever before. It is being
attacked, moreover, in the name of a new regulatory ethic promulgated by anti-business critics in the academy and in government,
and implemented by the ever-expanding bureaucracy in Washington. The new regulatory ethic has turned the old presumptions
on their heads.

It was once understood that our economy functioned best and
for the good of the greatest number when it was left to the inter-
action of a million daily decisions by private investors, manufacturers, sellers, and consumers, each pursuing his own private gain
and fulfillment. It was understood that government would inter-
fere in these decisions only where necessary to protect an overriding and clearly defined public need; and then, only to the extent
required to meet that need. It was understood that the primary role
of government in economic affairs was not to control the private

sector, but to preserve the free, competitive environment in which that sector could operate with the greatest efficiency.

But now, the new regulatory ethic is in the ascendant on a broader scale than anyone could have believed just a year or two ago. It takes as indisputable doctrine the desirability and even the absolute necessity for the government to regulate on an ever-wider scale. It has its own propagandists, such as John Kenneth Galbraith; its own shock troops, typified by Ralph Nader; and, as is typical of all essentially ideological movements, its own rallying cry: "the public interest."

Professor Galbraith, the high priest of the planned economy, has written:

> [S]ocial pressures build up, politicians respond, so the kinds of actions which are required get taken. The action may be disguised by the semantics. It will be some time before we get around to talking about planning. It will be longer, no doubt, before we get around to using so obscene a word as "socialism." I sometimes use the phrase "social action," which is more benign. Even talk about income redistribution seems to many people still very odd and dangerous. But circumstances are in the saddle, not theory.

Professor Galbraith at least has the virtue of candor.

That the distrust of business has reached dangerous levels is to me beyond dispute. A 1973 Harris survey showed that 77 percent of those polled wanted the government to be "tougher on business." As recently as 1966, 70 percent of Americans thought that business was at least striking a fair balance between making a profit and providing a service to the public; but last year, only 29 percent did. In 1966, 28 percent thought big business was dangerous to our way of life; last year, 46 percent did.

As the oil and gas business remains indelibly identified in the public mind as the biggest of big businesses, the more than five thousand independent producers notwithstanding, it is hardly surprising that recent polls show that of all U.S. industries, oil and gas commands the next-to-lowest public respect. If it is of any comfort to you, you are outranked in the low-esteem derby by the tobacco industry, whose products the U.S. surgeon general has gone to great lengths to advertise as dangerous to the public's health. I know how you must feel. I am advised that only garbage collectors and journalists are held in lower esteem than politicians. What the public has against garbage collectors, I don't know.

Whether public opinion has affected congressional attitudes, or vice versa, it is clear that today the petroleum industry is Congress's favorite whipping boy. But in sharpening its knives, Congress is doing far more than merely making it harder and more expensive for the industry to develop the new sources of energy required to liberate us from an unhealthy dependence on the OPEC cartel. Legislation in the congressional hoppers today would pioneer new frontiers of federal intervention and control that ought to be of profound concern not only to this industry, but to all American business—and to all consumers as well, as it is they, in the end, who must bear the cost of government-induced inefficiencies.

These new proposals reflect a general ignorance of business economics, a growing hostility to business as a whole, and a passion to regulate that in the case of oil and gas can verge on the punitive. Bills affecting the energy industry have been introduced this year, or are in the last stages of preparation, that are awesome in their sweep. They can only be described as revolutionary in their potential impact on traditional concepts of the appropriate role of government in our economic affairs. Unfortunately, they are attracting growing support among the most influential members of Congress.

Let me describe just a few that I believe have a chance of being enacted by this Congress if effective opposition isn't mobilized. Henry Jackson, chairman of the Senate Interior Committee, is expected shortly to introduce his long-awaited bill for the national chartering of companies engaged in the oil and gas business in the United States. Chartered companies would be required to accept on their boards of directors the equivalent of a Ralph Nader, who would be given the mandate to go rummaging through corporate files for practices he deemed contrary to the public interest. The bill would also require that various refinery products be priced on the basis of cost rather than market. In other words, it would extend public-utility concepts to manufactured goods sold in competitive markets, thereby destroying the market mechanism by which shortage-induced profits serve to channel investment capital where it is needed to increase supply.

The next exhibit in my gallery of horrors is the bill that Senator Adlai Stevenson III has just introduced to establish a federal oil and gas corporation. Its underlying rationale is that a public corporation ought to be formed to develop the public's resources, and never mind the performance of national oil companies in Argentina, Mexico, and elsewhere. This is bad enough, but there is now talk of establishing federally organized "competitive public enterprises" in various industries. Their objective would be to develop yardsticks for determining the extent to which private corporations are operating—you guessed it—in the public interest.

Senator Jackson and Senator Ernest Hollings have both introduced more modest proposals that would authorize the federal government to engage in offshore exploration and production on our outer continental shelves. These bills are about to be marked up by the Interior Committee and should be on the floor of the Senate within a month or so.

I have saved the most astonishing and by far the most dangerous proposal for the last. This one is Senate bill 740, Senator Jackson's proposal for a National Energy Production Board. The board would be authorized not only to tell the petroleum industry where to drill, but also to engage in exploration and production on public lands. The board would be empowered, among other things, to manufacture tubular goods, own and operate coal mines, and nationalize the rail facilities serving them. Although the bill was introduced for what Senator Jackson describes as "discussion purposes," it must be taken seriously. The various recently issued congressional energy reports all contain recommendations favoring the creation of some sort of energy production board.

These proposals, as I say, present a clear and present danger not only to the oil and gas business, but to all business. If refinery products are to be priced on the basis of cost rather than market, why not chemicals, or paper, or computers? If a federally organized company can be justified as providing a basis for determining whether private oil and gas companies are operating in the public interest, how do you draw the line on pharmaceuticals? Tomorrow's whipping boy may well be steel, or insurance, or the banks. These proposals would have been unthinkable just a few years ago; but today they are not only being thought, they are being advocated by members of the Senate who wield important influence. They do violence to our traditional understanding of the respective roles and rights of government and private citizens. But as Professor Galbraith reminds us, "circumstances are in the saddle, not theory."

The time has come, I suggest—in fact, the time is long overdue—for the oil and gas business, indeed for American business as a whole, to take an effective hand in shaping the circumstances of which Professor Galbraith speaks. It seems that there is no challenge that the ingenuity of American business has not been able to meet except that of ensuring the survival of the economic institutions that have provided our people with greater opportunities and a higher standard of living than have been enjoyed by any other in the history of the world. These institutions are under attack, but the captains of industry are too preoccupied with seeking special favors to do anything about it.

As far as I know, there is nothing in our antitrust laws that would prohibit a combination among American businesses in restraint of a headlong plunge into a socialized society; and I submit that nothing short of this sort of combination may be required if we are to avoid one. But if our business community is to harness its enormous resources and talents in a successful rescue operation, every component of American business must learn to work together for the common good by seeking to protect our economic system rather than seeking to achieve parochial advantages.

How is this to be done? First of all, business leaders must become more directly concerned over the general level of public understanding of how that system works. Secondly, business men and women who care about the future must involve themselves in the political process—to advance not their own personal ends, but the nation's ends. Finally, the Washington representatives of every sector of American business must begin lobbying first and foremost for the preservation of a political environment in which our economy can continue to prosper. They should be directed to work against the adoption of any legislation, whomever it directly affects, that would establish new precedents dangerous to our economic system. And who knows, in the process they may even help our legislators gain a better understanding of how our economy operates and why, if left essentially alone, it will continue to serve the best interests of the American people.

Whether we are now living in the twilight years of the most creative and fruitful economic system the world has ever known or whether we will turn the corner and preserve the conditions in which it can continue to flourish may well depend on the will and understanding of those who now head our business community. I fervently hope that they will rise to the challenge. The one thing I know is that they can set for themselves no task better designed to serve their enlightened self-interest as well as the best interests of all Americans.

The petroleum industry is particularly subject to public outrage because it is not only huge, it is hugely visible. The major oil companies are the primary sources of a commodity that is essential to virtually every American, and their names are rubbed in our faces every time we fill our tanks. If anything goes wrong, we know—or think we know—whom to blame. So when oil markets went haywire in the 1970s, Congress indulged in an orgy of Big Oil–bashing, even though it was the Arab oil embargo and OPEC supply trimming that were largely responsible for the long lines and erratic prices at the gasoline pumps.

This is not to suggest that oil companies are beyond reproach. Quite the contrary. During my last conversation with my father, he repeated a familiar warning: "Never trust a major oil company." That advice was based on long experience. I am sure he would have said the same thing of the major players in any other business he might have engaged in, because whether in private or public hands, power breeds arrogance. Corporate giants are quite capable of cutting corners and ignoring the rules that apply to lesser folk.

That may well have been the case with BP's Gulf of Mexico oil-spill disaster in 2010. If so, BP deserved the opprobrium and liabilities it incurred.

Your Energy Regulators at Work

It is one thing to speak of regulation and regulators in general terms. It is quite another to see how the latter's faithful application of the former can trump common sense. I spoke about this in two of the fortnightly commentaries I delivered during 1977 and 1978 on National Public Radio's program All Things Considered.

Natural Gas and Theology

Here are my January 19, 1978, comments on the exasperating subject of natural-gas shortages—exasperating because the solution to that problem had been known for years. All that was required was the elimination of price controls on the interstate sales of natural gas, a solution that was being blocked by ideology, not theology.

When the Senate conferees on the energy bill broke for the holidays empty-handed, a number of commentators noted, in tones ranging from mild to severe disapproval, that their efforts to reach a compromise had run aground on the shoals of "theology." The theologians in question were those who argued that the only way to address growing shortages of natural gas was to phase out federal controls over the wellhead price of natural gas in order to restore incentives for new discoveries by allowing the marketplace to establish the price of this, as well as of every other, commodity.

If a belief in the virtues of a free market is indeed a matter of theology, then it is one worth going to the mat for, and for the most pragmatic of reasons. If the marketplace is kept free and competitive, it is nothing more than a clearinghouse for transactions between willing buyers and willing sellers, and the price agreed upon reflects the classic factors of supply and demand. Under normal circumstances, shortages result in higher prices, which, in turn, provide the incentive for the capital investment required to increase supply. The natural floor for the price of any commodity is the cost of replacing it. The ceiling, in the case of natural gas, is roughly what it would cost consumers to buy the same amount of energy in a different form, namely oil or coal.

We suffer from domestic natural-gas shortages today because, for too many years, government price controls have held the cost of gas committed to interstate pipelines so low, in comparison with the cost of other fuels, that we have created an artificial demand that has depleted existing gas reserves at far too fast a rate. At the same time, the low price imposed by government has destroyed the incentive to make the risky investments required to find and develop new reserves. Yet in the face of all this, the Carter administration still stubbornly insists on keeping the price of natural gas committed to interstate pipelines at below its natural level.

Nothing could better illustrate the idiocy of the Carter policy than the Mexican government's recent announcement that it was suspending its plans to complete a $1.5-billion pipeline to the Texas border—a pipeline that would deliver 2.2 billion cubic feet of gas per day to our interstate system, which is enough to heat between two and four million American homes. Why the suspension? Because the Carter administration refused to approve the sales price that had been negotiated between Mexico and a half-dozen American gas-distribution companies.

Was the price unreasonable? Not by any objective standard. The Mexican government had declared its willingness to commit its huge, newly discovered reserves to the U.S. market at a price that represented no more than the commercial value of the gas as measured by the price of the fuel oil required to yield an equivalent amount of energy. This comes to about $2.60 per thousand cubic feet, which is approximately the same as the current free-market price of natural gas sold intrastate in Texas and Louisiana.

What this tells us is simply this: If we insist on retaining an artificial price lid on new natural gas, we not only retard the development of needed domestic reserves, but we also cut ourselves off from large potential sources now being developed in Mexico and Canada. In the meantime, in order to avoid crippling shortages, gas distributors in the Northeast are busily increasing their production and importation of synthetic and liquefied natural gas at costs significantly higher than the price the Mexicans were asking.

Yes, if gas deregulation is a matter of theology, then let us cheer on the theologians: for what they are promising us is not comfort in the next world, but a sufficiency of gas in this one.

This lament had a happy ending. Soon after this commentary was delivered, the Carter administration yielded to reality and began a staged deregulation of natural gas that culminated in the lifting of all price controls after Ronald Reagan took office. The result? An abundance of natural gas at prices people were happy to pay.

An Alaskan Oil Odyssey

This commentary was broadcast on August 17, 1978.

A recent news item offers a fascinating insight into the tangled web our federal regulators have woven as they meddle in the energy marketplace.

It seems that the government proposes to replace up to 50,000 barrels per day of Ecuadorian and African oil now being refined in Puerto Rico with Californian crude, under a program designed to encourage the movement of surplus Californian oil to other U.S. markets. To cover extra transportation and other expenses, the government proposes to pay the Puerto Rican refiner an additional $4.41 per barrel in "entitlement subsidies" under its "crude oil cost equalization program."

Now let's try to thread our way through this bureaucratic maze. First we need to ask ourselves, why is there a surplus of Californian crude? The answer is because the West Coast is now being flooded with Alaskan crude. Alaskan producers had wanted to sell their oil in its logical market, Japan, and to use the proceeds to help pay for foreign oil imported into the eastern United States, but Congress would have none of it.

Oil produced in the United States, wherever located, must be sold in the United States, at whatever cost. And so, instead of using the dollars earned by exporting the Alaskan oil to finance the purchase by the Puerto Rican refinery of oil from its logical sources in Ecuador and Africa, the government insists that the Alaskan crude be dumped into West Coast markets, creating the surpluses which the government proposes to take care of by offering over $80 million a year in subsidies to induce a Puerto Rican refiner to import its oil all the way from California.

[*The above is from the first two pages of a four-page commentary. Unfortunately, I have lost the third page. I am left, however, with the following teaser from the fourth.*]

. . . different classes of users. All of this will require a bewildering number of classifications of gas—seventeen, to be precise—which are to be subject to twelve different pricing formulas.

This is an example of the labyrinthine extremes to which the regulatory mind is capable of going. In this case, it was an attempt to restore incentives for the production of new gas while stubbornly retaining price controls.

BEYOND THE
WATER'S EDGE

My reference to "the water's edge" here has to do with America's turning her face to the world. Its classic use, of course, is in the venerable axiom that "Politics stops at the water's edge." That precept has been honored mostly in the breach, and with reason. Despite a president's constitutional primacy in the areas of national security and foreign policy, Congress has legitimate responsibilities in respect to both those areas. The problem arises when, in exercising those responsibilities, a politicized Congress refuses to consider the consequences of its actions beyond the water's edge. That was the case with Vietnam.

Vietnam and Its Aftermath

There are lessons to be drawn from our Vietnam experience: We should be very, very reluctant to become involved in conflicts abroad; but once engaged, we should be equally reluctant to turn tail because of political pressures at home. That doesn't mean that we must remain engaged forever in a no-win situation; only that any withdrawal must be managed in a manner that will not endanger vital American interests elsewhere. The following is taken from my 1974 book, If Men Were Angels.

On the afternoon of August 21, 1974, I stood on the floor of the Senate, listening to the clerk intone the litany of familiar names as he called the roll. Amid the usual clatter that marks the Senate chamber during a roll-call vote, I sensed a serious mood. This vote was one that you know is different, one that is symbolic of issues larger than the specific question being voted on.

When my name was called, I cast my vote against the proposed reduction in military aid to South Vietnam. As other senators came into the chamber to answer "Aye" or "No," it soon became apparent that my negative vote was going to be one of a distinct minority. The final vote was an overwhelming 86 to 5 in favor of an appropriations bill slashing by more than half the administration's $1.5-billion request for military aid to South Vietnam.

The Senate had repudiated our undertaking, as expressed in the Paris Accords of January 1973, to replace "armaments, munitions, and war matériel which have been destroyed . . . or used up after the cease-fire, on the basis of piece-for-piece," and in the process created doubt as to the continuing ability of the South Vietnamese to repel the mounting attacks by the well-equipped forces of the North.

I will not re-examine the old arguments as to whether we should have become actively involved in the Vietnam conflict in the first place; or, having become engaged, how we ought to have conducted the war. I would only observe that there was nothing impulsive about our involvement in Vietnam. We went in, on a steadily expanding scale, as a result of decisions by three presidents, the first a Republican, the next two Democrats. These decisions were concurred in by the leaders of our military forces and by majorities in both houses of Congress. The critical expansion in the magnitude, though not in the essential character, of our involvement took place under the authority of the Tonkin Gulf Resolution, which was adopted by a near-unanimous vote. Although it is charged that President Johnson engaged in deception to secure approval of the resolution, Congress nevertheless continued for many years thereafter to appropriate the funds required to support our involvement in the war.

The military aid appropriations bill that sealed the fate of the Republic of South Vietnam, the one adopted by so lopsided a vote on August 21, 1974, was not surreptitious. There had been sufficient advance notice to allow every member of the Senate to reach a deliberate decision on how he would vote. While the other "patron" signatories to the Paris Accords—the Soviet Union and China—had violated the spirit of the accords by the exuberance with which they supplied Hanoi with the most modern weapons even as the North Vietnamese were busily building roads and airports and expanding their forces south of the demilitarized zone in direct violation of the accords, the U.S. Congress also violated their spirit by placing the South Vietnamese on half rations.

Barry Goldwater made a rhetorical point by proposing an amendment (which he never actually introduced) that would have eliminated military aid to South Vietnam altogether. His argument was simple. South Vietnam could not possibly survive on a starvation diet. Therefore the cost of the reduced aid provided for in the Senate appropriations bill could not be justified. Senator Goldwater was, of course, correct. No matter how brave you are, it is impossible to win a battle against a well-armed enemy if you are not kept supplied with weapons and fuel, if you have to hoard your ammunition (towards the end the South Vietnamese infantrymen in the Fourth Military Region were allotted two grenades per day instead of the usual ten, and twenty-five rounds of artillery ammunition per gun instead of the usual two hundred), and if you find you cannot concentrate your forces to meet an attack because more than 60 percent of your aircraft are grounded for lack of spare parts.

I say "No matter how brave you are" because of the prevalent myth that the South Vietnamese were unwilling to fight. The wonder is that they continued to fight so long after it became clear that Congress had decided to abandon them. We find it oh so easy to overlook the fact that in the two years between January 1973 (when the Paris Accords ushered in a "cease-fire") and January 1975 (when the North Vietnamese launched major attacks in the highlands in flamboyant violation of the same accords), the South Vietnamese forces had suffered more than 59,000 men *killed* out of a population of less than one-tenth that of the United States.

The Republic of South Vietnam has now slipped into history, and its more than twenty million people are now under the Communist rule that so many of them had fought against for more than twenty years at an incalculable cost. It will always be arguable whether the South Vietnamese could in the end have maintained their independence even with unstinting material aid from the United States. What cannot be argued is the role Congress played in sealing their fate.

Whether we like it or not, the world viewed the Vietnam War as far more than a fratricidal conflict in a remote corner of Asia. It was seen as a test of wills between the United States on the one hand and the Soviet Union and China on the other, one which we ultimately failed. We can protest that we ought not to have become involved in Indochina, or that we had already expended more in blood and treasure than ought to have been expected of any outsider. But, unfortunately, the world is more interested in results than explanations, especially those parts of the world that have been asked to place their reliance on America.

The point was made with characteristic tact and clarity in a statement that caught my attention during my 1970 campaign for the Senate. Abba Eban, then foreign minister of Israel, had this to say during the course of a televised interview:

> There are two trends in American history: there is a trend towards responsibility and commitment—and there is a trend towards withdrawal and isolation. . . . Now if the argument is for a withdrawal and for saying that it doesn't matter if a little country goes under, then this can become an epidemic. . . . On the other hand, if there is a line of principle which says that if there are engagements for the protection of independence of countries, these engagements must be honored to the fullest possible effective extent, then all small countries will be the beneficiaries of that approach. Now, it may be that Vietnam is not a very happy arena in which to put this principle to the test. I'm not answering that question, but I do understand those who say that if you want America to show a spirit of commitment and responsibility in one area, then you should be careful not to take an attitude of withdrawal and folding up the tent in another. Or, if you do, you should establish this distinction very carefully and with much logical rationality.

Once Congress decided not to honor our engagement, under the Paris Accords, to replace expended matériel on a one-for-one basis, did we make the necessary distinctions with "logical rationality"? The answer is no, or at least the rationale proved too obscure for the leaders of the countries who must try to anticipate

American intentions, as witness the following reactions to the debacle in Vietnam:

"The United States does not have any morals at this point. They have already pulled out from Cambodia and South Vietnam, so we are going to have to depend on ourselves."
                    —Thai Foreign Minister Chatichai Choonhavan

"I believe the danger of the North Korean Communist clique playing with fire is greater this year than ever before."
                    —South Korean President Park Chung Hee

"Japan, too, must rectify her position of having relied excessively on the United States."
                    —Foreign Ministry official in Tokyo

"Rather than go through the mincing machine, it makes more sense to seek political and diplomatic solutions."
                    —Singaporean Prime Minister Lee Kwan Yew

"Close links with the Communist states are the only ways to ensure our security and survival."
                    —Philippine President Ferdinand Marcos

"If Berlin were attacked tomorrow I am not absolutely certain that the United States would intervene."
                    —Kurt Biedenkopf, Secretary General of West
                    Germany's Christian Democratic Union

These statements were made within a week or two of the fall of Saigon. Asian nations wasted no time in accommodating to what they perceived to be the new realities. Thailand formally requested that the United States close down its air bases within a year, beginning with the immediate withdrawal of 7,500 men.

Stating candidly that his country could no longer afford the luxury of relying on American guarantees, President Marcos ordered a renegotiation of American basing rights in the Philippines. Indonesia declared a policy of neutrality, while North Korea's President Kim Il Sung started rattling sabers while demanding a withdrawal of American forces stationed in South Korea. Japan sent a special delegation to the United States as part of a major reassessment that some believe could even lead to a decision by Japan to build nuclear arms, an option that the South Koreans are rumored to have under active consideration as the only reliable means of self-defense. The rollback of American forward bases to the Marianas and Hawaii may come sooner than anticipated by the most avid advocates of the domino theory.

I do not suggest that we can never change either the form or the substance of our relationships with other nations. What I do suggest is that those changes we do make must be made deliberately with their long-range consequences well in mind, and that if we intend to continue a major role in the affairs of Asia or anywhere else, we must place a high premium on maintaining the confidence of those on whose goodwill and cooperation we must rely in our own self-interest.

In Vietnam, we failed a major test; and as a result we may invite other, even more difficult ones, in other areas—Korea, the Middle East, Africa, or even in our own hemisphere. It may take such a test to restore confidence in our ability as a nation to sustain a role of leadership. We may well have to redefine the engagements we are now prepared to honor. But having done so, we will have to persuade friends and foes alike that we can be relied on to keep them. Unless we do, we will most assuredly undermine the network of alliances on which our foreign policy and world stability have so long depended.

Those tests weren't long in coming; and, in time, they did reach into our hemisphere. Our failure of will in Vietnam encouraged the Soviets to launch a series of initiatives in the 1970s, some of them military, that brought South Yemen, Ethiopia, Angola, and Nicaragua within their orbit. This experience suggests the likely responses in the Middle East and elsewhere should we be perceived as having abandoned Iraq or Afghanistan under pressure.

The Mexico City Population Conference

In the spring of 1984, I was asked by President Reagan to serve as chairman of the American delegation to the UN Conference on Population that was to take place that summer in Mexico City. The American position was highly controversial because (a) it urged the adoption of free-market economics as the most effective way of achieving long-term reductions in fertility rates and (b) the administration had announced that the United States would no longer make contributions to organizations that promoted or funded abortions in other countries. The latter, now known as the "Mexico City policy," caused a furor in pro-choice circles here at home, and it continues to be controversial. President Bill Clinton shelved the prohibition on funding on his first day in office; his successor, George W. Bush, restored it shortly after he assumed the presidency; and it took his successor, Barack Obama, only two days to banish it again. The following report was published in the December 14, 1984, issue of National Review.

As has become depressingly typical of too many UN affairs, the International Conference on Population in Mexico City last August operated on two quite different planes, each with its own agenda and dynamics. The first involved the substantive matters the conference had been called to address, all in one way or another broadly related to the twin subjects of population and economic-development policies and their interrelationship. The second was purely political.

In theory, conferences sponsored by specialized agencies of the UN are supposed to deal with problems of universal concern, problems that transcend politics. But in practice, they have tended to have a second, unstated agenda forced upon them by the Soviet Union and various Third World factions intent on exploiting them as targets of opportunity for the pursuit of highly political and often inflammatory objectives.

At the substantive level, the United States accomplished far more than anyone had a right to expect, especially in the light of the near hysteria with which the United States' statement on population policy had been received by the press and birth-control activists here at home. On the eve of the conference, Robert McNamara assured a national NBC audience that the American delegation would be laughed out of Mexico City. Instead, we emerged with some significant achievements.

As the result of our initiatives, the report adopted by the conference reaffirmed the primacy of parental rights in determining the size of individual families, condemned the use of coercion to achieve state-defined population objectives, and acknowledged that government is not the sole agency for the achievement of social objectives. It also adopted a far more balanced presentation of the progress already achieved by the developing world in advancing individual well-being and reducing birth rates. Also, given the intensity of the attacks on the U.S. position on abortion ("the United States does not consider abortion an acceptable element of family planning programs"), we took considerable satisfaction from the adoption, by a conference consensus, of an almost identical position; namely, that abortion "in no case should be promoted as a method of family planning."

Where we did not succeed, nor would it have been anything but romantic for us to think we could have succeeded, was in securing an explicit endorsement of the American proposition that the best way for developing nations to achieve the twin objectives of economic development and population stability would be through the adoption of freer, market-oriented economic policies. To have succeeded in that would have required that a significant number of delegations acknowledge that their own countries' centralized controls were responsible for much of the misery experienced by their people.

Nonetheless, raising the issue of economic policy enabled us to cite a compelling historical linkage between rising income and declining birth rates, and to draw on the examples of such developing countries as Singapore, South Korea, Colombia, and Botswana to demonstrate the linkage between economic freedom and economic growth. And we weren't laughed out of town for having made the attempt.

As the UN Fund for Population Activities itself acknowledges, "It has been clear for a long time that family planning campaigns are largely ineffectual in producing a lower rate of population growth." The UNFPA also observes: "While family planning programs . . . will help couples to have the number of children they wish, other economic and social factors lie behind their ideas of desired family size." On the record, rising income is the most important of those factors.

Nor did our advocacy of freer economies make us pariahs. In fact, many statist nations tacitly acknowledge the need for change. As a Kenyan journalist admitted in a *Newsweek* article attacking the U.S. position, many countries, especially in Africa, "that opted for socialist systems soon after independence are now gradually shifting their economic policies towards free enterprise." Perhaps it was for that reason that the U.S. delegation can be credited with the revolutionary achievement of insinuating the phrase "entrepreneurial initiatives" into a UN document as having some relevance to economic growth.

By the sheer mobilization of statistics, we were also able to pierce the Malthusian gloom with which so many wanted the proceedings to be wrapped. We demonstrated, for example, that over the last thirty years, birth rates in the developing world have fallen more than halfway towards the goal of population stability, that human life expectancy had dramatically increased, and that caloric intake had improved, literacy soared, disease diminished, and per capita income grown substantially. At the same time, we helped to focus attention on those nations—particularly in sub-Saharan Africa and portions of the Indian subcontinent— that had not shared in this undoubted progress, and therefore required particular attention. Although these tender rays of sunshine were not universally welcomed, they did help illuminate the true dimensions of the problems that remain to be resolved and place them in the unhysterical perspective that is essential to intelligent analysis.

In retrospect, this is not a bad track record for what the American press almost unanimously predicted would be an American disaster. And I believe we could have accomplished even more had so much of our delegation's time and energies not been preempted by the conference's second, unofficial agenda; namely, the political agenda.

This consisted of two extraneous proposals. The first was sponsored by the Soviet Union. In essence, it would have committed the conference to the proposition that no progress was possible in dealing with economic and population matters unless and until nuclear arms were dismantled, the threat of nuclear devastation eliminated, and the West's investment in armaments redirected to the production of plowshares. The second proposal was introduced by a group of Arab countries. It contained a statement that "the establishment of settlements in territories occupied by force is illegal and condemned by the international community." Although no names were mentioned, it was amply clear from the proposal's history and sponsorship that it was aimed not at Soviet settlements in the occupied Kuriles, not at the Vietnamese colonization of Cambodia, but, in exclusive intent, at Israeli settlements on the West Bank.

We did our best to eliminate these wholly irrelevant and politically disruptive proposals because, if allowed to stand, they would feed the cancer that is already plaguing the entire UN system and making it increasingly difficult for serious people to conduct a rational discussion of important matters in any forum sponsored by a UN agency. Working with a number of other delegations that shared our concern, we were ultimately able to neutralize the Soviet thrust, but we failed on the issue of settlements. Israel, it is clear, has far fewer friends within the United Nations than does the Soviet Union, and it has none of the latter's leverage.

This, of course, is precisely the kind of political corruption that caused the United States to notify UNESCO, earlier this year, of its intention to withdraw from that body; the kind of corruption the Reagan administration has been fighting throughout the UN system these past four years. This solicitude for the well-being of the United Nations seems ironic, to say the least. Perhaps no American administration has been more skeptical of the ultimate value of the United Nations; yet, none in recent years has taken it more seriously. In fact, today, the United States may be the only Western nation to do so.

Unlike our sophisticated European brethren, we no longer treat the excesses and presumptions of UN resolutions as "mere words" that give developing countries a chance to blow off steam, words that have no meaning in the real world. On the contrary, we believe that Third World formulations, if they are repeated often enough and left unchallenged, will achieve a cumulative effect that can damage our fundamental interests and erode traditional concepts of international law.

In private meetings, more often than not with other Western delegations, we hammered away at the point that unless a stop was put to the practice of converting every international conference into an ideological battlefield, the United Nations would soon lose its utility as a forum for the discussion and settlement of prob- lems that clearly lay outside the realm of politics. When speaking with other Westerners, we generally met with strong support on the matter of principle and with simultaneous explanations as to why it would be either inconvenient or impossible for a particular nation to draw the necessary line at that particular time.

This experience is an example of the differences in perspective within the Atlantic alliance that so often take Americans by sur- prise. When an American meets with his European counterparts at an international conference, he is apt to find the experience marvelously seductive. European professionals tend to be intelligent and urbane; we and they speak the same intellectual language, and share the same values. But any time the conversation goes much beneath the surface, the fundamental differences that distinguish the American experience from the European will reveal themselves. By and large, America has retained a sense of purpose, self-confidence, and hope. Beneath the European surface, however, one can detect the symptoms of tired societies unable or unwilling to think through to ultimate consequences, societies for which there are few causes that will justify the risk of confrontation.

At one meeting attended by delegates from several Western nations, I looked around the room and thought about the latent political and economic power represented there. As I listened to the rationalizations, I concluded that the problem with the United Nations lies not with the Third World countries (which can hardly be blamed for asserting bloc leverage so long as they can get away with it) nor with the ability of the Soviet bloc to exploit their tensions, hopes, and resentments. The problem lies with the West. If the half-dozen countries that provide more than half the UN's total revenues chose to do so, they could put an end to the abuses we were then witnessing. All that is required to achieve reform is for the major Western nations to announce that henceforward they will withdraw from any UN conference that allows politically divisive, non-germane business to be placed on the agenda; and, then, to demonstrate that they mean it.

The compulsion to politicize it is by no means the only problem undermining the UN system, although it is the one that could be most easily corrected. Others are imbedded in the UN Charter itself. The structural problems range from the UN's voting rules to its mandate to promote human rights and fundamental freedoms. The former, in which each sovereignty is accorded an equal vote despite the vast disparities among them, encourages an irresponsibility and a cynicism that too often serve to heighten tensions rather than dissipate them. The latter requires the UN to square the circle in vain attempts to find common ground between the free world and the Communist world on such matters as democracy and the freedoms to speak, worship, and assemble. The result too often is a resort to Orwellian Newspeak that debases the rights and freedoms the UN is supposed to champion.

These and other flaws will not be corrected by spontaneous action on the part of the member states that have learned to turn them to their advantage. The initiative can only come from the West. Only the West has the power to compel a fundamental re-examination of the UN's structure, mission, and practices. But if the will isn't there, if the West is not in fact ready to take the UN seriously and save it from its own suicidal tendencies, then the time may soon come for the United States to face the ultimate option; and that is to acknowledge the UN's failure, provide it with the sad eulogies appropriate to lost causes, and give it a quiet burial.

Because one thing is clear: If allowed to continue on its current course, the UN will prove itself a forum not for the analysis and resolution of technical problems, but for endless political warfare; an advocate not of basic human rights, but of their subordination to the superior rights claimed by the majority of member states; an instrument not for peace, but for aggravating tensions.

Sophisticates were dismayed by our delegation's insistence that economic development held the key to bringing population growth under control. So I chuckled when, twenty-five years later, I perused the October 31, 2009, issue of The Economist. *Its cover showed a diapered baby in free fall over the legend, "Falling fertility. How the population problem is solving itself." The text underscored the role of, yes, economic development in triggering record declines in developing-world fertility rates. The Economist noted that "By about 2020, the global fertility rate will dip below the global replacement rate for the first time." A future UN conference will no doubt be called to consider the plight of nations with population implosions.*

REFORMS

U.S. Senator Roscoe Conkling once quipped, "When Dr. Johnson defined patriotism as the last refuge of a scoundrel, he did not have in mind the possibilities of the word *reform.*" Bearing that in mind, I offer some thoughts on one reform that should be repealed and others that should be adopted if we are to improve campaigns for and the functioning of Congress. My recommendations are based on my experiences both as a candidate for elective office and as a member of the Senate.

On Limiting Campaign Contributions

I became involved in the issue of campaign financing when the Campaign Reform Act of 1974 reached the Senate floor. Among other things, the legislation placed limits on both campaign contributions and spending in federal elections. I questioned the 1974 act's merits as a matter of public policy and challenged its constitutionality in court. The result was the case of Buckley v. Valeo, in which the Supreme Court declared that the limits on expenditures were unconstitutional but sustained those on contributions. I discussed the consequences of that decision in the following article from the September 27, 1999, issue of National Review.

I think it is time for the Buckley of *Buckley* v. *Valeo to* say a word about today's debate on campaign-finance reform. Recently, the Twentieth Century Fund released a 140-page report entitled "*Buckley* Stops Here: Loosening the Judicial Stranglehold on Campaign Finance Reform." As the title suggests, the report proposes a legal strategy for persuading the Supreme Court to reverse certain of its holdings in the *Buckley* decision. The authors of the report are particularly concerned with the Court's conclusion that the First Amendment forbids any limitation on what a campaign committee or an independent citizen may spend in support of a candidate for federal office or on what a candidate may expend on his own campaign. For them, meaningful reform requires stringent restrictions on the amounts that may be contributed *or* spent by all players in the election game. As a federal judge, I accept the Court's construction of the Constitution; but as the Buckley in *Buckley*, I feel obliged to offer a dissenting view as to what constitutes true reform as a matter of public policy.

At the outset, it is instructive to take a look at the *Buckley* plaintiffs. They were political underdogs and outsiders. Although I was a United States senator at the time, I had squeaked into office four years earlier as the first third-party candidate in forty years to be elected to the Senate. My co-plaintiffs included Senator Eugene McCarthy, who had bucked his party's establishment by running a sufficiently effective challenge in 1968 to cause President Lyndon Johnson to withdraw his candidacy for re-election; the very conservative American Conservative Union and the equally liberal New York Civil Liberties Union; New York's Conservative Party and the national Libertarian Party; and Stewart Mott, a wealthy sponsor of liberal causes who had contributed $220,000 to the McCarthy presidential campaign.

What we all had in common was a concern that the 1974 amendments to the Federal Election Campaign Act would effectively squeeze independent voices and political reform movements out of the political process by making it even more difficult than it already was to raise effective challenges to the political status quo. That legislation established, among other things, an elaborate system of public financing for presidential elections, and it placed ceilings on what could be spent by presidential and congressional campaign committees. It also restricted independent spending in support of a candidate to $1,000 and limited individual campaign contributions to $1,000. However, it permitted contributions of $5,000 to political-action committees (the notorious "PACs"), which, in turn, could contribute up to $5,000 to a candidate.

We believed that these restrictions were fundamentally flawed both constitutionally and as a matter of public policy. The core value protected by the First Amendment's Speech Clause is the freedom of political speech. It is incontrovertible that, in today's world, it takes money—and a great deal of it—for political speech to be heard. Therefore, we opposed the 1974 amendments' limits on contributions and spending as unlawful restrictions on political speech. We found the legislation equally objectionable on grounds of public policy because a healthy democracy should encourage competition in the political marketplace rather than increase the difficulties already faced by those challenging incumbents or the existing political establishment. Incumbents enjoy enormous advantages over challengers. These include name recognition, the use of the frank to communicate with constituents, automatic access to the media, and the goodwill derived from handling constituent problems.

Given this fundamental political reality, a challenger who is not a celebrity in his own right must be able to persuade both the media and a broad base of potential contributors that his candidacy is credible. This requires a substantial amount of seed money. As I testified in *Buckley*, I could not have won election in 1970 if the present $1,000 limit on individual contributions had been in place. Thanks to substantial gifts from a handful of individuals, my campaign was able at the outset to hire key personnel, print campaign literature, and rent strategically located space for our New York City headquarters. This caused the media to take my candidacy seriously; and that, in turn, enabled me to raise (largely through mass mailings) the $2 million required for a competitive campaign. Nor could Senator McCarthy have launched a serious challenge to an incumbent president without the more than $1 million that was provided by fewer than a dozen early supporters.

We won a number of our arguments before the Supreme Court, but lost the critical one. The Court agreed with us that the restrictions placed on what could be spent in support of a congressional candidate were unconstitutional. It held, however, that the limitations placed on contributions by individuals and PACs was constitutional because of Congress's expressed concern for avoiding the appearance of improper influence in federal elections. But because an individual cannot corrupt himself, the Court overturned the limits that Congress had placed on what candidates could spend on their own campaigns.

In the wake of the Supreme Court's decision, we are left with a package of federal election laws and regulations that have distorted virtually every aspect of the election process. The 1974 amendments were supposed to de-emphasize the role of money in federal elections. Instead, by limiting individual contributions to a thousand dollars of diminishing value, that law has made the search for money a candidate's central preoccupation. When I ran in 1970, I never made telephone calls requesting money, and I doubt that I attended as many as a dozen fundraising functions. Passing the hat was the exclusive concern of my finance committee. Today, the need to scrounge for money has proven so burdensome that two senators have recently cited this as a major reason for their decision to retire from public life.

The federal regulation of campaigns has virtually driven grass-roots action from the political scene. The rules have become too complex, the costs of a misstep too great. In 1970, when on campaign tours around New York State, I would often run into groups that, on their own initiative, had rented storefronts from which to dispense my campaign literature, man the phones, and deploy volunteers. Today, anyone intrepid enough to engage in that sort of spontaneous grass-roots action is well advised to enlist the counsel of an election lawyer and an accountant; and even then, he must be prepared to prove his independence in court. In the case of my storefront volunteers, the mere possession of my campaign handouts would have been cited as proof enough of collusion.

The restrictions on giving are also at the root of the alarums in recent times over the uses of "soft" money, a term of art used to describe money raised by political parties that is not subject to federal-election-law limits, and sometimes used to describe all unregulated money. This includes, for example, the use of funds to advocate positions with which a particular candidate is identified—known as "issue advocacy." Such expenditures are perfectly legal and, in fact, constitutionally protected if one is to take the Supreme Court's holdings in *Buckley* at face value. Nevertheless, reformers are demanding the closing of what they describe as the loopholes in present law that permit such egregious abuses of political speech.

Today's reformers also complain about the power of PACs, and there is some justification for those concerns. PACs can have very specific objectives and they may make contributions conditional on a candidate's commitment to vote this way or that on future legislation. But these committees are the beneficiaries of the restrictions placed on individual giving by the reformers of 1974. A citizen who would have contributed $25,000 to one or two candidates in whom he believes, but who is limited to a gift of $1,000 to each, will find other ways to deploy the rest of the money he has earmarked for political purposes.

But perhaps the most disturbing consequence of the 1974 amendments has been the way they have consolidated the political power of favored establishment forces. By compounding the difficulties faced by challengers, they have enlarged the advantages already enjoyed by incumbents. By restricting the political speech of political outsiders, they have enhanced the power of the two major parties. By discouraging individual action, they have enhanced the political influence of trade associations and labor unions. And if current efforts to control issue advocacy succeed, the result will be to increase still more the political power already exercised by the mass media.

There is general agreement that the current state of the law governing federal campaigns is worse than unsatisfactory. The answer, however, is not to place further restrictions on the freedom of speech but to re-examine the premises on which the existing ones have been based. In the first instance, it has been amply demonstrated in a dozen recent races that money cannot "buy" elections. The voters have the final say. What money can do is buy the exposure without which no candidate, however meritorious, has a chance. This is the major reason why sound public policy would not place artificial obstacles in the way of challengers trying to launch a viable campaign.

Second, while it is of course true that large contributions can corrupt, the likelihood that a candidate will be seduced by such contributions is vastly overstated. The overwhelming majority of wealthy donors back candidates with whom they are in general agreement, and they are far more tolerant of differences on this point or that than are the PACs or other single-issue organizations to which a candidate will otherwise turn for necessary financing. It is true, of course, that a major financial contributor will have readier access to a candidate he has helped elect than someone else might have, and with access comes the opportunity to persuade. But corruption occurs only when a legislator casts a vote that violates his convictions in exchange for financial support; and virtually every study of actual voting patterns suggests that this kind of corruption is too rare to warrant the distortions created by the present law in its attempt to avoid appearances of impropriety.

This is not to deny the importance of such appearances in a cynical age. A less damaging remedy is available, however, and that is full and immediate disclosure. Campaign committees can and should be required to record contributions on a daily basis and to make that information immediately available over the Internet. The opposing campaign can be relied upon to publicize any gift that could give rise to an adverse inference. The public can then judge whether the contribution is apt to corrupt its recipient. What makes no sense is to retain a set of rules that make it impossible for a Stewart Mott to provide a Eugene McCarthy with the seed money essential to a credible challenge to a sitting president, or that make politics the playground of the super-rich who can finance their own campaigns.

The greater the government's involvement in our lives, the more important it is that participation in political debate be unhampered by artificial restraints. The problem today is not that too much money is spent on elections. It isn't. Procter & Gamble spends more each year in advertising its products than all political campaigns and parties do in extolling the merits of theirs. The problem is that the electoral process is enmeshed in a tangle of campaign laws and regulations that restrict the ability of citizens to make themselves heard and that rig the political game in favor of the most privileged players. And because congressional incumbents are the beneficiaries of the tilted playing field (the advantages of Senate incumbency are worth well over $1 million in some states), it is fanciful to believe that Congress will rewrite the rule book to give outsiders an even break. (I know because I tried. The 1974 campaign-financing bill placed a cap on spending in congressional elections. I submitted an amendment that would have allowed challengers to spend 20 percent more than incumbents. It was tabled, of course, without discussion—as was a proposal that challengers at least be granted franking privileges comparable to those enjoyed by incumbents.)

The road to true reform lies not in trying to persuade the Supreme Court to permit further restrictions on political speech, as the authors of the Twentieth Century Fund report are seeking to do, but in trying to persuade Congress to rescind those that now exist while requiring the immediate disclosure of contributions. We have nothing to fear from unfettered political debate and everything to gain. If artificial restraints are lifted, viable candidates will not lack the funds with which to be heard, because no side of the policy debates has a monopoly on money. American democracy can ill afford government control of the political marketplace; but that is where today's reformers would lead us. [Vide *Congress's enactment, in 2002, of the McCain-Feingold bill outlawing varieties of independent political speech for various periods prior to federal elections.*]

Justice Clarence Thomas's concurring opinion in Citizens United v. FEC, *the Supreme Court's most recent ruling on campaign-reform laws, has given me serious second thoughts on the merits of requiring the instant identification of contributors to political campaigns. Justice Thomas describes in chilling detail the organized harassment of individuals who had made contributions in support of a California referendum and the effect of that harassment on others. He then concludes that he "cannot endorse a view of the First Amendment that subjects citizens of this Nation to death threats, ruined careers, damaged or defaced property, or pre-emptive and threatening* warning letters as the price for engaging in 'core political speech, the "primary object of First Amendment protection."'" I am no longer sure that I can either. Which raises the question: Is there another way of defusing the fact or appearance of corruption that can arise from large expenditures in support of a political candidate? One that comes to mind is a law requiring that all contributions be made anonymously. To be effective, however, such a law would have to require the execution of anyone who divulged the identity of a contributor. But it may be worth a try.

An Alternative Reform:
Term Limitations

In January 2000, I was the speaker at an American Conservative Union dinner celebrating the twenty-fifth anniversary of Buckley v. Valeo. The dinner was attended by my co-plaintiff Senator Eugene McCarthy and by Ira Glasser, executive director of the American Civil Liberties Union, whose New York affiliate had also served as a co-plaintiff.

In my remarks, I offered substantially the same critique of campaign-financing limitations that I had advanced in my National Review *article, but I then addressed the subject of term limitations—the reform I believe we need most urgently, at least at the national level. I led into the subject by noting that . . .*

The kind of corruption the media talk about, the kind the Supreme Court was concerned about, involves the putative sale of legislative favors in exchange for campaign contributions. But virtually every study of actual voting patterns suggests that this occurs far too rarely to warrant the distortions of the political process that are the product of the present law. What people fail to appreciate is that the currency of corruption in elective office is not money, but votes. Witness, for example, the extraordinary leverage exercised by Iowa farmers during the quadrennial caucus season and, it seems, by the Miami Cuban community in just about any season.

This source of corruption, alas, is inherent in the democratic system itself; and it can be controlled only, if at all, by finding ways to encourage legislators to subordinate ambition to principle. The oath of office required by the Constitution represents one such attempt. Before taking office, members of Congress must swear that they will support the Constitution and faithfully discharge the duties of the office they are about to assume, which duties presumably include the duty to vote one's conscience. Unfortunately, in today's world we have to be reminded that the power of an oath derives from the fact that in it we ask God to bear witness to the promises we make, with the implicit expectation that He will hold us accountable for the manner in which we honor them. This understanding of the meaning of an oath is as old as our civilization. In a passage on the role of religion in the Roman Empire, Edward Gibbon noted that the Roman magistrates "respected as the firmest bond of society, the useful persuasion that, either in this or in a future life, the crime of perjury is most assuredly punished by the avenging gods."

I suspect there are few positions in public life in which it is easier to keep faith with an oath of office than the one I now occupy. Thanks to life tenure and the cloistered environment in which appellate judges work, none of us is exposed to the temptations to depart from perceived duty that routinely confront our senators and representatives. I am persuaded that in the case of elected officials, the overwhelming temptation is to conclude that it is more important for your constituents that you be re-elected than that you deal honestly with them. Hence the frequency with which legislators will yield to political pressures or expediency and vote against their convictions, especially when they can salve tender consciences by persuading themselves that a principled vote would not have affected the outcome. Given the difficulty of resisting such temptations over the longer run, a proper concern for the welfare of congressional souls may well be the ultimate argument in favor of term limitations.

In the last analysis, of course, an oath will encourage fidelity in office only to the degree that officeholders continue to believe that they cannot escape ultimate accountability for a breach of faith. In a footnote to the passage I quoted earlier, Gibbon observed that by around 100 A.D., the poet Juvenal would lament that the Roman world had lost the fear of punishment in the afterlife that had given oaths their special force. I suspect the same may now be said of ours.

It would seem, therefore, that this constitutional safeguard may no longer serve its original purpose, especially when, as we learned last year in the Clinton impeachment proceedings, some acts of perjury may now be acceptable—in this world, at least, if not the next. Under the circumstances, I suggest the adoption of term limitations as an alternative means of encouraging probity in elective office. Once it becomes impossible for members of Congress to make a career of legislative service, the temptation to bend a vote for whatever reason may yield to the better angels of their nature. They may then be willing to cast principled votes based on an educated understanding of the public interest in the face of polls suggesting that the public itself may have quite a different understanding of where its interest lies.

I reached this conclusion towards the end of my service in the Senate, and I have observed nothing since then that has done other than reinforce my conviction that, under today's conditions, nothing short of term limitations can be counted upon to liberate the best in the very fine men and women who continue to be elected to Congress. Our old tradition of citizen legislators was a great one, and I recommend espousal of term limitations to both the ACU and the ACLU as another cause in which they may confidently cooperate.

My epiphany on this subject occurred in November 1970. President Nixon had invited me to meet with him shortly after my election to the Senate. When I was ushered into the Oval Office, Nixon was standing behind his desk. He was completing a meeting with George Shultz, who was then director of the

Office of Management and Budget. As I entered, I heard the president say, ". . . but Milton Friedman doesn't understand that an election will be coming up." It seemed clear that they had been discussing Friedman's advice on a particular economic matter, that they agreed with that advice, but that the president was reluctant to act on it because of its possible impact on his 1972 re-election campaign. That persuaded me that a president should be limited to a single six-year term. I felt (and continue to feel) that six years is long enough to give a president a fair opportunity to deliver on his campaign promises, but not so long as to enable him to inflict irreparable harm on the Republic should he prove a disaster. After a couple of years in the Senate, I was persuaded that limits should be placed on congressional service as well.

Reforming the Senate

In my article "On Becoming a United States Senator" (see p. 26, above), I describe the huge pressures under which senators now have to operate and the impact these have on their work. The following (which originally appeared in that article) suggests ways in which the Senate might reorganize its operations in order to provide its members with more time to think through the difficult decisions they are required to make.

What, if anything, can be done about the ever-increasing workload that is at the heart of so many of the Senate's problems? I am not so romantic as to believe that we can dismantle the Departments of Education, Health and Human Services, and Housing and Urban Development in the immediate future and return most of their functions to the states and localities. Therefore, another approach to restructuring the work and the flow of business in the Senate must be considered if senators are to be able to use their scarce time more efficiently, and if they are to bring a maximum degree of thought to bear on legislation.

One approach might be to place as much legislative business as possible on a two-year cycle. One year might be devoted to debate and action on bills reported out of committee the prior year and to the holding of public hearings to assemble information for committee consideration in the succeeding one. The alternate years would then be available for detailed consideration of new legislative proposals—without arbitrary deadlines requiring a hurried, patchwork approach to important bills—and for the important work of legislative oversight.

A system that required legislation to be reported out of committee one year and debated and voted on the next would allow ample time for special-interest groups, and for the public at large, to weigh in on the matter, and for members of individual senatorial staffs to digest what it is that their senator will be asked to vote upon when the legislation reaches the floor. It would also provide a period within which amendments could be introduced sufficiently far in advance of debate to enable the members of the relevant committees to study them and to give the Senate as a whole the benefit of their expert assessment.

Whether the appropriation process could also be placed on a biennial basis, I don't know; and of course, any fundamental reordering of business would have to make special provision for the handling of emergencies. But if the work of the Senate could be organized in such a manner—and I see no reason why it is necessary to enact routine legislation every year instead of every other year—then the conflicts among committee hearings could be greatly reduced, members of the Senate would have time to participate more fully in floor debate, and it ought to be possible—at least every other year—to adjourn Congress early enough to provide senators with a greater opportunity to return to their states to listen and to observe.

Given their central role in the work of the Senate, there is also a need to examine how committees are composed and how they operate. One problem derives from the fact that there is no assurance that the membership of a committee will reflect the views of the Senate as a whole. Thus it will very often happen that highly controversial legislation will be reported out unanimously, or with appended minority views that are more concerned with details of the legislation than with its basic merit. This means that in too many cases the report that accompanies a new bill is not nearly as informative as it ought to be, and fails to alert the Senate as a whole to its controversial features.

This is especially true of committees that have a tradition of trying to iron out all differences of opinion so that legislation may be reported out unanimously. This practice has a certain utility, in that it results in a genuine effort within the committee to reach reasonable compromises among conflicting views. Yet I wonder if the interests of the Senate, and of the country, are necessarily best served by this drive to consensus, for it encourages a sense of commitment to the end product which inhibits public expression of misgivings by individual committee members. Thus the Senate is apt to be deprived of the candid insights of those senators who are best informed about the weaknesses of the legislation in question.

CULTURAL DRIFT

The 1960s brought us a cultural revolution in which young radicals rebelled against just about every restraint on behavior. In Berkeley, California, students engaged in sit-ins to proclaim a right to pot and obscene speech; in Woodstock, New York, crowds wallowed in mud in an orgy of sex and drugs; and coast to coast, students bombed college buildings in protest against the Vietnam War.

Those stories grabbed the headlines, but they were just the most visible manifestations of a deeper, seismic shift from age-old standards that has taken place in America over the past fifty years. Most Americans once shared the same understanding of right and wrong, of acceptable and unacceptable behavior. Now, just about anything goes; and if anyone raises an eyebrow, he is condemned for being judgmental. The following offerings touch on some of the ways, big and small, in which this cultural drift has affected American life.

Vietnam and the Cultural Revolution

In the late 1990s, I was invited to participate in a symposium on "The Unintended Consequences of the Vietnam War." The other participants included high-ranking military officers (among them a former prisoner of war), historians, a former under secretary of the Air Force (from the Johnson administration), and a journalist who had covered the war and written a book about it. As they could be counted upon to discuss the military and political aftermaths of Vietnam, I decided to explore a possible consequence that had long intrigued me—the ultimate impact on higher education of a provision of the military-draft law that permitted young men to postpone military service by prolonging their stays in academe.

Unlike the other participants in this symposium, I have not studied the Vietnam War, nor did I participate in it. Nevertheless, I am able to certify one incontrovertible and wholly unintended consequence of the war; namely, my election, in 1970, to the United States Senate as a third-party candidate.

That year was marked by massive and often violent student antiwar demonstrations, exemplified by the burning of a campus library in Berkeley and the demonstrations at Kent State and Jackson State Universities in which six students were killed. My Republican and Democratic opponents sympathized with the protestors and excused their excesses, while I suggested that they be expelled or jailed, preferably both. As a consequence, traditional, socially conservative Democrats who were appalled by the behavior of flag-burning, bomb-throwing students provided me with the margin of victory.

Perhaps that is why, when I was invited to participate in this panel, my first thought was of the impact of the student antiwar movement on the home front, and so I decided to leave for my co-panelists the dozen or more devastating consequences of our conduct of the war in the areas of foreign affairs and defense. What I offer today is a hypothesis; namely, that the war proved critical to the success of the cultural revolution launched by student radicals in the 1960s, a revolution that has resulted in the degradation of much of American life and corrupted large areas of our higher education.

I see the progression of causes and effects as follows. In the early 1960s, small groups of student revolutionaries, such as Berkeley's "Free Speech" (meaning dirty speech) Movement and Students for a Democratic Society, emerged on campuses across the country and engaged in often outrageous acts to advance equally outrageous demands. These initially centered on such subjects as sex, drugs, and America's alleged oppression of blacks and women. Their cultural/social agenda was characterized by an abandonment of traditional standards, a rejection of authority, and a hatred of America and its institutions as racist, sexist, and repressive.

Around 1965, the SDS and other groups that made up the New Left added Vietnam to their agenda and co-opted an antiwar movement that had earlier been launched by traditional pacifists. Because it sought confrontation, the SDS replaced the pacifists' "Build, not burn," slogan with "Burn. Not build," and it proceeded to burn a college library here and an auditorium there. As Judge Bork notes in *Slouching Towards Gomorrah*, "Vietnam was more an occasion for the outbreaks [of violence] than their cause. The war at most intensified into hatred a contempt for American civilization that was already in place. . . . Vietnam was a convenient metaphor for what was in reality the belief that America's culture, society, economy, and polity were corrupt." Peter Collier and David Horowitz, who were editors of the New Left journal *Ramparts* for part of that period, have described Vietnam as "a gift of chance that allowed radical leaders to convince others of the need for a social apocalypse and the necessity of their destructive strategies."

Although these strategies were responsible for literally thousands of fires and bombings, the New Left came to be seen by the liberal establishment as a moral force whose most violent acts must be condoned as the response of idealistic youths to the violence in Vietnam and whose radical cultural and social demands must be treated as legitimate expressions of that idealism. Thus a former chancellor of the University of Chicago, Robert Hutchins, would state that "students . . . not only should be granted full amnesty for taking over five [Columbia University] buildings for six days but should be honored at special graduation ceremonies for forcing open the door to university reform," and he would quote John D. Rockefeller IV—then governor of West Virginia, and now senator—as saying that "instead of worrying about how to suppress the youth revolution, we of the older generation should be worrying about how to sustain it. The student activists . . . perform a service in shaking us out of our complacency. We badly need their ability and fervor in these troubled and difficult times." It would appear from the above that the New Left's adoption of the Vietnam War as an issue had the effect of moving major portions of its agenda from the unthinkable to the thinkable; and because Gresham's law applies to manners as well as money, the debasement of social and cultural standards we see today was sure to follow.

Although the radicals were not able to sell their ideological baggage to mainstream America, they provided cover for students who wished to escape the draft; and because the pursuit of advanced degrees proved a ready way to avoid military service, the more affluent members of that generation entered graduate schools in record numbers. Graduate degrees conferred in the fields of English, journalism, foreign languages, and the social sciences rose from roughly 22,000 in 1965 to 44,000 in 1970; they were still at 40,000 in 1975, and did not settle back to 29,000 until 1980. It is in these fields that the post-Vietnam politicization of higher education has been most pronounced.

There is reason to believe that a disproportionate number of the more radical graduate students found academic life congenial and stayed on to become tenured professors. As Stephen H. Balch and Herbert I. London noted in a 1986 article in *Commentary* entitled "The Tenured Left," "Given the skewed sensibilities of its liberal guardians, and given, too, the intellectual proclivities and gentrified tastes of many '60s radicals, the academy provided a safe, even pleasant, haven for ideological rest, recuperation, and regrouping. [As a consequence,] the American campus is now the nesting place for a significant population of political extremists."

It is important to note the distinction made by Messrs. Balch and London between the liberal professors who once dominated academia and the ideologues who have taken charge of so much of it in recent years. It is the latter who have been responsible for the multiculturalism, race- and gender-centered programs, and codes of politically correct behavior that deform so much of American higher education today. Unlike the liberals, who acknowledged the importance of objective standards and welcomed discussion, the ideologues will not tolerate any idea that does not conform with the new orthodoxy.

Finally, there can be no doubt that the ideologues have become the dominant force in many of our institutions of higher learning, especially in such disciplines as English and modern languages, ethnic and area studies, sociology, anthropology, and social welfare. This politicization has been documented in an interesting analysis by Will Morrisey of articles appearing at ten-year intervals, and then five-year intervals, between 1930 and 1990 in the Modern Language Association's official journal. Although the percentage of what he called "tendentious" articles rose from less than 5 percent in 1930, 1940, and 1950 to 15.5 percent in 1960, those labeled "ideological" because of their overt political bias rose from an average of less than 4 percent between 1930 and 1975 to 41.5 percent in 1980, 50.0 percent in 1985, and 52.5 percent in 1990. While Morrisey noted that the fastest growth of politicized scholarship did not occur until after 1975, he observed that "it took that long for students, politicized in the Vietnam era, to move through graduate school into the professoriate and to begin publishing in academic journals." He added: "The continued growth in the number of ideological articles in the 1980s may reflect the further progress of the same generation into positions where they can influence editorial decisions, or it may reflect their success in recruiting the next generation of scholars to their cause." Anyone who has read Christina Hoff Sommers's *Who Stole Feminism?* will accept both explanations.

I recognize that this recitation falls short of confirming my hypothesis. The historian Stephen Ambrose, however, has written that "The permanent influence of the antiwar movement was not to shorten the war but to pave the way for and extend the boundaries of the counterculture"; and David Horowitz, one of the founders of the New Left, has asserted that the war was "the absolutely crucial event" in bringing about the politicization of the academic professions. I suggest that if it is established that the Vietnam War served as the catalyst for the profound changes that have occurred in American social and academic standards over the past two decades, then these will in the longer term prove the most devastating of the unintended consequences of that conflict.

Abortion and the New Ethic

I have always considered the traditional prohibition against abortion to be a matter of biology rather than theology. For aeons, our civilization had opposed the taking of innocent human life. Biology tells us when that life comes into existence, a simple proposition the Supreme Court tried to sidestep, in Roe v. Wade, by pleading biological ignorance: "We need not resolve the difficult question of when life begins. When those trained in the respective disciplines of medicine, philosophy, and theology are unable to arrive at any consensus, the judiciary, at this point in the development of man's knowledge, is not in a position to speculate as to the answer." The following PBS commentary, delivered on June 23, 1977, puts that "speculation" in perspective.

This week's Supreme Court decisions on abortion [*Maher* v. *Roe*, *Beal* v. *Doe*, and *Poelker* v. *Doe*] represent no more than a tactical victory for those opposed to abortion on demand. They have come no closer than did the original ones to coming to grips with what it is that takes place in a non-therapeutic abortion; namely, an election to exterminate a human life for reasons of convenience.

And so the controversy is allowed to wallow through a sea of emotion in which the pro-abortionists neatly avoid the hard scientific facts that we must ultimately confront if this divisive issue is ever to be put to rest. This is regrettable, because infinitely important questions are at stake that we as a society ought to be able to decide in a thoughtful and deliberate manner.

An unusually candid statement of what is really involved in this controversy was presented in an editorial, entitled "A New Ethic for Medicine and Society," that appeared a few years ago in a journal published by the California Medical Association. The thrust of the editorial is simply this: The current controversy over abortion represents the first phase of a head-on collision between the traditional Judaeo-Christian ethic, with its reverence for human life, and a new ethic which permits the taking of human life for what are held to be the social, economic, or psychological needs of others. The critical point made in that editorial is the following:

The process eroding the old ethic and substituting the new has already begun. It may be seen most clearly in changing attitudes towards human abortion. In defiance of the long-held Western ethic of intrinsic and equal value for every human life regardless of its stage, condition, or status, abortion is becoming accepted by society as moral, right, and even necessary. . . . Since the old ethic has not yet been fully displaced, it has been necessary to separate the idea of abortion from the idea of killing, which continues to be socially abhorrent. The result has been a curious avoidance of the scientific fact, which everyone really knows, that human life begins at conception and is continuous whether intra- or extra-uterine until death. The very considerable semantic gymnastics which are required to rationalize abortion as anything but taking a human life would be ludicrous if they were not often put forth under socially impeccable auspices. It is suggested that this schizophrenic sort of subterfuge is necessary because while a new ethic is being accepted, the old one has not yet been rejected.

Lest there be any ambiguity as to the ultimate thrust of the "new ethic," the editorial, which discusses the growing role of physicians in deciding who will and will not live, goes on to state the following: "One may anticipate further development of these roles as the problems of birth control and birth selection are extended inevitably to death selection and death control whether by the individual or by society."

That editorial is a powerful, eloquent, and compelling statement of the ultimate questions involved in the controversy. The question at issue, the Supreme Court to the contrary notwithstanding, is not when life begins, for that is a matter of scientific fact. The question, rather, is what value we shall continue to place on human life in general, and whether unborn human life in particular will be granted legal protection.

Whether our society will continue its historical commitment to the old ethic, or will transfer its allegiance to the new, is a question to be decided not by a transitory majority of the Supreme Court, but by the people acting through their political processes. That is why the American people should be granted the opportunity, through the painfully difficult process of amending the Constitution, to determine for themselves which ethic will govern this country in what is, after all, quite literally a matter of life or death.

Although recent polls indicate that a majority of Americans now identify themselves as "pro-life," I fear that an attempt to overturn Roe v. Wade by amending the Constitution would prove futile. As I noted above ["The Constitution and the Courts," p. 82], Supreme Court decisions have a powerful impact on culture. Although the great majority of Americans still disapprove of the reasons most women give for having an abortion, too many of them have come to accept it as a right, however repugnant its exercise might be. In the meantime, the new ethic's utilitarian view of human life is slowly gaining acceptance. Two states have now legalized medically assisted suicide, and there are growing pressures for the acceptance of Netherlands-style voluntary euthanasia, which, in practice, is not always voluntary.

Government-Sponsored Gambling

While riding a New York City subway one day, I was struck by the juxtaposition of two advertisements. The first invited fortune seekers to patronize state-operated "Off-Track Betting" emporia; next to it was one that provided the location of a clinic for the cure of gambling addiction. I discussed the consequences of government-sponsored gambling in a PBS radio commentary broadcast on July 20, 1978.

Caught between rising budgets and increasingly mutinous taxpayers, public officials are turning more and more to legalized gambling as a source of new revenues. New Jersey, for example, recently became the first state outside of Nevada to offer casino gambling, and others may soon follow suit. State lotteries are now a widespread phenomenon; and in New York, state-run Off-Track Betting parlors are well-advertised fixtures in the urban landscape.

Years ago, most Americans found it morally wrong for governments to exploit the weaknesses of their citizens through the establishment of government monopolies over gambling. Fiscal imperatives, however, plus the seductive argument that the money not bet with state agencies would otherwise find its way into the underworld's channels, have finally won the day. Government-sponsored gambling is now a common fact of American life. A question we still should be asking, however, is, "At what cost?"

It is a gross oversimplification to claim that the money poured into the slot machines in Reno or used to purchase lottery tickets in New Hampshire, or to place bets at OTB parlors in New York City, would otherwise be handed over to illegal bookmakers or numbers-game operators. Enough experience has now been accumulated to demonstrate that state-sponsored gambling—which is readily accessible and accompanied by mass advertising campaigns—has the effect of introducing new people to gambling, whetting their appetite for it, and causing illegal gambling to grow even larger than it otherwise would.

There are two good reasons for the last effect. Illegal gambling is a highly competitive, free-market business in which profit margins are kept low. This means that the customer is afforded significantly better odds than those offered by a state monopoly. Secondly, no record is kept of winners, so winnings don't have to be shared with tax collectors.

It is now widely recognized that gambling can be as addictive as alcohol. There is even an organization, equivalent to Alcoholics Anonymous, that helps victims deal with this addiction. New York State tries to salve its conscience, in its ads urging the public to "Get a horse at OTB and let him run for you," by admonishing readers, in small print, to "Bet with your head—not over it," and giving, in still smaller print, the address and telephone number of the National Council for Addictive Gambling.

No doubt about it, government-sponsored gambling increases the incidence of gambling; and, over time, the players are bound to lose. As a consequence, state-sponsored gambling represents, among other things, a heavy tax on the poor, and it should be recognized as such. The poor are often the most anxious to believe that they can get something for nothing. Encouraged by the few well-publicized winners, they continue to pour dollars from paychecks and welfare checks into the coffers of both governments and the underworld.

Criminals benefit from gambling. Governments benefit from legalized gambling. And the people? Whether it's legal or illegal, they always lose; and those who can least afford to are the poor.

Recessions, especially great ones, can undermine societies in more than the obvious ways. The Wall Street Journal *notes that since the 2008 meltdown, a number of states are expanding state-sponsored gambling in frantic attempts to balance their books. Others are contemplating easing restrictions on strip clubs and legalizing pot in their search for new sources of tax revenues. Sin and sleaze obviously pay. In all these cases, the question that needs to be asked is: "At what social cost?"*

WOMEN'S RIGHTS

One evening in 1973, while I was walking down New York City's Avenue of the Americas, a woman on the other side of the street yelled my name, gave me the "finger," and shouted, "Take that, you male chauvinist pig!" What had a mild, inoffensive man like me done to warrant such public abuse? The only thing I could think of was that I had had the temerity to oppose two of hard-line feminists' favorite causes—the Equal Rights Amendment and the right to abortion on demand. To be specific, I had voted against the ERA, which would have imposed a rigid unisexism on American law that, in the view of male sentimentalists like me, would have deprived women of privileges and benefits to which they were entitled for reasons biological as well as cultural. I had also proposed a constitutional amendment that would have restored an unborn child's right to live by reversing the Supreme Court's proclamation that its mother had the right to kill it.

The Case against the Equal Rights Amendment

In the early 1970s, feminists were on a roll, and one of their prime objectives was to secure the adoption of a constitutional amendment outlawing discrimination on the basis of sex. When the Equal Rights Amendment was adopted by Congress in the spring of 1972, it was assumed by friend and foe alike that it would soon become the law of the land. When it came to a vote in the Senate, I was one of only nine who opposed it. As expected, state ratifications began to roll in. By the spring of 1973, thirty states had ratified the ERA. But then, thanks in substantial part to the efforts of Phyllis Schlafly, the American public, particularly women, began to have second thoughts about the amendment. They questioned whether every legal distinction based on sex constituted discrimination in a pejorative sense, and the wind went out of the ERA's sails. The following is a condensed version of my Senate remarks in opposition to the amendment.

Mr. President, I have studied the committee report in support of the Equal Rights Amendment with care and agree with its finding that discrimination against women still exists in our country in forms that cannot be justified and ought not to be tolerated. As to this, there is virtually no disagreement, either within the Senate or in the United States as a whole. Therefore, the only question to be resolved is whether the proposed amendment is the appropriate way to right this wrong.

The text of the ERA is deceptively simple: "Equality of rights under the law shall not be denied or abridged by the United States or by any State on account of sex." But what does that seductive language really mean, and how would it be applied in practice? In America today, three types of factors affect the relative rights, prerogatives, duties, immunities, and obligations of men and women. Some of these are cultural, others social, and the balance economic. I speak of distinctions based on sex, deferences conferred because of sex, and prejudicial discrimination predicated on sex. Only the last, I submit, is the proper target of the amendment now under consideration and of the enormous effort by the women of America to redress their long-standing grievances. Yet the proposed Equal Rights Amendment would have the inevitable effect of obliterating all of these differentiations—these distinctions, deferences, and discriminations—in the name of an abstract equality, regardless of whether they in fact infringe upon the substantive rights of women.

It is because of this—and because of my deep respect for women—that I cannot support the amendment; and I cannot support it because whatever the intentions of its sponsors, we will inevitably find it tugged and twisted and extended far beyond the limits of common sense and reason. I oppose the amendment because, in its attempt to eliminate discrimination against women, it will at the same time inevitably strike down the benign distinctions and deferences that our society now extends to them. It seems to me that the discriminations which all of us want to see ended can be more effectively ended in other ways.

I recognize that many militants regard the deferences and distinctions that are imbedded in our social customs as discriminatory per se. Yet, if these customs and attitudes do not harm women, I cannot see why we should be forced to abandon them.

According to the analyses provided by the amendment's proponents, however, that is precisely what would happen to many of our existing conventions.

Let me cite a few of the effects of the Equal Rights Amendment as described in the committee report and in an article in *The Yale Law Journal* that has been cited by the principal proponents of the ERA as best describing its consequences. One of the most immediate of them would be to make women subject to being drafted into military service; more than that, "they will be eligible for combat duty." I cannot see why we should adopt a constitutional amendment that would preclude American society from determining that the obligation to serve in combat forces will be restricted to men. I cannot, for the life of me, see why this distinction would make second-class citizens of women.

The proponents also advise us that it would nullify "[s]tatutory rape laws, which punish men for having sexual intercourse with any woman under an age specified by law"—even though "the singling out of women probably reflects sociological reality," and even though, in our society, "the bad reputation and illegitimate child which can result from an improvident sexual liaison may be far more ruinous to a young woman's psychological health than similar conduct to a young man's." Thus legislation intended to address injuries experienced unilaterally by women will be outlawed because "the Equal Rights Amendment forbids finding legislative justification in the sexual double standard."

We are also told that the ERA would overturn laws dealing with parental and family obligations if (as is generally the case) they provide women with preferential treatment. Thus, although mothers are currently awarded custody of their children in 90 percent of divorce cases, the amendment "would prohibit both statutory and common law presumptions about which parent was the proper guardian based on the sex of the parent." Although the laws of all states now hold men primarily liable for the financial support of their children, under the ERA "the child support sections of the criminal non-support laws . . . could not be sustained where only the male is liable for support. . . . The Equal Rights

Amendment would bar a state from imposing greater liability for support on a husband than on a wife merely because of his sex."

These, then, are some of the admitted practical consequences of the adoption of the proposed amendment. On the basis of our experience with the sometimes extravagant extension of newly defined rights in other fields, if the ERA is adopted, we can surely expect future courts to strike down as unconstitutional a host of other customary provisions favoring women today.

Mr. President, this entire debate rests on certain assumptions about the meaning of a singularly elusive word, "equality." It is therefore incumbent upon Congress to make the amendment's purpose and limitations absolutely clear. Unfortunately, from the outset, its proponents both in and outside of Congress have oscillated between two conflicting interpretations of the word. The first, which derives from a "unisex" understanding of "equality," holds in effect that any legal classification based on sex would be per se unconstitutional under the proposed amendment. As Professor Thomas I. Emerson put it in the *Yale Law Journal* article cited by proponents as authoritative:

> The basic principle of the Equal Rights Amendment is that sex is not a permissible factor in determining the legal rights of women, or of men. This means that the treatment of any person by the law may not be based upon the circumstance that such person is of one sex or the other.

The second interpretation, which seeks to avoid the rigidities of a per se rule, holds that sexual classifications are valid provided that they are applied equally to both sexes. Even now, on the eve of the vote, proponents seem uncertain as to which understanding ought to be controlling.

These may appear to be distinctions without a difference, but the Coast Guard has obliged us by providing an example of how they might be applied in practice. A recently promulgated Coast Guard regulation fits the unisex model by converting shipboard washrooms and toilets into facilities open to both female and male members of a ship's crew. The alternative understanding would permit the establishment of separate facilities, each restricted to a given sex—something that the Emersonian approach would not allow.

It is not easy to say, on the basis of the record to date, which view ought to be ascribed to Congress. But if Congress's intention is ambiguous with respect to the use of washroom and toilet facilities, how can we expect the courts to find clarity of intention with respect to a whole host of prospective problems of construction that may arise if this amendment is adopted? I pity the judge who will be obliged to wallow through the legislative history in search of clarity where there is none.

I rarely agree with the editorial writers of the *New York Times*, but when the House passed the Equal Rights Amendment, the *Times* said something that badly needs saying:

> Equal rights for women is a proposition so unarguable in principle and so long overdue in practice that it is a pity to have it approached by the House of Representatives in an exercise in political opportunism. For 47 years that body regularly rejected out of hand all proposals for a women's rights amendment to the Constitution. Now it approves, without committee hearings and after only an hour's debate, a constitutional change of almost mischievous ambiguity.

Despite extended hearings, and despite debate here on the floor, the Senate is indulging precisely the same kind of mischievous ambiguity that possessed the House. At its root is a fundamental confusion between the concept of "equal rights" (which, as we have seen, has its own internal tensions) and that of "women's rights." The former would tend to obliterate any law that is based on sex; the latter seeks to eliminate only those laws which discriminate against women as such and relegate them to an inferior legal status. If the latter were the sole objective of the ERA, and if it were certain that the courts would limit themselves to that purpose and refrain from indulging unisex excesses, I could support it.

I am convinced, however, that the present amendment is not so limited; but more to the point, I am also satisfied that adequate remedies exist today to correct the inequities that would be the appropriate targets of a properly constructed women's-rights amendment. The most important of these is the Fourteenth Amendment. In the past, some have doubted whether its guarantee of "equal protection of the laws" provided a basis for the elimination of unreasonable classifications based on sex. Last December, however, the Supreme Court held that it did. In the case of *Reed* v. *Reed*, the Court struck down an Idaho statute that granted preference to males over females in the appointment of administrators for decedents' estates, holding that the discrimination bore no reasonable relationship to the purpose sought to be accomplished by the law governing the administration of estates.

The Fourteenth Amendment, moreover, is not the only legal remedy available to aggrieved women. Title VII of the Civil Rights Act of 1964, which Congress recently amended to provide greatly enlarged enforcement powers for the Equal Employment Opportunity Commission, provides another powerful tool for the relief of women discriminated against in the field of employment. Litigation under the Fourteenth Amendment and under Title VII should provide adequate remedies in the great majority of cases in which women are relegated to an inferior legal status, and other statutory remedies can be adopted to target types of discrimination not adequately addressed by existing law.

This approach, of course, is unlikely to appeal to the leaders of the women's-liberation movement, who seek instant cures and view themselves as the duly appointed representatives of the women of America. Whether American women want or need this kind of representation is, of course, another matter altogether. The dramatic changes in existing laws and practices that would be brought about by the ERA might delight militant feminists, but they are not necessarily in the interests of most American women. As Professor Philip Kurland, of the University of Chicago, has pointed out:

> There remains . . . a very large part of the female population on whom the imposition of such a constitutional standard could be disastrous. There is no doubt that society permitted these women to come to maturity not as competitors with males but rather as the bearers and raisers of their children and the keepers of their homes. There are a multitude of women who still find fulfillment in this role. This may be unfortunate in the eyes of some; it remains a fact. It can boast no label of equality now to treat the older generations as if they were their own children or grandchildren. Nor can women be regarded as unified in their desire for this change. Certainly the desire to open opportunities for some of them can be achieved without the price of removal of the protection of others.

This is not an argument for retaining the legal status quo. Feminist activists have made a compelling case for changing laws and practices that unjustly discriminate against women, especially in the area of job opportunities. I have the greatest sympathy with many of their grievances; but those objectives can be met without the adoption of a mischievous amendment. I am not at all convinced that the "liberation" of some women requires the removal of legal protections from others or the imposition of greater legal burdens upon those who do not share the goals of the liberationists. I recognize that as more and more women enter the workplace and establish independent earnings, the time may come to re-examine their preferential treatment as mothers and wives. But again, legislative bodies are in the best position to make the necessary adjustments in response to changing social conditions.

I do not believe that the best way to deal with these complex issues is to adopt an ideologically rigid constitutional amendment. I am prepared to examine each case as it arises, and I am persuaded that the Constitution as it now stands, supplemented as required by state and federal statutory remedies, can achieve the necessary reforms. There are many injustices in this world, but a constitutional amendment is not always the best way to eradicate them. Should the ERA be ratified, I fear that victory for some women will have been bought at the expense of others. I will therefore vote against its adoption.

Calls for an ERA are still heard, but women now have the best of two worlds: protection against invidious discrimination, thanks to the development of Fourteenth Amendment jurisprudence, and the deference that the mothers of our children deserve—a statement that no doubt brands me as a sexist.

An ERA Progress Report

The legislation proposing the Equal Rights Amendment required that it be ratified by the states within seven years in order to take effect. By 1978, when this PBS commentary was broadcast, the amendment was still short of the thirty-eight ratifications required for its adoption, and women activists were pressing for an extension. Congress ultimately extended the period by three years, but to no avail. The ERA died in 1982.

Women activists claim that seven years is insufficient time to educate the public as to the merits of the Equal Rights Amendment, so they are lobbying for an unprecedented seven-year extension of the time within which the amendment may be ratified. The fact is that the arguments for and against the ERA are now widely known, which is why the amendment is in trouble. In the last few years as many states have rescinded their earlier ratifications of the ERA as have ratified it. And in 1975, when the voters of New York and New Jersey were asked to approve equal-rights amendments to their state constitutions, they rejected them by substantial majorities. What made those votes particularly interesting is that the amendments were rejected by larger percentages of women than of men.

Why this opposition? Quite clearly, it stems from a growing understanding that the ERA goes far beyond the stated goal of eliminating discrimination. The Senate debate made it abundantly clear that the amendment would have the inevitable effect of obliterating all distinctions and deferences based on sex, whether or not they in fact impinged upon the substantive rights of women— all in the name of an abstract unisex view of equality. Sponsors of the ERA stated specifically that its adoption would render the exemption of women from compulsory military service unconstitutional, and would end the presumption, in the case of a divorce, that the mother should be granted custody of the children and the father required to provide for their financial support.

The list of practices whose constitutionality would be challenged under the amendment would not stop with those cited on the Senate floor. To see the future under the ERA, one need merely observe the pattern emerging in the interpretation of existing laws forbidding discrimination on the basis of sex. The federal government has issued edicts forbidding all-girl choirs and father-son picnics at schools receiving federal aid; a Pennsylvania court has ruled that girls must be allowed to participate with boys in such contact sports as football; and a prominent New York lawyer, who is mentioned from time to time as a potential candidate for the federal bench, has declared that the ERA would require the legalization of homosexual marriages.

But what about the admittedly discriminatory practices that in years past have relegated women to a second-class status? The ironic fact here is that over the past half-dozen years, a series of Supreme Court decisions interpreting the Equal Protection Clause of the Fourteenth Amendment has evolved a constitutional doctrine that prohibits discrimination against women. Thus women today are constitutionally protected against any practice or law that discriminates against them. Their constitutional rights, in short, will not be improved through the enactment of the ERA, but its adoption could well jeopardize the special protections they now enjoy. What ratification of the amendment would achieve is the unisex society that is the ideal of some women, but hardly the majority.

The fact remains that the public has had adequate time to assess the amendment's implications. By March of next year, its advocates will have had their constitutional day in court, and they ought to be willing to abide by the verdict.

Introducing the Human
Life Amendment

On May 31, 1973, I proposed a constitutional amendment that would protect human life "at every stage of [its] biological development." Two years later, the Senate Committee on the Judiciary held hearings on my proposal, but the committee never acted on it. The following is the statement I made on the Senate floor when I introduced my Human Life Amendment.

In a pair of highly controversial, precedent-shattering decisions, the Supreme Court has held that a pregnant woman has a constitutional right to destroy her unborn child. Not only do the Court's rulings in *Roe* v. *Wade* and *Doe* v. *Bolton* contravene the express will of every state legislature in the country; not only do they remove every vestige of legal protection hitherto enjoyed by the child in the mother's womb; but the Court reached its decisions through a curious and confusing chain of reasoning that, logically extended, could apply with equal force to the genetically deficient infant, the retarded child, and the insane or senile adult.

After reviewing these decisions, I concluded that, given the gravity of the issues at stake and the way in which the Court had carefully closed off alternative means of redress, a constitutional amendment was the only way to remedy the damage wrought by the Court. My decision was not lightly taken, for I believe that only matters of permanent and fundamental interest are properly the subject for constitutional amendment. I regret the necessity for taking this serious step, but the Court's decisions leave those who respect human life in all its stages from inception to death with no other recourse.

To those who argue that an amendment to the Constitution affecting abortion and related matters would encumber the document with details more appropriately regulated by statute, I can only reply that the ultimate responsibility must be borne by the Court itself. With Justice Byron White, who dissented so vigorously in the abortion cases, "I find nothing in the language or history of the Constitution to support the Court's judgment."

The Court simply carved out of thin air a previously undisclosed right of "privacy" that is nowhere mentioned in the Constitution, a right of privacy which, oddly, can be exercised in this instance only by destroying the life and, therefore, the privacy of an unborn child. As Mr. Justice White remarked last January, "As an exercise of raw judicial power, the Court perhaps has authority to do what it does today; but, in my view, its judgment is an improvident and extravagant exercise of the power of judicial review that the Constitution extends to this Court."

In the intervening weeks since the Court's decisions, I have sought the advice of men and women trained in medicine, ethics, and the law. They have given me the most discriminating and exacting counsel on virtually every aspect of the issues involved and have provided invaluable assistance in drawing up an amendment that reflects the latest and best scientific facts, and that comports with our most cherished legal traditions.

Before discussing the specific language of my proposed amendment, I believe it necessary first to analyze the effect and implications of Roe and Doe, and then to place them in the context of current attacks on our traditional attitudes towards human life. At the outset, it is necessary to discuss with some care what the Court in fact held in its abortion decisions. This is not an easy task, because parsing the Court's opinions in these cases requires one to follow a labyrinthine path of argument that simultaneously ignores or confuses a long line of legal precedent and flies in the face of well-established scientific fact.

The Court's labored reasoning in these cases has been a source of considerable puzzlement to all who have the slightest familiarity with the biological facts of human life before birth or with the legal protections previously provided for the unborn child. The Court's substantial errors of law and fact have been so well documented by others that it would be superfluous for me to attempt to add anything of my own.

The full import of the Court's action is as yet incompletely understood by large segments of the public and by many legislators and commentators. It seems to be rather widely held, for example, that the Court authorized abortion on request in the first six months of pregnancy, leaving the states free to proscribe the act thereafter. But this is far from the case. The truth of the matter is that, under these decisions, a woman may at any time during pregnancy exercise a constitutional right to have an abortion provided only that she can find a physician willing to certify that her "health" requires it; and as the word "health" is defined in *Doe*, that in essence means abortion on demand.

The Court attempts to distinguish three stages of pregnancy, but, upon examination, this attempt yields, in practical effect, distinctions without a difference. In the first three months, in the words of the Court, "the abortion decision and its effectuation must be left to the medical judgment of the pregnant woman's attending physician." This means, for all intents and purposes, abortion on request. During the second trimester, a state may— but it need not—regulate the abortion procedure in ways that are reasonably related to maternal health. The power of the states' regulations here is effectively limited to matters of time, place, and perhaps manner.

Thus, through approximately the first six months of pregnancy, the woman has a constitutionally protected right to take the life of her unborn child, and the state has no "compelling interest" that would justify prohibiting abortion if a woman insists on one. Once the unborn child is "viable," which the Court puts at six, or alternatively seven, months of pregnancy, a state "may"—but, again, it need not—proscribe abortion except "where necessary . . . for the preservation of the life or health of the mother." This provision, which appears at first glance to be an important restriction, turns out to be none at all, as the Court defines health to include "psychological as well as physical well-being," and states that the necessary "medical judgment may be exercised in the light of all factors—physical, emotional, psychological, familial, and the woman's age—relevant to the well-being of the patient." The Court, in short, has included under the umbrella of "health" just about every conceivable reason a woman might want to advance for having an abortion.

It is clear, then, that at no time prior to natural delivery is the unborn child considered a legal person entitled to constitutional protection; at no time may the unborn child's life take precedence over the mother's subjectively based assertion that her well-being is at stake. In reaching these findings, the Court in effect wrote a statute governing abortion for the entire country, a statute more permissive than that enacted by the hitherto most permissive jurisdiction in the country; namely, my own state of New York. Nor is that all. In the course of its deliberations, the Court found it necessary to concede a series of premises that can lead to conclusions far beyond the immediate question of abortion itself. These premises have to do with the conditions under which human beings, born or unborn, may be said to possess fundamental rights. I will touch briefly on one or two basic points.

First, it would now appear that the question of who is or is not a "person" entitled to the full protection of the law is a question of legal definition as opposed to practical determination. Thus, contrary to the meaning of the Declaration of Independence, contrary to the intent of the framers of the Fourteenth Amendment, and contrary to the previous holdings of the Court, to be created human is no longer a guarantee that one will be possessed of inalienable rights in the sight of the law. The Court has extended to government, it would seem, the power to decide the terms and conditions under which membership in good standing in the human race is determined. This statement of the decisions' effect may strike many as overwrought, but it will not appear as such to those who have followed the abortion debate carefully or to those who have read the Court's decisions in full. When the Court states that the unborn are not recognized by the law as "persons in the whole sense," and when it uses as a precondition for legal protection the test of whether one has a "capability of meaningful life," a thoughtful person is necessarily invited to speculate on what the logical extension of such arguments might be.

If constitutional rights depend on being "persons in the whole sense," where does one draw the line between "whole" and something less than "whole"? Is it simply a question of physical or mental development? If so, how does one distinguish between the child in his twenty-third week of gestation who is lifted alive from his mother's womb and allowed to die in the process of abortion by hysterotomy, and the child who is prematurely born and rushed to an incubator? It is a well-known scientific fact that the greater part of a child's cerebral cortex is not formed, that, in other words, a child does not become a "cognitive person," until some months after normal delivery. Might we not someday determine that a child thus does not become a "whole" person until sometime after birth, or that he never becomes "whole" if born with serious defects? And what about those who, having been born healthy, later lose their mental or physical capability? Will it one day be found that a person, because of mental illness, or a serious accident, or senility, ceases to be a "person . . . in the whole sense," that he ceases to have a "capability of meaningful life," and as such is no longer entitled to the full protection of the law?

The list of such questions is virtually endless. The Court, in attempting to solve one problem, has ended up by creating twenty others. One can read the Court's opinions in the abortion cases from beginning to end and back again, but one will not find a glimmer of an answer to these questions; indeed, one will not even find a glimmer of an indication that the Court was aware that such questions might be raised or might be considered important.

A second general consideration has to do with the Court's definition of "health" as involving "all factors—physical, emotional, psychological, familial, and the woman's age—relevant to the well-being of the patient." It is a little-remarked but ultimately momentous part of the abortion decisions that the Court, consciously or unconsciously, has adopted wholesale the controversial definition of "health" popularized by the World Health Organization. According to the WHO, "health" is "a state of complete physical, mental, and social well-being, not simply the absence of illness and disease." In this context, the Court's definition acquires a special importance, not only because it can be used to justify abortion any time a woman feels discomfited by pregnancy, but because the Court made a pointed reference to the "compelling interest" of the state in matters of health in general and maternal health in particular. One is bound to wonder whether a state's interest in maternal health would ever be sufficiently "compelling" to warrant an abortion against a pregnant woman's will. This is no mere academic matter. An unwed, pregnant teenage girl was ordered by a lower court in Maryland just last year to have an abortion against her will. That girl was able to frustrate the order by running away. The order was later overturned by a Maryland appellate court; but the important point is that an analogue to the compelling-state-interest argument was used by the lower court to justify its holding.

Let us consider, for example, the case of a pregnant mental patient. Would a state's compelling interest in her health ever be sufficient to force an abortion upon her? What of the unmarried mother on welfare who is already unable to cope with her existing children? Again, I am not raising an academic point for the sake of argument. In the abortion cases, the Supreme Court breathes life into the notorious precedent of *Buck* v. *Bell* (1927). That case, it will be recalled, upheld the right of a state to sterilize a mental incompetent without her consent. The Court held that "The principle that sustains compulsory vaccination is broad enough to cover cutting the Fallopian tubes."

One is necessarily bound to wonder whether, by an analogous extension, the principle that sustains compulsory sterilization of mental patients is broad enough to cover compulsory abortion for mental patients; and if for mental patients, then why not, as the lower court in Maryland suggested, for unwed minor girls? And if for unwed minor girls, then why not for any other woman? Just how "compelling" is the state's interest in matters of "health"? Where does the power begin or end? In the abortion cases, *Buck* is cited, curiously, for the proposition that a woman does not have an unlimited right to her own body, whence the only inference to be drawn is that the reason she doesn't have such a right is that the state may qualify that right because of its "compelling interest" in her "health." I find that a strange doctrine to be celebrated by the proponents of women's liberation.

These larger and deeply troubling considerations may in the long run be as important to us as the special concern that many of us have with the matter of abortion itself. Every premise conceded by the Court in order to justify the killing of an unborn child can be extended to justify the killing of anyone else if, like the unborn child, he is found to be less than a person in the "whole" sense or incapable of "meaningful" life. The removal of all legal restrictions against abortion must, in short, be seen in the light of a changing attitude regarding the sanctity of individual life, the effects of which will be felt not only by the unborn child who is torn from his mother's womb but by all those who may some day fall within the arbitrary boundaries of the Court's definition of humanity.

This wider context of the abortion controversy was brought to my attention most forcefully by an unusually candid editorial entitled "A New Ethic for Medicine and Society" that was published two and a half years ago in *California Medicine*, the official journal of the California Medical Association. It was occasioned, as I understand it, by the debate then taking place in our largest state regarding the liberalization of its abortion law.

The thrust of the editorial is simply this: that the controversy over abortion represents the first phase of a head-on conflict between the traditional Judaeo-Christian medical and legal ethic, in which the intrinsic worth and equal value of every human life is secured by law, regardless of age, health, or condition of dependency, and a new ethic according to which human life may be taken for what are held to be the compelling social, economic, or psychological needs of others.

I concur in Justice White's condemnation of the abortion decisions as "an exercise of raw judicial power" that is "improvident and extravagant." I concur in finding unacceptable the Court's action in "interposing a constitutional barrier to state efforts to protect human life and [in] investing mothers and doctors with the constitutionally protected right to exterminate it."

The majority of the Court, however, has rendered its decision. We as a people have been committed by seven men to the "new ethic"; and because of the finality of their decisions, because there are now no practical curbs on the killing of the unborn to suit the convenience or whim of the mother, those who continue to believe in the old ethic have no recourse but to resort to the political process. That is why I intend to do what I can to give the American people the opportunity to determine for themselves which ethic will govern this country. That is why I send my proposed Human Life Amendment to the desk and ask that it be printed and appropriately referred.

In doing so, Mr. President, may I say how deeply gratified I am to be joined in introducing this amendment by my distinguished colleagues from Oregon, Iowa, Utah, Nebraska, Oklahoma, and North Dakota. Senators Hatfield, Hughes, Bennett, Curtis, Bartlett, and Young are known in this body and elsewhere as exceptionally thoughtful and dedicated men whose day-to-day political activities are informed by devotion to first principles. When such a geographically, ideologically, and religiously diverse group of senators can agree on a major issue like this, it suggests that opposition to abortion is truly ecumenical and national in scope. These senators honor me by their co-sponsorship, and I consider it a privilege to work together with them in this great cause. I would simply like to take this occasion to extend to each of them my personal gratitude for their help and cooperation and to say how much I look forward to working jointly with them in the months ahead.

The text of our amendment reads as follows:

Section 1. With respect to the right to life, the word "person," as used in this Article and in the Fifth and Fourteenth Articles of Amendment to the Constitution of the United States, applies to all human beings, including their unborn offspring, at every stage of their biological development, irrespective of age, health, function or condition of dependency.

Section 2. This Article shall not apply in an emergency when a reasonable medical certainty exists that the continuation of the pregnancy will cause the death of the mother.

Section 3. Congress and the several States shall have the power to enforce this Article by appropriate legislation within their respective jurisdictions.

The amendment's central purpose is to create, or rather, as will be made clear below, to restore, a constitutionally compelling identity between the biological category "human being" and the legal category "person." This has been made necessary by two factors. The first is the more or less conscious dissemblance on the part of abortion proponents by virtue of which the universally agreed-upon facts of biology are made to appear as questions of value—a false argument that the Supreme Court adopted wholesale. The second is the holding of the Court in *Roe* and *Doe* that the test of personhood is one of legal rather than of biological definition. The amendment addresses these difficulties by making the biological test constitutionally binding, on the ground that only such a test will restrain the tendency of certain courts and legislatures to arrogate to themselves the power to determine who is and who is not human and, therefore, who is and who is not entitled to constitutional protections. The amendment is founded on the belief that the ultimate safeguard of all persons, born or unborn, normal or defective, is to compel courts and legislatures to rest their decisions on scientific fact rather than on political, sociological, or other opinion.

Such a test will return the law to a position compatible with the original understanding of the Fourteenth Amendment. As the debates in Congress during consideration of that amendment made clear, it was precisely the intention of Congress to make "legal person" and "human being" synonymous categories. By so doing, Congress wrote into the Constitution that understanding of the Declaration of Independence best articulated by Abraham Lincoln; namely, that to be human is to possess certain rights by nature—rights that no court and no legislature can legitimately revoke. Chief among these, of course, is the right to life.

On the specific subject of abortion, it is notable that the same men who passed the Fourteenth Amendment also enacted, in April 1866, an expanded Assimilative Crimes Statute, which adopted the substance of anti-abortion statutes recently passed in various states. These statutes, in turn, had been enacted as a result of a concerted effort by medical societies to bring to legislators' attention the recently discovered facts of human conception. The Court's opinion in *Roe* totally misreads—if the Court was aware of it at all—the fascinating medico-legal history of the enactment of the nineteenth-century anti-abortion statutes, and ignores altogether the fundamental intention that animated the framers of the Fourteenth Amendment.

Section 1 of our proposed amendment would restore and make explicit the biological test for legal protection of human life. The generic category is "human being," which includes, but is not limited to, "unborn offspring, at every stage of their biological development." What constitutes a human being is a question of biological fact, as is the question of when "offspring" may be said to come into existence. While the basic facts concerning these matters are not in dispute among informed members of the scientific community, the ways in which they are to be ascertained in any particular case will depend on the specifications contained in implementing legislation passed consistent with the standard established by the amendment. Such legislation would have to consider, in the light of the best available scientific information, the establishment of reasonable standards for determining when a woman is in fact pregnant and, if so, what limitations are to be placed on the performance of certain medical procedures or the administration of certain drugs.

Section 1 also reaches the more general case of euthanasia. This is made necessary because of the widespread and growing talk of legalizing "death with dignity," and because of the alarming dicta in the *Roe* opinion by which legal protection seems to be conditioned on whether one has the "capability of meaningful life" and whether one is a "person . . . in the whole sense." Such language in the Court's opinion, when combined with the Court's frequent references to the state's "compelling interest" in matters of "health," is pointedly brought to our attention by the revival in *Roe* of *Buck* v. *Bell*, which upheld the right of the state to sterilize a mentally defective woman without her consent. Taken as a whole, the *Roe* and *Doe* opinions seem to suggest that unborn children are not the only ones whose right to life is now legally unprotected. Thus, the proposed amendment explicitly extends its protections to all those whose physical or mental condition might make them especially vulnerable victims of the "new ethic."

Regarding the specific subject of abortion, Section 2 makes an explicit exception for the life of the pregnant woman. There seems to be a widespread misimpression that pregnancy is a medically dangerous condition, when the truth of the matter is that under most circumstances a pregnant woman can deliver her child with minimal risk to her own life and health. There is, however, an exceedingly small class of cases where continuation of pregnancy is likely to cause the death of the woman. The most common example is the ectopic or tubal pregnancy. It is our intention to exempt this unique class of pregnancies without opening the door to spurious claims of risk of death.

Under the amendment, there must be an emergency in which reasonable medical certainty exists that continuation of the pregnancy will cause the death of the woman. This is designed to cover the legitimate emergency cases, such as the ectopic pregnancy, while closing the door to unethical physicians who in the past have been willing to sign statements attesting to risk of death when in fact none exists or when the prospect is so remote in time or circumstance as to be unrelated to the pregnancy. Contrary to the opinion of the Supreme Court, which assumes that pregnancy is a pathological state, modern obstetrical advances have succeeded in removing virtually every major medical risk once associated with pregnancy. As Dr. Alan Guttmacher [*a strong advocate of "abortion rights"*] himself remarked nearly a decade ago, modern obstetrical practice has eliminated almost all medical indications for abortion. In certain limited instances, however, a genuine threat to the woman's life remains, and it is felt that excepting such situations is compatible with long-standing moral custom and legal tradition.

I profoundly believe that whatever acceptance abortion has acquired derives largely from the ability of its proponents to dissemble the true facts concerning the nature of unborn life and the true facts concerning what is actually involved in an abortion. I further believe that when these facts are fully made known to the American people, they will reject abortion save under the most exigent circumstances; that is, those in which the physical life of the mother is itself at stake. In recent weeks, in discussing this matter with friends and colleagues, I have found that, like many of the rest of us, they labor under certain misimpressions created by the proponents of permissive abortion. I therefore believe that it would be useful to call our colleagues' attention to clinical evidence upon these points.

I will begin with a particularly felicitous description of the biological and physical character of the unborn child by Dr. A. W. Liley, research professor in fetal physiology at National Women's Hospital, Auckland, New Zealand, a man renowned throughout the world as one of the principal founders and masters of the relatively new field of fetology. Dr. Liley writes:

> In a world in which adults control power and purse, the foetus is at a disadvantage being small, naked, nameless and voiceless. He has no one except sympathetic adults to speak up for him and defend him—and equally no one except callous adults to condemn and attack him. Mr. Peter Stanley of Langham Street Clinic, Britain's largest and busiest private abortorium with nearly 7,000 abortions per year, can assure us that "under 28 weeks the foetus is so much garbage—there is no such thing as a living foetus." Dr. Bernard Nathanson, a prominent New York abortionist, can explain that it is difficult to get nurses

to aid in abortions beyond the twelfth week because the nurses and often the doctors emotionally assume that a large foetus is more human than a small one. But when Stanley and Nathanson profit handsomely from abortion we can question their detachment because what is good for a doctor's pocket may not be best for mother or baby.

Biologically, at no stage can we subscribe to the view that the foetus is a mere appendage of the mother. Genetically, mother and baby are separate individuals from conception. Physiologically, we must accept that the conceptus is, in very large measure, in charge of the pregnancy, in command of his own environment and destiny with a tenacious purpose.

It is the early embryo who stops mother's periods and proceeds to induce all manner of changes in maternal physiology to make his mother a suitable host for him. Although women speak of their waters breaking or their membranes rupturing, these structures belong to the foetus and he regulates his own amniotic fluid volume. It is the foetus who is responsible for the immunological success of pregnancy—the dazzling achievement by which foetus and mother, although immunological foreigners, tolerate each other in parabiosis for nine months. And finally it is the foetus, not the mother, who decides when labor should be initiated.

One hour after the sperm has penetrated the ovum, the nuclei of the two cells have fused and the genetic instructions from one parent have met the complementary instructions from the other parent to establish the whole design, the inheritance of a new person. The one cell divides into two, the two into four and so on while over a span of seven or eight days this ball of cells traverses the Fallopian tube to reach the uterus. On reaching the uterus, this young individual implants in the spongy lining and with a display of physiological power suppresses his mother's menstrual period. This is his home for the next 270 days, and to make it habitable the embryo develops a placenta and a protective capsule of fluid for himself. By 25 days the developing heart starts beating, the first strokes of a pump that will make 3,000 million beats in a lifetime. By 30 days, and just two weeks past mother's first missed period, the baby, one-quarter inch long, has a brain of unmistakable human proportions, eyes, ears, mouth, kidneys, liver and umbilical cord and a heart pumping blood he has made himself. By 45 days, about the time of mother's second missed period, the baby's skeleton is complete, in cartilage not bone, the buttons of the milk teeth appear, and he makes his first movements of his limbs and body—although it will be another 12 weeks before his mother notices movements. By 63 days he will grasp an object placed in his palm and can make a fist.

Most of our studies of foetal behavior have been made late in pregnancy, partly because we lack techniques for investigation earlier and partly because it is only the exigencies of late pregnancy which provide us with opportunities to invade the privacy of the foetus. We know that he moves with a delightful easy grace in his buoyant world, that foetal comfort determines foetal position. He is responsive to pain and touch and cold and sound and light. He drinks his amniotic fluid, more if it is artificially sweetened and less if it is given an unpleasant taste. He gets hiccups and sucks his thumb. He wakes and sleeps. He gets bored with repetitive signals but can be taught to be alerted by a first signal for a second different one. Despite all that has been written by poets and songwriters, we believe babies cry at birth because they have been hurt. In all the discussions that have taken place on pain relief in labour, only the pain of mothers has been considered— no one has bothered to think of the baby.

This then is the foetus we know and indeed each once were. This is the foetus we look after in modern obstetrics, the same baby we are caring for today and after birth, who before birth can be ill and need diagnosis and treatment just like any other patient. This is also the foetus whose existence and identity must be so callously ignored and energetically denied by advocates of abortion.

This issue is of paramount importance. As we stand here today, thousands of unborn children will be sacrificed before the sun sets in the name of the new ethic. Such a situation cannot continue indefinitely without doing irreparable damage to the most cherished principles of humanity and to the moral sensibilities of our people. The issue at stake is not only what we do to unborn children, but what we do to ourselves by permitting them to be killed. With every day that passes, we run the risk of stumbling, willy-nilly, down the path that leads inexorably to the devaluation of all stages of human life, born or unborn. Just a few short years ago, a moderate liberalization of abortion was being urged upon us. The most grievous hypothetical circumstances were cast before us to justify giving in a little bit here, a little bit there; and step by step, with the inevitability of gradualness, we were led to the point where, now, we no longer have any legal constraints on abortion.

What kind of society is it that will accept this sort of senseless destruction? What kind of people are we that can tolerate this mass extermination? What kind of Constitution is it that can elevate this sort of conduct to the level of a sacrosanct right, presumably endowed with the blessings of the Founding Fathers, who looked to the laws of nature and of nature's God as the foundation of this nation?

Abortion, which was once universally condemned in the Western world as a heinous moral and legal offense, is now presented to us not as a necessary evil, but as a morally and socially beneficial act. The Christian counsel of perfection, which teaches that the greatest love consists in laying down one's life for one's friend, has now become, it seems, an injunction to take another's life for the security and comfort of one's own. Doctors sworn to apply the healing arts to save lives now dedicate themselves and their skills to the destruction of life.

To enter the world of abortion on request, Mr. President, is to enter a world that is upside down: it is a world in which black becomes white, and right wrong; a world in which the powerful are authorized to destroy the weak and defenseless; a world in which the child's natural protector, his own mother, becomes the very agent of his destruction.

I urge my colleagues to join me in protecting the lives of all human beings, born and unborn, for their sake, for our own sake, for the sake of our children, and for the sake of all those who may someday become the victims of the new ethic.

A SELECTION OF RADIO COMMENTARIES

I was the house conservative for National Public Radio's *All Things Considered* program during most of 1977 and 1978. My commentaries were broadcast every other week. The following sampler covers a range of subjects that do not fit easily within the headings I have chosen for my other writings. The frequent mention of Jimmy Carter reflects nothing more than the fact that he happened to be president during the years when I was a radio commentator. His policies in the areas I touch upon were probably little different from those that would have been followed by the candidates he defeated in his race for the Democratic Party's presidential nomination.

Public and Private Morality

This, the first of my All Things Considered *commentaries, was broadcast on March 3, 1977. Unfortunately, scandals among public officials have only become more common since then.*

The newspapers are filled with tales of scandals involving crimes and immorality in public office. But perhaps the greatest scandal of all is the one we hear too little about, and that is the growing incidence of crime and immorality and the debasement of standards throughout the entire spectrum of American society. A recently concluded study estimates, for example, that one-third of the juveniles in the state of Illinois have committed a serious crime. In Washington, D.C., signs on city buses read: "Shoplifting is Dumb"—not "illegal," mind you, not "wrong," but "dumb": dumb because shoplifters might be put to the inconvenience of an arrest.

Sexual promiscuity is now commonplace; and sex-education courses consider taboo any suggestion that sexual activity should be subject to moral constraints. Businessmen routinely pad their expense accounts, and well-to-do students brag of the ease with which they qualify themselves for food stamps—shrugging off the cold fact that, in so doing, they are stealing from their taxpaying neighbors. Cheating in schools has grown so commonplace that the honor system at West Point has been attacked as, in effect, cruel and unusual because it seeks to impose on cadets a standard of behavior so much higher than that currently practiced by their contemporaries.

All of this suggests that we are drifting into an age that accepts the philosophy that anything goes, without ever pausing to calculate the cost in terms of our ability to maintain a free and ordered life. For, as the Founders of this nation were keenly aware, there is a vital relationship between the quality of the people and the democratic process. That is why they repeatedly warned that only an essentially virtuous, law-abiding, self-disciplined people could preserve its freedom.

A perceptive student of the current American scene, Irving Kristol, reminds us in a recent essay of what he calls

> an older idea of democracy. . . . This idea . . . declares that, if you want self-government, you are only entitled to it if that "self" is worthy of governing.
>
> And because the desirability of self-government depends on the character of the people who govern, the older idea of democracy was very solicitous of the condition of this character. It was solicitous of the individual self, and felt an obligation to educate it into what used to be called "republican virtue."

We may today complain about the quality of morality in public life; but after all, in a democratic society, elected representatives are apt to do no more than mirror the essential values and virtues of their constituents.

And so I believe it is time that we once again feel that obligation to concern ourselves with the virtue of our people. We need to concern ourselves once again with fundamentals, with inculcating in our children a deeper sense of right and wrong, with standards of behavior, with such outdated notions as "honor" and "duty." We need to concern ourselves far more than we now do with the contents of the textbooks our children are required to study in order to make sure that they support rather than undermine the traditional values of our society. Above all, we need to be strengthening rather than undercutting the role of the family, of parents, in supervising the moral and ethical education of their children.

A year or so ago, parents in certain fundamentalist communities in West Virginia were widely criticized and ridiculed for boycotting schools that used textbooks that subverted certain of their religious beliefs. I suspect that those West Virginians understood far better than their condescending critics the true responsibilities of parents and their role in maintaining the quality of a people and the integrity of a civilization.

In Defense of the Electoral College

In 1977, President Carter suggested abolishing the consti-
tutionally mandated Electoral College and relying instead on
a straight head count for the election of our presidents. In the
wake of the 2000 election, reformists are again calling for the
substitution of a plurality vote for the Electoral College. Indeed,
some states have recently amended their laws towards that end:
they will order their electors to cast their votes for whichever
candidate receives a plurality of the votes cast nationally. If
states selecting a majority of the electors follow their example,
they will have achieved their objective without having to amend
the Constitution. In this April 28, 1977, commentary, I explain
why that is a very bad idea.

President Carter's proposal that we abolish the Electoral College and elect our presidents by direct popular vote is deceptively appealing, but it is an insidious one that would reshape our
political institutions and undermine their stability. It is based on
the assumption that it would be intolerable, in these enlightened
times, for a president to ever again be elected (as has happened
a few times in the past) by less than a plurality of those voting.
But the genius of the American Constitution is that it tempers

majority rule with mechanisms designed to ensure a stable society in which diversity can exist, and minority and regional interests can be protected against domination by a naked majority.

We divide the powers of the federal government among three branches, each existing in a degree of tension with the others. A non-elected Supreme Court can declare the actions taken by elected officials to be unconstitutional; and Congress and the president act as restraints on each other. Congress itself is structured to allow sparsely populated states a disproportionate voice in the shaping of the nation's laws. In the Senate, Alaska has the same two votes as New York, even though New York has more than forty times the population. And the Senate acts as a check on the House of Representatives, which has resulted in the enactment of laws that have tended to represent a broader national consensus; for the most part, no region of the country feels itself victimized by another that happens to be more populous.

So it is with the mechanism by which we choose our chief executive. As John F. Kennedy once put it when stating his reasons for opposing the direct election of the president, the existing mechanism "provides a system of checks and balances to ensure that no area or group shall obtain too much power." The Electoral College system has the practical advantage of limiting the strength of any one region or class of Americans, and this in turn encourages the selection of presidential candidates on the basis of a broader, more national appeal. Under the existing system, for example, a president can't be elected simply by concentrating his campaign on the perceived self-interests of a few highly industrialized and populous states at the expense of the rest of the country.

There is another, admittedly accidental aspect of the Electoral College device that should make us think twice before abandoning it. We are accustomed to congratulating ourselves on the stability we have derived by virtue of ours being an essentially two-party system. Yet too few people ever stop to wonder why this system has prevailed, as there is nothing in the Constitution or in our laws that mandates that our politics should be so organized. What accounts for this distinctive characteristic of the American political scene is that as the winner in each state is awarded all of that state's electoral votes, viable presidential candidates must have the support of political parties that have a broad national base. What this means is that it is virtually impossible for candidates or parties with a purely regional appeal, however strong, to compete successfully in a presidential campaign. It is this institutional peculiarity of the American system, rather than any unique character trait of the American people, that has been largely responsible for the essentially stable two-party system we have enjoyed since our earliest days.

There are undoubtedly a number of ways in which we can improve our political institutions, but abolishing the Electoral College isn't one of them. The Electoral College is part and parcel of the system of checks and balances by which we achieve a consensus that all can accept. It is one of the features of our Constitution that make us a republic and not a democracy; and the difference between the two may well be the difference between the political stability we have enjoyed and the factionalism that has plagued so many other experiments in self-government.

Security vs. Freedom

The siren song of today's politics is the promise of protection from all of life's vicissitudes. The public-welfare safety net was first constructed to help the truly down-and-out. It is now beginning to be viewed as a middle-class entitlement—and no one seems to ask at what cost. Jefferson warned us that a government big enough to give us everything we want is also big enough to take everything we have. This commentary was broadcast in April 1977.

In a recent article on the future of the Republican Party, Clare Boothe Luce concludes that the party has none. Her thesis, simply stated, is that Republicanism is a dying cause because in America today, individual freedom is a dying cause.

Mrs. Luce rejects the notion that the Republican Party is the victim of a bad press, or of an inability to project a clear understanding of the principles for which it stands. Not at all, she maintains, and I quote:

> Consciously, or unconsciously, the voters know quite well that the GOP stands for a certain set of principles: for political and economic freedom, for the liberty of the indi-

vidual, for a free-market economy, for fiscal and financial responsibility in government, and for limited government. And most of the voters also know that these are the principles on which the Republic itself was founded. The real reason that Americans have been leaving the GOP in droves is that most of them just don't give a damn any more for these principles.

It is Mrs. Luce's thesis that over some indeterminate period, we have evolved from a Republic, with its restraints on the power of a majority, to what she calls a "pure democracy." In her view, in a pure democracy, a majority coalition of the have-nots, the want-mores, and the envious will inevitably use its political power to milk the economic system to the point where it will collapse; and with that collapse will inevitably come authoritarian rule.

Few, I suppose, will agree with so pessimistic a view of the American future, but no one seriously concerned about that future can afford to dismiss it out of hand. History has not been kind to free societies; and Mrs. Luce is entirely correct in her underlying thesis that we have witnessed, in recent years, a most disturbing development in American political life. It is one that has seen a dramatic shift in what is perceived to be the appropriate relationship between government and the individual.

The federal government was viewed by the Founders as a necessary evil. But during the New Deal years, it increasingly took on the role of a benevolent provider, intent on freeing us from every care, from every risk; and ever since, we have seen a gradual shift in the role of the state from that of servant towards that of master. The results have been deeply damaging. People have been damaged by promises easily made but seldom kept. The economy is being damaged by excessive taxation and inflation. But most serious of all is the damage that has been done to the human spirit. Politicians out to build permanent constituencies have encouraged people to retreat from self-reliance by singing that old siren song of total security.

It is a disturbing trend, one that brings to mind the haunting passage that Edward Gibbon wrote about the ancient Athenians.

"In the end," wrote Gibbon, "more than they wanted freedom, they wanted security. They wanted a comfortable life and they lost it all—security, comfort, and freedom. When the Athenians finally wanted not to give to society, but for society to give to them, when the freedom they wished for was freedom from responsibility, then Athens ceased to be free and was never free again."

I pray that that tragic epitaph will never be read over this Republic of ours. And I don't believe it will be. But the possibility is nevertheless there, and I think that in those words Gibbon delineated the choice facing Americans in the years immediately ahead, the choice between security and freedom as our primary political goal. And the irony here, of course, is that the choice is really no choice at all, for ultimate security can in the end be realized only through freedom.

Mrs. Luce may be far too pessimistic about the future of the Republican Party and, what is infinitely more important, the future of the American Republic. But she will be proven wrong only to the degree that Americans consciously understand the dangerous waters into which we have been drifting and decide once again to assert the principles of individual and economic freedom and of limited government on which this nation was founded.

Competition and the
Postal Service

There are countless areas in which governments at every level have saved money and improved services by placing them in the hands of private for-profit corporations. Prisons and toll roads are just two examples of this. As the following April 1977 commentary suggests, allowing private competition in the delivery of first-class mail would be the surest way to improve that vital service—something that Belgium, Britain, Finland, Germany, New Zealand, and Sweden have found to be true.

G overnor Jerry Brown of California recently described the distinction between government and private enterprise in this way: "The difference between the private sector and the public sector is that in the public sector when something goes wrong with the enterprise, it doesn't go bankrupt, it just gets bigger."

The U.S. Postal Service would seem to be a case in point. Even though, under its recent reorganization, it is supposed to become self-supporting, and even though the price of first-class mail has been rising at twice the rate of the overall cost of living, and even though services are steadily being curtailed, Congress has been called upon to provide almost $3 billion in postal subsidies for the current fiscal year.

Now, when presented with a problem such as this one, Congress has what has become an almost automatic response: appoint a commission. And so last September, a Commission on the Postal Service was appointed to determine what, if anything, could be done to improve the delivery of mail while holding costs to humane levels. A few weeks ago, the commission filed its report. It recommended that federal subsidies be increased and that service be decreased still further, by dropping Saturday deliveries. It also recommended that the Postal Service consider cutting its losses by expanding into the field of electronic communication—presumably at the expense of the private companies that are rapidly developing new and better ways of transmitting letters and transferring money over telephone lines.

The one cure that the commission did not prescribe for the admitted ills of the Postal Service is a large dose of competition. Private carriers, by the grace of Congress, are currently permitted to compete in the delivery of every kind of mail except the one that most citizens use; namely, first-class mail. These poor people— you and I—are routinely milked through excessive charges; and under present law, there is precious little that we can do about it. Anytime a free-spirited, red-blooded American entrepreneur tries to give us better service at a lower price, he is apt to find the clammy hand of the law on his shoulder. This was the case with an enterprising young couple in Rochester, New York, who last year committed the crime of offering same-day delivery within the city at ten cents a letter. [*First-class postage at the time was thirteen cents.*] Existing law even forbids utilities to save their customers a few dollars by having meter readers do double duty, delivering bills into the mailboxes paid for and owned by those same customers.

Until the law is changed, we are condemned to live with the usual consequences of a monopoly—excessive cost and deteriorating service—because the enterprise is spared the kind of competitive prod that can induce efficiency. It is interesting to note that last year, when the president's Council on Wage and Price Stability looked into the causes of the startling rise in first-class postage, it concluded that a little competition could retard and even reverse the upward push of postal rates while introducing higher productivity within the Postal Service.

The postal lobby, of course, is opposed to this suggestion. It comes up with the standard objection offered by all monopolists when defending their privileges; namely, that competitors would skim the cream in the most profitable markets, leaving the monopolists to service the unprofitable ones. Who, they ask, would look after rural communities? This raises at least a couple of questions. Why should the 70 percent of Americans living in urban areas be deprived of the possibility of better and cheaper service just so that their rural cousins can enjoy hidden subsidies? It would be far fairer and cheaper to provide six or seven hundred million dollars in direct subsidies to keep rural post offices open than to continue to overcharge the users of first-class mail by more than twice that amount.

And why should we conclude that private carriers would leave rural America unserved? Here it is instructive to look at the record of the United Parcel Service. Today, this private, taxpaying carrier serves the entire population of every state except Alaska. It provides its customers more deliveries, with less breakage, and at lower prices, than does the tax-subsidized Postal Service. And to cap it all off, it does so at a profit.

But even if private letter carriers couldn't serve all portions of the country, we as taxpayers and consumers would still be far better off allowing competition to cut costs and improve efficiency where it can, while relying on direct subsidies where necessary to maintain essential services. America's taxpaying, letter-writing consumers can do themselves a favor by taking to the mails to encourage Congress to open the Postal Service to the test of competition. It could be a liberating experience.

Free Trade vs. Protectionism

Hard economic times will always create pressures for protectionism, even though the experience of the Great Depression demonstrates that trade barriers offer a sure way of prolonging a recession. But, as I explained in this commentary, broadcast in May 1977, the political class tends to be blind to economic causes and effects and will seek any opportunity to protect favored constituencies from foreign competition. So it is no surprise that the depressed economy of the late Seventies should have revived protectionism—or that Congress in the economic turmoil of 2008–09 should insert trade barriers into its "stimulus" legislation.

There are few areas of public policy that better test the mettle of political leadership than that of international trade. If statesmanship consists of the ability to rise above politics in pursuit of the greatest good for the greatest number, then we shall soon have the measure of Jimmy Carter in an area where rapidly mounting political pressures are on a collision course with the ultimate public good.

The high command of the AFL-CIO is demanding a return to protectionism on a half-dozen fronts; the garment industry in

New York City closed down for a day in protest against rapidly increasing imports of foreign goods; and within weeks of President Carter's inauguration, the U.S. International Trade Commission handed him a bundle of hornets' nests in the form of recommendations that he restrict the importation of shoes and TV sets while relaxing restrictions on foreign-grown sugar. In each of these cases, the president has been called upon to make agonizingly difficult decisions, whether measured in human or political terms. There is no question but that competition from these and other imported goods threatens the jobs of thousands of Americans in dozens of communities throughout the country. And it is to be expected that those affected will mobilize every possible political pressure to reduce the competition from abroad.

But the job that Jimmy Carter worked so hard to win requires him to weigh the long-term interests of all Americans against the undoubted hardships faced by some. What he and we must always remember is that Americans are consumers as well as producers, exporters as well as importers, and that we live in an economy that is no longer even close to being self-sufficient. As consumers, it is in the interest of every American to be able to choose from among the widest variety of goods and to be able to buy them at the lowest possible prices, irrespective of the country of origin. As exporters, Americans have a very significant stake in freedom of access to foreign markets; and we have to export if we are to earn the tens of billions of dollars we need in order to pay for the imported oil and other raw materials on which our economy increasingly depends.

To illustrate the conflicting interests that must be taken into account in weighing the immediate consequences of protectionism, let us take the case of the International Trade Commission's recommendations with respect to the importation of shoes. About 170,000 people are employed in the American shoe industry. Many of these jobs remain secure, because some American lines, such as higher-quality men's shoes, remain competitive. But cheaper lines are being undersold by foreign manufacturers, and many plants will have no alternative but to go out of business unless competition from abroad is curtailed.

There can be no doubt that the import quotas and higher tariffs recommended by the commission would safeguard thousands of jobs in the domestic shoe industry. But they would also increase the cost of shoes to American consumers, especially the poor, by an estimated half-billion dollars a year. More than that, this kind of protectionism, if it becomes widespread, could trigger retaliatory restrictions by other nations against American goods, thereby causing layoffs of American workers in our export industries. Thus, in order to save jobs in some industries, we would endanger jobs in others, while increasing the cost of goods to all consumers. At the same time, we would be depriving ourselves of the foreign earnings we need to pay for such essential imports as oil.

Enlightened policy will recognize that economic relationships are anything but static. Changing technologies and changing standards of living will require changing patterns of production within the countries that are linked together as trading partners. A dozen years ago, the American textile industry was demanding protection from cheaper goods produced in Japan. Today, the Japanese textile industry is in shambles because of the cheaper goods that are now being produced in places like Taiwan. Protectionism is not the answer. What we need is fairer trade, not less trade. We have the right to demand fair access to the domestic markets of our trading partners, and we have the right to protect our industries against competition from goods exported to us at artificially low prices. The president's initiatives in the area of international trade must therefore seek an end to export subsidies and import barriers that impede honest competition in world markets.

This will still leave us with the trauma of individual industries suddenly faced by the impact of foreign competition. We have programs designed to afford a degree of short-term protection and assistance to help them and their employees make the transition to new products and jobs. This limited degree of protectionism is appropriate. But on every rational balance, the president can best serve the long-term interests of all Americans by working to reduce existing barriers to world trade rather than erecting new ones of our own.

Tuition Tax Credits

Despite documented evidence of the educational value of school choice, most comprehensively in Milwaukee and most recently in Washington, D.C., our national education system remains an underperforming monopoly controlled by teachers' unions and their political allies. This commentary from April 13, 1978, describes that year's attempt to give parents economic assistance so that poor and middle-class families might enjoy some of the educational opportunities taken for granted by wealthy politicians who decline to give them that choice.

When I was in the United States Senate, I found that a usually reliable guide to sound policy was to search out the *New York Times*'s position on a particular issue and then to take the opposite side. When the *Times*'s editorial voice verged on the hysterical, my rule of thumb proved infallible. Over the years the paper has shown an absolute genius for coming down on the wrongheaded side of virtually every important issue.

Today, the *Times* is leveling its editorial Big Berthas at what is probably the most important consumer-protection bill on our national agenda, if you share my belief that the quality of American education is supremely important to America's future. I speak of the Tuition Tax Credit Bill, which has the sponsorship of half the Senate. Its basic soundness is attested to not only by the stridency of the *New York Times*'s attacks on it but also by the hysteria it has stirred up at the *Washington Post* and in the United Federation of Teachers. UFT President Albert Shanker, for example, warns in somber tones that the bill "threatens to do incalculable damage to this country's public schools. . . . The bill will engender conflict and bitterness of the kind created by the Civil War." The *Washington Post* shakes its editorial head and deplores the bill for supposedly abetting "ethnic and social separatism." The *Times* concludes that the bill is "deplorable on all counts."

It is time to throttle down the rhetoric and examine the facts. This excellent legislation (I declare my bias by admitting that I offered an earlier version three years ago) was introduced by Senators Packwood of Oregon and Moynihan of New York to help parents exercise what for too many of them is only a theoretical right of choice where the education of their children is concerned. It would entitle them to take a tax credit for 50 percent of tuition bills paid, up to limit of $500. Because it incorporates a negative-tax feature, it extends its benefits to the poor, who are often in the most desperate need to find alternatives to deteriorating public education.

The critics of the bill claim that private schools are undemocratic institutions. In fact, most private schools in the United States today incorporate, as a matter of policy, a broader spectrum of ethnic, financial, and social backgrounds than do the public schools, most of which serve reasonably homogeneous neighborhoods.

The Tuition Tax Credit Bill, we are told, is a devious device designed to preserve parochial schools. Sure, these schools, along with all other private institutions, will benefit, in that more people will be able to afford to send their children to them. But the aid provided by the bill is to parents, not to religious institutions; and the beneficiaries are the children of all religions and of no religion who attend those schools. Between 33 and 50 percent of all black students in Catholic parochial schools are non-Catholic. Although only 1 percent of American Lutherans are black, blacks make up

10 percent of the student body at Lutheran elementary schools, and 18 percent at the secondary level. The reason their parents are sending them to those schools at substantial sacrifices is not for religious education but for quality education of a kind that unfortunately is increasingly hard to find in public institutions.

The bill, we are told, will represent an indiscriminate raid on the public treasury. To this there are two answers. First, the parents in question are already supporting public education with their tax contributions, and will still be digging into their own pockets to pay the other half, and more, of private-school tuition bills. It is an act of justice to allow them some relief from a double burden as they exercise their responsibilities as parents. Second, because private schools operate at a significantly lower cost per student than their public-school counterparts, every child sent to a private institution represents a net saving to the taxpayers.

The Tuition Tax Credit Bill is important because it allows parents to reassert some choice over the kind of schooling their children will have. In too many cases, they have seen their tax money poured into public schools that have become educational laboratories where dubious experimentation and lowered academic standards cheat children of their future. The bill will not destroy public schools. Rather, it will improve them. By encouraging competition, it will force them to be more responsive, not to the endless schemes of bureaucratic experts, but to the parents' desires that their children receive a sound education.

Surely this is an objective that national policy should support, the editors of the *New York Times* notwithstanding.

Barriers to Entry

This May 25, 1978, commentary explains why so many men and women in the lower strata of American society find it so hard to work up the economic ladder and realize the American dream.

There are many dangers that can flow from the development of a seemingly permanent welfare population in the United States. But the most insidious of them is that it will feed the gut assumption already shared by too many Americans that this new dependent class is inherently shiftless, unwilling to get out there and fight its way up the economic ladder to a full participation in American life. If the Irish, and the Jews, and the Poles, and the Italians could make it all on their own during the first half of this century, so the reasoning goes, why can't these most recent immigrants into our inner cities do the same in the second half?

A growing number of studies are documenting a very real reason for the contrast, which is simply this: the rules of the game have been changed. Governments at all levels have erected barriers to entry into the mainstream of American life that didn't exist sixty years ago when, for example, sociologists were despairing over the abysmally low IQs of Jewish immigrants being drafted into the armed services in World War I. These earlier inhabitants of our inner cities didn't face the obstacles of a permissive education that denies children a working command of the three Rs; they didn't have to cope with urban-renewal programs that destroyed the housing they could most easily afford; they didn't enjoy levels of public assistance that might have tempted them to remain on welfare instead of seeking work; and they weren't confronted with minimum-wage laws that priced jobs beyond the reach of the least skilled. Moreover, those earlier urban immigrants weren't facing a battery of licensing restrictions that denied them access to trades and priced them out of opportunities to begin their own small businesses. They weren't required to earn a plumber's equivalent of a Ph.D. in order to take on the less demanding plumbing work they could readily master.

In most of the country a half-century or so ago, all that an ambitious person needed in order to go into the taxi business was a driver's license, a clean police record, and the down payment on a car. In most cities today, however, restrictive licensing is in place to limit the number of cabs that can be legally operated. An individual must therefore be prepared to pay as much as $50,000 to buy the privilege—an entry fee clearly beyond the reach of the poor, however qualified. The same holds true for individuals wishing to operate a truck across state lines. The Interstate Commerce Commission has imposed restrictions on new entries into interstate trucking that few newcomers are able to meet.

The demonstrable fact is that the people who today occupy the bottom of the economic totem pole are deprived by well-intentioned laws and regulations of too many of the traditional opportunities to make it on their own; and because today a disproportionate percentage of those people are black, these laws and regulations disproportionately hurt black Americans, feeding the swamp fevers of a latent racism.

This is a phenomenon that is enormously important for us to understand, for the most obvious political as well as moral reasons. True, recent studies indicate that we are making progress in narrowing the gap between the earnings of white and black Americans, which reflects the narrowing of the educational gap. But we aren't making progress fast enough; and whole populations are being left outside, looking in. It is time we launched a concerted drive to dismantle the man-made barriers that today deny too many of our citizens a fair access to the American dream.

Conservatives vs. Corporate America

During my Senate years, I felt a constant frustration over corporate America's self-interested myopia. Its skilled lobbyists worked diligently—and effectively—to secure special tax and other advantages for their clients, but never to protect the economic system to which they owed their success. This commentary was broadcast in September 1978. Unfortunately, it made little impression on corporate boardrooms.

Among the many burdens that American conservatives bear is the widespread assumption that they are knee-jerk apologists for corporate America.

As a self-confessed conservative, I acknowledge a bias in favor of the system of private, competitive enterprise, which experience has demonstrated to be the most fruitful way of harnessing man's economic energies. I have an abiding suspicion of any concentration of power, whether in political or private hands; but I am neither shocked nor will I moralize over the fact that most human beings tend to act more on the basis of perceived self-interest than on the basis of altruism. I also accept as self-evident Lenin's observation that a capitalist will sell the rope with which the last capitalist is hanged, as well as Adam Smith's observation to the effect that any time five men engaged in the same business come together, they will soon be conniving to limit competition. Hence my approval of government action to enjoin any conspiracy to impose restraints on trade.

Today's conservative is pro-business in the sense that he favors our economic system of private, competitive enterprise and wants it to be able to operate with the maximum freedom consistent with the freedom and rights of others; and it is this principled commitment to a free economy that places American conservatives increasingly at odds with so much of corporate America. Regulated businesses, for example, tend to become so accustomed to being sheltered against the rigors of competition that they are among the most ferocious opponents of any attempt to liberate them from their regulators—witness the strenuous opposition of the major airlines to legislation designed to curb the regulatory power of the Civil Aeronautics Board, and of the trucking industry to proposals for the deregulation of interstate trucking.

Moreover, too many of our larger corporations are now in the hands of professional managers whose conception of corporate self-interest is apt to extend no further than their own retirements. As a result, with a few honorable exceptions, large corporations have shown themselves singularly reluctant to stick their collective necks out and risk the displeasure of government officials by taking stands on important questions of economic principle on which the long-term welfare of their companies—and of society at large—ultimately depends. And so we see the dismaying phenomenon of corporate political-action committees playing it safe by giving their major financial support to incumbent congressmen who devote the bulk of their energies to finding new ways of harassing business.

This is in sharp contrast to the leaders of organized labor, who know which candidates favor their objectives, and then go about giving them effective support. Corporate managers, by contrast, tend to take the road of expediency. And so today, the political levers are all being applied in favor of still greater intervention in the economy despite the massive resources that major American businesses have the power to bring to bear in defense of a free economy.

It is small wonder, then, that conservatives today are tending to view big business more as members of the enemy than as friends and allies, even as conservatives continue to work to preserve the economic freedom that permitted those businesses to grow and prosper in the first instance.

It is ironical that as Congress focused on the measures that would be required to prevent a repeat of the 2008 financial meltdown, congressional conservatives were routinely tarred as the lackeys of Wall Street, when in fact big Wall Street bankers were contributing far more to Democratic candidates than to Republicans. The bankers were being expedient. Congressional conservatives, however, were doing their best to make sure that a new regulatory regime wouldn't lead to further Wall Street bailouts or strangle sources of capital that will be required to restore the vitality of the American economy. Nothing has changed since I wrote this commentary thirty years ago.

OF HISTORICAL INTEREST

The writings in this section shed little light on today's head-line issues, but they do have something to say about a period that affected the shape of the world today. They describe the frustrations that high-minded but misguided citizens can cause those responsible for deterring a war, the role shortwave radios can play in winning one, and how to achieve a hapless presidency.

Freezing the Chances for Peace

Feel-good sentiments should never be allowed to divert us from the enduring truth that credible strength is the surest guarantee of peace. In the early 1980s, some wonderfully well-intentioned and influential citizens were urging a freeze in spending on our nuclear arms. This October 1982 address to the Commonwealth Club of California explains the folly of their position.

I want to talk to you today about nuclear arms and the Reagan administration's policies for reducing the risks of nuclear war. It is a subject replete with paradox. Nuclear war is too gruesome to contemplate—or to ignore. The intricacies of the nuclear balance require great expertise to master; and yet we don't always trust the experts. No subject places so great a demand on calm, rational thought; but few subjects so stir our emotions.

Let me begin with two simple but often overlooked truths. First, we all want peace. Yet in the intensity of the current debate over nuclear policy, it sounds at times as if some groups believe they hold a monopoly on the abhorrence of nuclear war. Let there be no such confusion here. We are all united in our desire to avoid a nuclear holocaust.

A second simple but often overlooked truth is that despite the outbreak of more than a hundred military conflicts in the thirty-seven years that have elapsed since World War II, the general peace has been preserved.

The policy that has maintained the general peace for so long is known as deterrence. It is not a Democratic or a Republican policy; it has been American policy in every administration since the Second World War. The basic premise of deterrence is simple. No matter how strong our enemies become or how successful a surprise attack they may launch, enough of our nuclear forces must survive to be able to inflict such terrible losses that no one could ever benefit from attacking us. [*A few months after I gave this speech, President Reagan made the radical suggestion that space-based missile defenses would provide a far more moral alternative to this kind of deterrence. The same people who were backing a freeze were appalled. Even though this initiative faced formidable obstacles at home, it presented the Soviets with a technological challenge they could not meet and helped bring the Cold War to a successful end.*]

Deterrence—the prevention of war by making the cost of aggression unacceptably high—is the only strategy that makes sense in the nuclear age. But while its premise is simple enough, it is not always so easy to determine whether we are, in fact, strong enough to successfully deter any attack. Because enough of our forces must be able to survive an attack to inflict unacceptable costs on our enemies, the sufficiency of our strength depends in part on how strong our adversaries become; and, because the stakes are so high, there must never be any room for doubt. Unfortunately, over the last decade the strength of our deterrent has steadily eroded. The balance that has kept the peace for more than thirty-five years is today endangered.

Our current danger—mankind's current danger—stems from two long-term trends: one well known, one more obscure. It is well known that over the last twenty years the Soviets have engaged in the greatest arms buildup the world has ever seen. It is less frequently appreciated that during most of this period, the United States chose not to keep pace. As the Soviets raced forward, we sat on our hands. As a result, while over three-quarters of Soviet strategic forces were built within the last five years, more than three-quarters of ours are fifteen years old or older.

Since 1972, the Soviets have developed and deployed three new types of intercontinental ballistic missiles (ICBMs) capable of a first strike—the SS-17, SS-18, and SS-19. The most destructive of these weapons carries up to three times the number of warheads our most powerful missile does. All of them pose a major threat to our land-based ICBMs. Yet it will be years before we begin deployment of the MX, the first new U.S. intercontinental ballistic missile in sixteen years.

Since 1972, the USSR has added more than sixty missile-firing submarines in four new or improved classes. The commissioning of the first U.S. Trident submarine earlier this year marked the end of a fifteen-year period during which the United States did not build a single new ballistic-missile submarine.

Since 1975, the Soviets have produced over 250 modern bombers, and they are continuing to build them at a rate of more than two a month. By contrast, the newest U.S. heavy bomber was built more than twenty years ago. Meanwhile, the Soviet Union has built a massive air-defense system, while the United States has no effective defense against Soviet bombers.

As a result of their massive buildup, the Soviets now surpass the United States in most significant measures used to judge nuclear weapons, including total number of systems, total number of ballistic missiles, and total destructive potential. For example, the Soviets possess 40 percent more delivery systems than we and surpass us in missile throw weight, an important measure of their nuclear punch, by a factor of more than two and a half to one. Their most advanced weapons have the capacity to destroy our land-based missiles and our command, control, and communication systems, while their own hardened installations remain relatively immune to U.S. counterattack.

Because for the first twenty-five years of the nuclear era America had the mightiest arsenal in the world, it is tempting to disbelieve the awesome change the last decade has witnessed. It is tempting to assume our technical advantages counterbalance Soviet advances. It is tempting to disbelieve claims that our land-based missiles and bombers are increasingly vulnerable to Soviet attack. Yet these are facts accepted even by groups that oppose the Reagan administration's policies.

The Soviets' massive buildup in their strategic forces, coupled with a similar buildup in their conventional forces, is significant in two major ways. First, to the degree that it damages the credibility of our deterrent, it increases the danger that the Soviets may see force as an attractive option. But what is just as important, the Soviets' increases allow them to exercise leverage over countries that once felt secure because of the assumed reliability of the American nuclear umbrella.

Thus the prices we pay for ignoring a twenty-year-long surge in Soviet strength are these: the nuclear balance has shifted greatly; our forces are less secure; and Soviet influence in the world has grown. These facts are undisputed by serious analysts. Where opinions differ is in our assessment of what we must do about these facts.

President Reagan's response to the challenge of the Soviet buildup has been twofold. One track of that response has been a vigorous commitment to reducing strategic arms; the other, to launching an overdue modernization of our strategic forces to protect our country and strengthen our ability to deter attack.

In a bold stroke in opening the Strategic Arms Reduction Talks (START) in Geneva, the president proposed, as an initial step, a one-third reduction in strategic-missile warheads together with reductions in the number of missiles per side to almost half the current U.S. levels, such reductions to be verifiable. I emphasize verification, because it is essential to the goal of long-term stability.

Trust, even in the best of situations, it is not an adequate safeguard where the safety of the world is concerned. But the critical reason we cannot rely on trust is that the Soviets so constantly prove themselves unworthy of it.

We have conclusive proof that the Soviets are currently violating international arms-control agreements by using chemical weapons in Afghanistan and supplying biochemical weapons for use in Southeast Asia. Ask an Afghan if Soviet agreements on arms control can be trusted. In March, the Soviets announced a temporary unilateral ban on further deployment of intermediate-range missiles—a not-so-grand gesture considering that the Soviets have raced to an advantage of more than six hundred missiles to none. Even so, we have conclusive evidence that the Soviets promptly violated even this undertaking. In other areas the Soviets have proven themselves equally unreliable. Soviet violations of the Helsinki Accords are only the most visible recent instances of Soviet disregard for international agreements.

The U.S. START proposal points the way to a more stable strategic balance at equal and reduced levels of strategic forces. Its terms would be verifiable and fair, and its limits in the mutual interest of both East and West. If the Soviets are indeed serious about seeking a substantial reduction in forces, there is much that they can work with here.

Moreover, an agreement along the lines of the U.S. proposal would be an historic first. No arms-control agreement to date— not SALT I, not SALT II [the Strategic Arms Limitation Treaties]— has ever led to such fundamental cutbacks in existing strategic forces. An agreement such as that outlined in the START proposals would be the first. Despite the necessarily cautious pace of the initial START negotiations, they offer the prospect for dramatic and fundamental progress.

But as sensible as the U.S. arms proposals are, there will be little progress in negotiations unless the Soviets are convinced that the United States has the will to restore and then maintain the nuclear balance. What is essential to remember is that in the past, the Soviets have made concessions in arms-control negotiations only when the United States has threatened to redress imbalances.

The Soviets agreed to negotiate an anti-ballistic missile (ABM) treaty only when the U.S. Senate approved an ABM system. Having unilaterally introduced new and revolutionary intermediate-range nuclear weapons into the European nuclear balance, the Soviets agreed to negotiate limits on such missiles only when it was made clear that NATO was prepared to deploy similar missiles. In 1977, the Soviets rejected out of hand U.S. proposals for deep reductions in nuclear forces. Only now, after the United States has shown its determination to modernize its forces, have the Soviets begun to take arms reductions seriously.

The president's proposal to modernize our forces in response to the massive Soviet buildup will maintain the effectiveness of our deterrent in years to come. Only the production of the MX—our first new type of intercontinental missile in sixteen years—and the proposed Trident II with its D-5 missile will give us survivable forces capable of destroying hardened military targets. Only the Tridents—our first new nuclear submarine in fifteen years—will ensure the continued viability of our sea-based forces. Only the B-1 and Stealth bombers—our first new models in more than twenty years—will protect our ability to penetrate Soviet airspace in the future. Only with these new forces can we revitalize the balance that has maintained the peace for three decades.

Thus do the two tracks of President Reagan's response to the massive Soviet arms buildup reinforce each other. The president's commitment to modernizing and strengthening U.S. nuclear forces is essential to the preservation of deterrence. At the same time, that commitment greatly enhances our prospects for achieving Soviet agreement to major reductions in our respective nuclear inventories.

Yet these twin objectives, which all Americans share, would be placed in jeopardy by a nuclear freeze of the kind now being urged as an alternative to the administration's policies. Freeze proponents argue that it is safe for both the United States and the Soviet Union to "stop where they are"—that is, freeze all testing, production, and deployment of missiles—and then proceed to negotiate reductions. While there are many versions of freeze proposals, all are based on three assumptions. First, they assume that the credibility of our deterrent would not be endangered by a freeze; second, they assume that the Soviets are eager to reduce the level of their nuclear arms but have been prevented from making such reductions by the arms race; and third, they assume that changes in nuclear forces will make the balance less stable and more destructive.

If any one of these assumptions were questionable, a nuclear freeze would prove not only unwise but dangerous. In fact, all three assumptions are not merely questionable, they are wrong.

Take, first, the assumption that the credibility of our deterrent would not be endangered by a freeze. Freeze proponents acknowledge the Soviets' massive buildup over the last decade but argue that even sizable inequalities are irrelevant given the vast destructive power at our disposal. If we simply considered the total of all our missiles, this is probably true. But the key to deterrence is the ability of our forces to survive a surprise attack in sufficient numbers to inflict unacceptable losses on the Soviets, and the plausible will to do so. Here the picture becomes more murky.

For more than three decades our strategy of deterrence has been based on a defensive triad of intercontinental missiles, bombers, and nuclear submarines. In the past, this triad has proven stable because any Soviet buildup or technological breakthrough that could defeat one element would still leave two able to carry out their missions. A freeze, however, would put the future of our triad in grave doubt.

Because of just such a technological breakthrough in missile accuracy, in combination with the huge size of the new Soviet warheads, the first leg of our triad—intercontinental missiles—is already in jeopardy. The Soviets could today destroy as much as 90 percent of our ICBMs. The second leg, bombers, may not fare much better. As I have noted, our intercontinental bombers are already more than twenty years old and rapidly reaching the point where they must be retired. In addition, the Soviets have invested huge sums in erecting air defenses.

Fortunately, the third leg of our triad—our submarine fleet— still remains relatively safe. But, with the exception of our two new Trident submarines, our current fleet of missile-launching submarines was built in the mid-1960s and will need to be replaced. If the Soviets should achieve a breakthrough in antisubmarine warfare, on which they are concentrating so great an effort, our nuclear deterrent would be fragile indeed.

Thus a freeze would leave us with one leg of our triad greatly vulnerable, one increasingly so, and our overall forces faced with dangerous deterioration. In short, we cannot assume that freezing our forces at current levels will be safe even in the near future.

The freeze proponents' second assumption concerns Soviet motivations. Their proposals assume that an arms race has forced the Soviets to build as many missiles as they have; therefore, once the arms race ends, they will be eager to reduce their forces. Unfortunately, Soviet deeds, as opposed to Soviet words, show that the freeze proponents are wrong in this assessment.

First, the Soviets' recent buildup is vastly greater than what would be required either by a policy of deterrence or by a need to "keep up" with American efforts. We voluntarily froze the number of our delivery systems in the mid-1960s. By 1972, the Soviets had achieved an equal number, except that theirs were substantially more powerful. Today, as a result of cutbacks in ours and increases in theirs, their delivery systems exceed ours by about 40 percent. The Soviets are not a reluctant party to the current arms race; they have a substantial lead.

Second, the character of the Soviet arms buildup belies a passive role. The Soviets have concentrated on developing land-based missiles that have a first-strike capability and, therefore, are the type most likely to intimidate. This is the effort not of a reluctant nation forced to build arms for defense but of a nation that seeks the political benefits of intimidating force.

Third, if the Soviets are building arms only to counter our buildup, then why did they introduce intermediate-range nuclear missiles into Europe? NATO has none there. Yet the Soviets have built six hundred of them, most of which are now deployed and targeted against Western European capitals. The Soviets did not reluctantly continue an arms race in Western Europe. They started one. They did so to garner the benefits of intimidation.

If we agree to a freeze, the Soviets are not likely to relinquish the advantages they have worked so hard to achieve. Far from speeding reductions, a freeze would preclude them.

The third assumption that underlies the proposed freeze is that technological improvements will increase both the quantity and the megatonnage of our nuclear forces, thus feeding visions of a reckless, runaway spiraling of destructive power. But in the case of the United States, new technology has actually resulted in a net decrease in the destructive power of our strategic forces. The technological advances of the past ten years have allowed us to reduce our total megatonnage by almost 30 percent, and by roughly 60 percent since the peak levels of the early 1960s—reductions, incidentally, which a freeze ten years ago would have made impossible.

Other advances that we contemplate would make our weapons safer and less vulnerable to attack or to unauthorized or accidental use. The freeze movement, for example, would have us forgo more survivable land-based missiles, the deployment of less vulnerable submarines, and other measures designed to ensure the survival of our forces and hence the continued credibility of deterrence.

In sum, a freeze makes sense only if it will preserve our security and lead to significant reductions in arms. This assumes that our deterrent would not be endangered by a freeze, that the Soviets would be willing to reduce their forces, and that further improvements in weaponry would make the peace less stable. As we have seen, these assumptions are not only questionable but false. As a result, a freeze would not only prove unwise, it could prove disastrous.

In 1934, England, paralyzed by the prospective horror of war, refused to maintain its defenses. Winston Churchill, then merely a member of Parliament, warned his country of the danger posed by a growing Nazi Germany in these words:

> Everyone would be glad to see the burden of armaments reduced in every country, but history shows on many a page that armaments are not necessarily a cause of war. Want of them is no guarantee of peace. . . . This truth may be unfashionable, unpalatable, no doubt unpopular, but it is the truth. . . . the only choice open is the old grim choice our forebears had to face, namely, whether . . . we shall submit to the will of a stronger nation or whether we shall prepare to defend our rights, our liberties and indeed our lives.

President Reagan's policy of force modernization will maintain the credibility of our deterrence and reduce the risk of war by accident. Deterrence is a proven, effective policy. It is our safest and wisest course. We cannot allow it to be jeopardized by a freeze, however well intended.

Although President Obama's wistful yearnings for a nuclear-free world are understandable, until that happy day arrives, our security will continue to require our possession of a credible nuclear deterrent. Those yearnings, however, may have had the upper hand in his negotiation of a new nuclear-weapons treaty with the Russians. Its reduction of strategic nuclear warheads is reasonable, but other aspects of New START raise a number of questions that senators will need to examine before they vote on ratification. In doing so, they must keep in mind that we face a new generation of potential nuclear mischief-makers—the North Koreans, Iranians, and any terrorists who may gain possession of a nuclear weapon. Thus provisions that could make eminent good sense if Russia were our only potential adversary might prove foolhardy in today's world.

These are among the questions that the Senate must consider: Does New START give the Russians an effective veto over the further development and deployment of our missile defenses? How will its limits on delivery systems (which can carry conventional as well as strategic weapons) affect our ability to respond to future crises? Why does the treaty fail to deal with Russia's huge superiority in tactical nuclear weapons? Will its restrictions on weapons and delivery systems raise sufficient questions about the credibility of our nuclear umbrella to trigger a new wave of nuclear proliferation? This last is not an idle question. The Japanese, for example, have expressed great concern that we might deal away the deterrent capabilities on which Japan has relied for its own security.

The objectives of New START are laudable. But in deciding whether to ratify the treaty, the Senate must make absolutely sure that we are not undermining the credibility of a deterrence that has guaranteed our security over the past half-century and enabled Japan and other allies to forgo the development of their own nuclear arsenals.

Radio Free Europe and Radio Liberty: Defending the Right to Know

I served as president of the Munich-based Radio Free Europe and Radio Liberty for three years, beginning in November 1982. These two radio services had been established in the late 1940s in response to the Soviet Union's rapid consolidation of its power over what came to be known as the "captive nations" of Eastern Europe, and they proved to be enormously effective weapons in our Cold War arsenal. The radios' mission was a simple one: to counter Communist censorship and internal propaganda by providing their Eastern European and Soviet audiences with the truth, and nothing but the truth, about what was happening within their own countries and in the world outside. The following remarks were delivered in September 1983 at New York City's Overseas Press Club.

A month ago, when this program was scheduled, I could not have anticipated that the Soviets would provide me with so graphic an example of the critical importance of the role played in today's world by international broadcasters such as Radio Free Europe and Radio Liberty. Without us, the tens of millions of men and women living in the Soviet Union and its Eastern European satellites would have had no knowledge of the basic facts about the Soviets' destruction of an unarmed Korean airliner or of the outrage this wanton killing caused around the globe.

Bear in mind that a totalitarian regime feels no need to inform its citizens of even the fiercest controversies in which it is involved. They are told only what the regime determines to be in its own best interest to tell. But Radio Free Europe, Radio Liberty, the BBC, Voice of America, Deutsche Welle, and the other major Western services can penetrate the most tightly controlled societies with factual descriptions of major world events.

We began our own hour-by-hour reporting of the KAL tragedy with the Korean government's first announcement of a missing airliner, followed in quick succession by Japanese fears and then the flat assertion that it had been shot down. During the following five days, before the Soviets finally made their first backhanded admission that they had ordered the "termination" of the flight (to use their chilling euphemism), our Russian-language service alone had carried 189 separate news items and 27 different commentaries, many of them repeated, detailing the facts and spelling out the significance of the unfolding story.

Our efforts, combined with the stream of broadcasts from other Western sources and the concrete evidence released by Western authorities, ultimately compelled the Kremlin to address the incident. That it did so initially in so evasive and clumsy a manner did more to spell out the essential nature of the Soviet system than anything our commentators might have been able to add. There could be no more classic example of the facts speaking for themselves.

Small wonder that Western broadcasters have been under such bitter and escalating attack for providing the peoples of the Soviet Union and Eastern Europe with the brutal truth about such recent events as the invasion of Afghanistan, the suppression of Solidarity (the Polish opposition movement), and the tragic fate of the 269 persons aboard the KAL flight. Moscow has denounced the more than one thousand dedicated souls who work for the stations in Munich as a "band of radio saboteurs" and the stations themselves as "mouthpieces which poison the airwaves with dirty slander against the Soviet Union" and as subversive instruments of American imperialism.

This hysteria has a more solid basis than the frustration of Communist censors, else why would the Soviets feel it necessary to spend $150 million or more a year to jam Western broadcasts? And why, for that matter, do financially straitened governments in Great Britain, France, West Germany, Canada, the Netherlands, the United States, and elsewhere feel it so important to expend the considerable sums required to reach out to foreign audiences?

Quite clearly, international broadcasting is serious business. We of the West are committed to the concept that human beings have an inherent "right to know"; the right to "seek, receive, and impart information and ideas through any media and regardless of frontiers," to use the words of the Universal Declaration of Human Rights, of which the Soviet Union is a signatory.

Moreover, we regard this right as more than an abstraction. We see its exercise as a fundamental stabilizer in human affairs, the best guarantee against the threats to peace that can occur from wholesale distortions of the truth. This position was reaffirmed a few months ago by Pope John Paul II, who declared that "one-way information imposed arbitrarily from on high, or . . . [by] monopolies . . . [and] manipulation of whatever kind . . . finish by injuring the rights to responsible information and by endangering peace." It is this explicit understanding of the need for, and the benefits to be derived from, an open flow of communications among the *peoples* of the world (as distinguished from their governments) that explains the importance the West has placed on the so-called Third Basket of the Helsinki Accords.

No one, of course, is surprised that the Soviets have shown such consistent hostility to the one medium able to frustrate their most persistent efforts to create hermetically sealed societies within which to manipulate the truth. Nor should one be surprised that they have reserved their greatest hostility for Radio Free Europe and Radio Liberty. While all the Western broadcasters to the Soviet Union and Eastern Europe share a common commitment to objectivity in the reporting of news, and balance in the presentation and discussion of ideas, only Radio Free Europe and Radio Liberty undertake to act as substitutes for the free domestic radio stations denied their people.

This is a functional distinction of fundamental importance. In common with other official government radio stations, the Voice of America has as its primary function reporting the news from its own national perspective and explaining its own country to the rest of the world. By way of contrast, although funded by the U.S. Congress, Radio Free Europe and Radio Liberty are essentially independent entities with a mission defined by their role as surrogate home services for the twenty-one nationalities in Eastern Europe and the Soviet Union to which they broadcast. It is indicative of their success that they are often referred to by their listeners as "our radio." Their primary job is to report on events in the countries to which they broadcast and to provide programs that address the particular interests of their citizens.

RFE and RL, in short, are focused on meeting the informational and cultural needs of more than three hundred million people trapped in societies in which the state exercises a monopoly control over every normal source of information, a monopoly that it is our mission to challenge every day of the year. Hence, we devote more hours a day to our target audiences in Poland, Czechoslovakia, Hungary, Romania, Bulgaria, and the Soviet Union, and we broadcast to them in more languages, than any other Western service. While the BBC, for example, broadcasts to the USSR in only two languages, Russian and English, we broadcast in fifteen, including seven spoken in the increasingly important Islamic areas of the Soviet Union.

We can be an effective home service because we are continually receiving and analyzing information from Eastern Europe and the Soviet Union. We monitor their radios and interview émigrés and visitors. Our research departments, which subscribe to hundreds of Eastern European and Soviet publications, provide our programmers with ongoing, up-to-date analysis of developments in economics, politics, culture, and other important aspects of life in our broadcast areas. In fact, we maintain the richest archives on postwar Eastern European and Soviet affairs to be found anywhere in the West.

We are, in short, our listeners' most reliable source of news and analysis, and they have come to know it. Moreover, our programs serve to frustrate official attempts to distort history and induce cultural amnesia. We air the works of banned authors, place historical events in perspective, provide extensive religious programming, and remind our listeners of the national and spiritual heritages that predate Marx by more than a thousand years and link them to the rich cultural life of the Western and Islamic worlds.

Finally, we provide dissidents with a forum. We report their activities and quote from their underground publications, thus helping maintain some semblance of debate of important public issues.

It is this unique identification with each of our audiences and our reputation for accuracy that give us such special access to them. Given the attacks leveled at Radio Free Europe and Radio Liberty by the Soviet and Eastern European regimes, let me stress *our* stress on the word "accuracy." I think it fair to say that few, if any, journalistic enterprises today exercise as great care as we do in determining what we can broadcast as fact. We have what we call the "two-source rule," which requires corroboration of a story before we put it on the air. Thus we did not carry the tempting report by one major wire service that the pope had told Secretary of State Shultz that he was personally convinced the KGB had engineered the plot on his life, a story that Shultz was later to deny. Nor will we broadcast stories that don't ring true, however numerous or pedigreed their Western sources.

Western media operating under deadlines and competitive pressures can afford to take some chances. If they make a mistake, other sources will quickly set the record straight, and little harm is done. In our case, however, we are often our listeners' sole source of uncensored news. We have a special responsibility to be accurate, and we would rather take a few extra hours to check out an item than make an error with which we could be hung.

Credibility is our stock in trade, the foundation of the relationship of trust we have established with our millions of listeners. We cannot succumb to the temptations of hyperbole; and to engage in distortions or misrepresentations would violate the confidence we have earned.

An undertaking not to lie implies of course a complementary commitment to tell the truth. In this skeptical age, however, this inevitably requires that one deal with Pontius Pilate's famous—or infamous—question: "What is truth?" For our purposes, truth exists at two levels. The first deals with facts, and our job is to report them accurately and objectively, what might be described as the classic "who, what, when, and where" school of journalism. But RFE and RL are not merely journalistic enterprises, and our commitment to objectivity in reporting the news is not to be confused with neutrality where human values are concerned. To the contrary, we are committed by our charter to respect for human dignity, to the rule of law, and to the principles of political, social, economic, and religious freedom that undergird democracy. In short, it is part of our brief to act as advocates for, or, perhaps more accurately, as witnesses to, the values that are central to the Western experience.

It is in this realm that the bone-weary cynicism of Pilate's question might seem appropriate, although I believe it not to be. After all, ours is a country whose founding document declared certain truths about the nature of man and his inalienable rights to be self-evident.

It goes without saying that in today's world the American assessment of what is self-evident is somewhat less than universally accepted. Nonetheless, although political and moral truths may not be capable of clinical proof, they are subject to the tests of human experience and intuition. Surely the millions who at great risk flee the Soviet empire or push off in flimsy boats into the South China Sea are making some sort of statement about the relative merits of today's major competing political systems.

Fortunately, oppression cannot destroy the human power to evaluate alternatives. It is therefore an essential part of our role to make sure they are known. When we are not broadcasting the news or filling informational voids created by the censorship of literature or the rewriting of history, we describe the alternatives to life under Communism as well as the stark realities of life under that system. In serving as spokesmen for the human values in which we so deeply believe, we offer our audiences what their rulers would deny them, intellectual choice. It is this, I suspect, that arouses such fury in those regimes. They fully understand that we need do no more, in our commentaries and programs, than simply state the case for freedom with meticulous attention to the accuracy of every fact we cite in its support and then leave it to our audiences to determine for themselves where the truth lies.

There is, of course, an infinite variety of ways in which facts can be presented in support of a position, ranging from the insipid to the inflammatory. There are those, I know, who fear that Ronald Reagan's ventures into public diplomacy might nudge us towards the latter. To them I would merely say this: The temptation undoubtedly arises from time to time to exaggerate or to attempt to make a point through the selective use of facts. But it would be sheer folly for us to yield to it, for there would be no surer way for us to forfeit the audiences it is our business to cultivate than by jettisoning our reputation for reliability.

That reputation is solidly based. By combining high standards of journalistic responsibility with the ability to deliver programs with solid content, we have clearly achieved our basic objective of establishing ourselves as thoroughly credible surrogates for free domestic radios.

Our Polish Service provides the most dramatic recent example of our resulting impact. With the rise of Solidarity after August 1980, we began to devote the great majority of our nineteen hours a day of Polish-language broadcasts to the internal situation in Poland, often providing the Polish people with their sole source of full and accurate information about events within their own country. Even though this was met by a sharp increase in jamming, our weekly audience increased from 54 percent of the adult population in 1979 to 66 percent in 1981.

But statistics about listenership tell only part of the story. Information will inevitably shape events. Collective action requires collective knowledge. The initial strikes that led to the formation of Solidarity were assiduously ignored by the Polish media. It was largely because of RFE's reporting of seemingly isolated actions that the emerging leadership of Solidarity realized the nationwide dimensions of the protests that were taking place. As one writer put it: "Without these programs, Poles certainly would not have been informed of the momentum of the Solidarity workers' movement, nor would other East Europeans have known of its existence." (In 1985, a Polish government spokesman, Jerzy Urban, paid RFE this backhanded compliment: "If you would close Radio Free Europe, the underground would cease to exist.")

It is equally true that Radio Free Europe's Polish broadcasts have served as agents of stability. By laying out the situation confronting our listeners—thoroughly and responsibly, without exaggeration or omission—and by countering rumors and distortions with hard facts, RFE broadcasts have provided listeners with the kind of full information needed for sound judgment and responsible action.

The Polish authorities, of course, place a less benign interpretation on our efforts. In fact, they have engaged in a series of quite extraordinary actions designed to discredit us and intimidate anyone who might cooperate with our efforts to keep the Polish people fully informed. These actions have ranged from a formal protest against our broadcasts as constituting part of "an aggressive and slanderous campaign" to destabilize Poland by inciting riots, to the charade of a secret trial in which the head of our Polish Service was condemned to death in absentia, to the passage of laws authorizing the imprisonment of anyone providing information to international broadcasters.

I am pleased to report that none of this has fazed us; and, if anything, this pattern of official harassment has only strengthened our standing with our listeners as the Polish drama continues to unfold. We remain their indispensable source of credible information about events at home. We alone reported every aspect of the pope's extraordinary tour of his homeland earlier this year, carrying to the Polish people, and to the people of other Eastern European countries as well, his soaring message about overriding human values and rights. We have also given careful coverage to every test of will between the Jaruzelski regime and the Solidarity underground. Where verified, we have reported the underground leaders' calls for participation in peaceful demonstrations as well as the regime's escalating threats of punitive action against anyone taking part in them. What we have not done is urge anyone to the barricades.

Some, I know, would argue that, as the mere reporting of facts to people living in a totalitarian society can prove provocative, Western broadcasters should in effect indulge in self-censorship. But to fail to broadcast legitimate news on the grounds that listeners might choose to act on that knowledge is to cooperate with and therefore condone the internal suppression of news. That we have proven indispensable in keeping our listeners informed of what is happening in their own countries is an indictment not of RFE and RL but of a system that requires citizens to rely on outside sources for information of the most vital importance to them.

We reject the notion that our listeners should not be trusted to make their own decisions as to how they should act and what risks, if any, they should be willing to take in attempting to bring about change. Where we draw the line is in presuming to tell them what to do. It is they, after all, not we, who must live with the consequences of their actions.

Needless to say, this self-restraint goes unappreciated in the Kremlin, which is increasingly concerned over the ability of international broadcasters to penetrate the barriers erected against uncensored information. As a consequence, the Soviets not only have intensified their jamming, but have also embarked on a tenacious campaign to promote legal restraints on Western radios and limit their physical ability to reach their audiences.

One area of attack goes to the most basic requirements of a free press: the freedom to gather information and the freedom to disseminate it. For several years now, the Soviet Union has been encouraging Third World delegates to UNESCO to seek enaction of a monstrosity called the "New World Information Order." If ever adopted, it would sanction the licensing of reporters and accord governments the right to censor incoming broadcasts. This last, in turn, would effectively legitimize jamming as an enforcement measure.

On another point, the Soviets are working through international fora to outlaw the use of satellites to broadcast programs into countries that declare their lack of interest in receiving them. Last November, they were able to secure a United Nations vote requiring prior approval by the governments of receiving countries of any TV program transmitted by satellite. How one makes the intellectual distinction between shortwave signals bounced off the ionosphere and televised programs relayed by satellite I do not know. But if the West accedes to the imposition of such a right of veto, it will have forfeited what may be the most promising means for maintaining open channels of communication among different societies—if need be, over the heads of their rulers.

If these and other Soviet challenges are successful, they could seriously restrict the reach of Western broadcasts. Because of the Soviets' demonstrated skill in marshaling Third World votes, democratic nations will have to exhibit an unusual degree of unity and tenacity if they are to surmount the attacks and protect their right to reach out to other societies.

This will not be easy, especially as we can expect the men in the Kremlin to supplement their parliamentary maneuvers with a certain amount of bluster. They know how to play on the fears of those predisposed to wonder whether an insistence on even an important point of principle is worth the displeasure it might provoke in Moscow.

Back in the early 1970s, after it had been revealed that Radio Free Europe and Radio Liberty had received their principal financing from the CIA, there was a move in the American Congress to eliminate them—even though the CIA connection had been completely severed. Some influential senators argued that the stations were obstacles to harmonious international relations and therefore should be abolished. Fortunately, those senators were in the minority, and the radios now enjoy broad bipartisan support.

But sentiments can always change, especially among those who seek accommodation at any cost, and the fact is that RFE and RL will always be targets for attack as potentially destabilizing forces. This is so not because they are less objective than other Western broadcasters but because their very effectiveness in identifying themselves so closely with the interests and needs of their audiences has earned them the special animus of the Kremlin. The Soviet leaders, of course, have a point. From their perspective, the major Western stations—but particularly Radio Free Europe and Radio Liberty, with their special mission of serving as surrogate domestic radios—are inherently subversive, because they act as conduits for the proscribed ideas and truths that challenge the legitimacy of the Communist system.

Those leaders to the contrary, however, Western radios are not the source of instability. For even if the radios did not exist, Soviet citizens would still seek a greater margin of freedom than the Kremlin clearly feels it can risk, and Eastern Europeans would still regard their governments and the system under which they are forced to live as illegitimate.

No, it isn't the open transmission of information and ideas that is the destabilizing force at work today, but their repression; a repression that, in closed societies, makes the peaceful discussion of change and therefore peaceful change itself impossible.

And this isn't the only reason to fear the suppression of information. In his Nobel Prize lecture in 1970, Alexander Solzhenitsyn referred to what he described as "a rampant danger: the suppression of information between the parts of the planet." In his words, "Suppression of information renders international signatures and agreements illusory; within a muffled zone it costs nothing to reinterpret any agreement—even simpler, to forget it, as though it had never really existed. . . . A muffled zone," he continued, "is, as it were, populated not by inhabitants of the earth, but by an expeditionary corps from Mars; the people know nothing intelligent about the rest of the earth and are prepared to go and trample it down in the holy conviction that they come as 'liberators.'"

Clearly, international broadcasting is an area in which both principle and the most immediate self-interest converge; principle requires that we keep all channels of communication open, however besieged. Our ultimate safety requires that we settle for nothing less.

The Soviet empire collapsed a few years after I delivered these remarks, but we continue to face long, twilight struggles against other totalitarian societies that rely on state control of news and communications. A new generation of U.S.-financed radios is currently broadcasting to China, Cuba, North Korea, and Iran. These services would do well to emulate the example of Radio Free Europe and Radio Liberty.

A Midterm Assessment of the Carter Presidency

In early 1975, Jimmy Carter was an obscure Southern governor known principally for his practice of approaching strangers, shaking their hands, and introducing himself with his trademark, "I'm Jimmy Carter and I'm running for president." Given that ambition and his persistence, one would have thought that he had some idea of what he hoped to accomplish were he to win the presidency. But it appears he had none. I presented this assessment in New York City at a January 1979 public-affairs luncheon at the Union League Club.

When I was asked to present a midterm appraisal of the Carter presidency, I almost demurred. I was not trying to be coy. My reservation simply reflected the extraordinary fact that even after two years, it is remarkably difficult to define that presidency in substantive terms—to get a feel for its underlying texture, its underlying philosophy, its central thrust. If indeed it has any.

One would have thought that a man who had devoted two years to stalking the presidency would have had some idea of what he intended to do with it. But on achieving office, Jimmy Carter did not devote his first hundred days to presenting us with a series of detailed proposals for transforming the quality of American life, taming the bureaucracy, enhancing our health and welfare, or banishing unemployment—all at no cost to the taxpayers; proposals that might have given us some clue to his central objectives and to how he intended to go about achieving them.

Instead, Mr. Carter devoted those initial months to demonstrating his mastery of the art of political theater. The systematic stagecraft to which he treated us was truly stunning. I refer to the way he went about dismantling the external trappings of the imperial presidency and giving the illusion of accessibility—his walk down Pennsylvania Avenue on Inauguration Day, his televised fielding of telephoned questions, his attendance at a town meeting, and the rest. He prepared the stage, built up expectations among the public . . . but for what?

The answer is that even two years after he was sworn in, no one really knows. There is no evidence I know of that Mr. Carter has yet evolved a comprehensive vision of what he hopes to achieve, or of a strategy for achieving it. More often than not, he gives the impression of responding to events rather than shaping them.

This seeming inability to get his act together has fed a visceral public disenchantment with Mr. Carter that continues to be reflected in public-opinion polls, the Camp David Accords notwithstanding. Mr. Carter's impressive success in persuading Begin and Sadat to agree to agree on a peace settlement cannot mask the serious erosion, under his presidency, of American influence and credibility around the globe. Even in his chosen arena of human rights, Mr. Carter may well end up setting back the cause in which he so deeply believes.

I am among those who applaud Mr. Carter's basic proposition that American foreign policy ought to reflect our ideals. But such a policy must be able to deal with the real world, and the issue of human rights abroad is far more complex than was the issue of civil rights in Georgia.

And so, in part because the principal instrument of Mr. Carter's human-rights policy is a former civil-rights activist [Andy Young] who apparently can see the problem only in terms of blacks and whites, we have so mortgaged our African policy to black regimes of the most repressive kind that we may well have frustrated the one hope for transferring political control of Rhodesia to the black moderates who represent the majority of its people; and we seem hellbent on doing the same in South West Africa.

This African policy seems to have rendered us helpless to counter the buildup of Russian and Cuban influence in the Horn of Africa, with consequences we are only now beginning to perceive as the turmoil in Iran causes us to take a new look at a map of the oil-producing areas of the Middle East, areas that are flanked by nations such as Ethiopia and Somalia to the west, the Yemens to the south, and Afghanistan to the east.

Our ability to win friends and influence the peoples of such strategically located nations of the Third World is hardly helped by substituting public moralizing for action; by publicly vacillating on the deployment of aircraft carriers; by withdrawing American troops from South Korea in the face of a growing military buildup in North Korea; or by repudiating our solemn undertaking to defend our oldest Asian allies, the Chinese Nationalists on Taiwan, a repudiation that was particularly unseemly because our total capitulation to Peking's demands gained us absolutely nothing.

The *New York Times* has tried to conjure up a Chinese quo for Mr. Carter's wholesale quids by applauding the latter's ability to secure the former's *permission* to continue to sell Taiwan selected defensive weapons, which permission, if ever confirmed, is of course subject to unilateral withdrawal.

If this non-concession represents Mr. Carter's negotiating prowess, God help us and anyone else who has staked his safety on the invulnerability of America's nuclear umbrella. The Soviets are currently punishing Mr. Carter for his China caper by declining to finalize the SALT II agreement for another few weeks. So we don't have access to its fine print. However, aside from the fact that Mr. Carter has publicly dealt away the B-1 bomber, an improved cruise missile, and the early development of the neutron bomb in the vain hope of reciprocal Soviet restraint, enough information has seeped out of the Geneva talks to confirm the net effect of what

Mr. Carter has achieved, to wit: (a) allowing the consolidation of the Soviets' superiority in every area of strategic weapons where they have achieved a clear advantage over us while (b) restricting our ability to develop new weapons to neutralize those advantages and, in the process, (c) bargaining away NATO's ability to develop its own sophisticated cruise-missile technology.

But enough of foreign affairs, other than to suggest that about all President Carter has been able to achieve on the foreign front, aside from his considerable achievement at Camp David and relinquishing sovereignty over the Panama Canal, is an infinite amount of confusion, and profound doubts about American leadership.

Unfortunately, that confusion is not limited to our brethren overseas. Even the most important domestic signals seem to be subject to change without notice—to the despair, we are told, of senior administration officials, who can never anticipate where the next presidential policy directives will lead. There has been a stop-and-go aspect to the Carter administration that has made it terribly difficult for anyone to plan, even for the worst.

Let me begin with the longest rhetorical limb on which the president has climbed in his celebrated moral equivalent of war. I will just touch on what was palmed off on the public as a natural-gas policy. It was based on the iron conviction that we are reaching the end of the line as far as the discovery and development of significant additional domestic reserves is concerned. The administration therefore concluded, in the words of the national energy plan issued in April of 1977, that "it is doubtful that even substantial price increases could do much more than arrest the decline in gas produced." From which the administration concluded that it should oppose deregulation of natural gas as a futile means of increasing supplies, and it ordered industrial America to switch from gas to oil or coal. And now, just twenty-one months later, price increases for gas sold in free intrastate markets in Texas, Louisiana, and Oklahoma having succeeded in producing substantial surpluses within said states, the administration is commanding industrial America to switch from oil to gas so as to cut back on imports of the former, the domestic production of which is still impeded by a complex of price regulations the administration is still unwilling to relax.

In the meantime, unable to emancipate itself from the notion that consumers are somehow entitled to buy pipelined gas at substantially less than its market value as measured by the BTU content of competing fuels, the administration vetoed a long-term contract for the purchase of enough Mexican gas to satisfy the needs of one-seventh of America's gas-connected homes over the next twenty years at half the price of the liquefied Algerian gas that is being delivered in New York City.

Then there is the area of tax reform. Beginning with his hastily withdrawn proposal of a $50 tax break in 1977, Mr. Carter has switched his signals faster than this chronicler has been able to record them. One can, however, perceive common denominators that will exist in whatever changes in tax laws he ultimately submits: (1) no three-martini lunches (either he doesn't like martinis, or he doesn't appreciate the magical way they can melt resistance to a deal); (2) they will make the IRS code more complex, not simpler; (3) taken as a whole, their net effect will be to increase the tax burden on the American people, not to lighten it; and (4) given Mr. Carter's evident innocence of the role of current tax policy in discouraging the capital investment so badly needed to produce jobs and increase our productivity, the net effect of his tax proposals will be to make the tax system still more progressive.

Today, of course, Mr. Carter's overriding domestic concern is inflation. Here it will be enormously interesting to see whether this represents merely another phase in his shifting economic concerns, or whether he has finally arrived at a firm policy behind which to concentrate his celebrated determination.

You may recall that during his first month in office it was widely assumed that he was a fiscal conservative because he had spoken so incessantly before and after his election of the need to curb inflation and balance the budget. Yet his first success with Congress was to induce it to accept a package of economic stimulants in the form of major public works and make-work programs that added tens of billions of dollars to subsequent federal deficits. He also introduced welfare and urban-aid proposals which, if adopted, would have added another $20 billion or more to the federal budget. Just last May, when he finally felt compelled to address a national TV audience on the subject of inflation, about the best he could do was to say that inflation was indeed a bad thing, but that there wasn't much that government could do about it. Then in October, after many suspense-building delays, Mr. Carter unveiled, in measured tones, his "voluntary" wage and price guidelines, with the plain suggestion that inflation is the product of private greed rather than public extravagance. The next day the stock market dropped and, overseas, the dollar fell through the floor.

Only then did Mr. Carter come up with meaningful proposals for fiscal and monetary restraint. Ever since, there has been every indication that he is totally serious about curbing the projected rise in the cost of domestic programs. Having said that, I would point out that his proposed cuts are not all that impressive when compared with social-spending levels in the 1976 and 1977 budgets, but they are nevertheless significant in the light of the predictable flak he has received from the Democratic Left.

Under the circumstances, one must ask: Does this new frugality represent just a tactical shift, or does it reflect a true breakthrough in Mr. Carter's understanding of both the dangers and the root causes of inflation? If the latter, does it suggest that his learning period is finally over and that a new president is about to emerge?

On both counts, I think it too early to say. On the now-substantial record, I still think it difficult to find any basis for predicting Mr. Carter's future direction; but I do believe we have learned something of the Carter approach to the problems that come his way. There seems to be a sort of mindset, one that was particularly apparent in his approach to energy.

These are its characteristics, as I see them: First, the energy program was improvised rather than thought through, and it was improvised virtually in a vacuum by brainstormers long on theory and short on experience. Second, Mr. Carter's approach to a problem—in this case, energy supply and demand—is basically authoritarian; and this, I believe, will prove especially characteristic. Government will decide what needs to be done, and how; government will issue the marching orders. The Carter program reflected no inclination to rely on private initiatives and risk-takers, and on a free market, to work their old-time magic in allocating resources where they are needed most. Third, there is a heavy reliance on the government's taxing powers, as carrot and stick, to impose the government's will. Mr. Carter's proposal for tax credits to protect cooperating workers against any rate of inflation over 7 percent is a recent case in point. Finally, throughout the resultant broth is stirred a heavy lacing of populism. We can expect just about any emergency or need to be used as a vehicle for a massive redistribution of income—in the case of Mr. Carter's originally proposed energy taxes and rebates, about $75 billion worth. Thanks to the Senate, most of the Carter energy program has gone down in flames. So much for the Carter generalship in what he has advertised as the most important battle in his moral equivalent of war.

His fumbling of energy and other issues, his misadventures abroad, and the tangle of contradictory signals emitted by the Carter administration have given rise to recurring questions as to his basic competence for his job.

About a year ago I attended a fascinating off-the-record symposium in Washington. It was presided over by three nationally known journalists, professional president-watchers whose politics would incline them to be sympathetic to a new Democrat in the White House. The first panelist set the stage by saying that based on his first year's performance, he would have to give the student a grade of C–, with some incompletes. Taking this cue, the second speaker said the best he could do was to award an F. The third stated that he didn't want to discourage the pupil so early in the game, so he would award him, reluctantly, a C. During the course of the morning, the following phrases were used to characterize Mr. Carter and his presidency: "moralism rampant," "militant amateur," "a loner in the classic sense." In short, he was generally pictured as a man who was temperamentally unprepared for the presidency. The consensus of these reporters can be summed up by the rhetorical question asked by one of them: "Is he constitutionally *able* to learn how to handle the presidency, how to go beyond his aloneness?"

A year has gone by since then, and I am not quite sure how that question should be answered. If it were to be phrased, "Has he learned how to use the *powers* of the presidency?" the answer would have to be yes. We saw the way he was able to use threats and promises to corral the votes needed to ratify the Panama Canal Treaty. He is using all the levers at the president's disposal to compel compliance with "voluntary" price restraints. He has intimidated the business opponents of the gas bill, and he played his China card in complete secrecy, in total defiance of the Senate. Quite clearly, Watergate has not put an end to the ability of a president to coerce cooperation.

But if the question is "Has he learned to exploit the potential for leadership inherent in the presidency?" I suspect the answer must be no. Leadership suggests, among other things, a sense of direction. In the case of Mr. Carter, however, I fear that we are destined for another two years of drift and uncertainty, with all that that suggests in terms of international hazards and the erosion of confidence at home.

Shortly after Mr. Carter was sworn in, one of his top aides was quoted as predicting that when he is running for re-election in 1980, people will still be asking, "What is the real Carter?" I suspect time will prove that aide right. During the intervening years, Mr. Carter will have made dozens of critical decisions, but they will leave no pattern—just a series of decisions, each isolated from the last, leading the nation nowhere.

Yet what we need more than anything else these days is a sense of direction, a sense of purpose. And here I unfurl my ideological colors, because I deeply believe that not only do we need a sense of direction, but we need a specific direction. I see nothing in the Carter record to suggest that he understands the dangers we have been courting in our drift towards a centralized, bureaucratized state, or that he has any plan to steer us away from them. Nor do I see anything in his stated goals, or in his evident love of command, that would lead me to believe that he will conclude that the best way to restore the economic vigor of our society, to liberate its creativity, to produce the wealth and jobs that will improve the lot of all our people, is to reduce the restraints and burdens we have imposed on them and on the economy.

And that is why this conservative continues to pray that Jimmy Carter will experience a second rebirth; this time a political one.

That rebirth did not occur. Jimmy Carter's next two years brought us "malaise," a record rate of inflation, 10 percent unemployment, long gasoline lines, and a botched attempt to rescue the American embassy personnel who were being held captive in Iran. But to his eternal credit, he negotiated the Camp David Accords, which established peaceful relations between Egypt and Israel.

Index